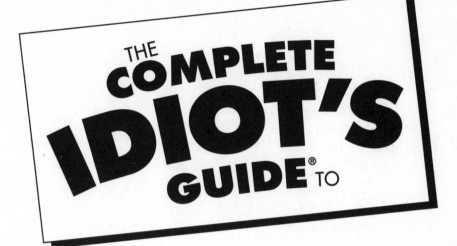

THE **COMPLETE IDIOT'S GUIDE** TO

The Perfect Resume

Fifth Edition

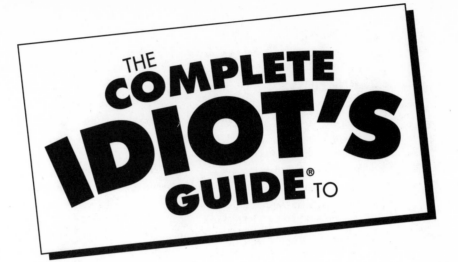

THE
COMPLETE
IDIOT'S
GUIDE® TO

The Perfect Resume

Fifth Edition

by Susan Ireland

ALPHA

A member of Penguin Group (USA) Inc.

To my dad, who taught me at an early age the value of building character through work.

ALPHA BOOKS

Published by the Penguin Group

Penguin Group (USA) Inc., 375 Hudson Street, New York, New York 10014, USA

Penguin Group (Canada), 90 Eglinton Avenue East, Suite 700, Toronto, Ontario M4P 2Y3, Canada (a division of Pearson Penguin Canada Inc.)

Penguin Books Ltd., 80 Strand, London WC2R 0RL, England

Penguin Ireland, 25 St. Stephen's Green, Dublin 2, Ireland (a division of Penguin Books Ltd.)

Penguin Group (Australia), 250 Camberwell Road, Camberwell, Victoria 3124, Australia (a division of Pearson Australia Group Pty. Ltd.)

Penguin Books India Pvt. Ltd., 11 Community Centre, Panchsheel Park, New Delhi—110 017, India

Penguin Group (NZ), 67 Apollo Drive, Rosedale, North Shore, Auckland 1311, New Zealand (a division of Pearson New Zealand Ltd.)

Penguin Books (South Africa) (Pty.) Ltd., 24 Sturdee Avenue, Rosebank, Johannesburg 2196, South Africa

Penguin Books Ltd., Registered Offices: 80 Strand, London WC2R 0RL, England

International Standard Book Number: 978-1-59257-957-0
Library of Congress Catalog Card Number: 2009930701

12 11 10   8 7 6 5 4 3 2 1

Interpretation of the printing code: The rightmost number of the first series of numbers is the year of the book's printing; the rightmost number of the second series of numbers is the number of the book's printing. For example, a printing code of 10-1 shows that the first printing occurred in 2010.

Printed in the United States of America

Note: This publication contains the opinions and ideas of its author. It is intended to provide helpful and informative material on the subject matter covered. It is sold with the understanding that the author and publisher are not engaged in rendering professional services in the book. If the reader requires personal assistance or advice, a competent professional should be consulted.

The author and publisher specifically disclaim any responsibility for any liability, loss, or risk, personal or otherwise, which is incurred as a consequence, directly or indirectly, of the use and application of any of the contents of this book.

Most Alpha books are available at special quantity discounts for bulk purchases for sales promotions, premiums, fund-raising, or educational use. Special books, or book excerpts, can also be created to fit specific needs.

For details, write: Special Markets, Alpha Books, 375 Hudson Street, New York, NY 10014.

Publisher: *Marie Butler-Knight*
Editorial Director: *Mike Sanders*
Senior Managing Editor: *Billy Fields*
Executive Editor: *Randy Ladenheim-Gil*
Development Editor: *Lynn Northrup*
Production Editor: *Kayla Dugger*
Copy Editor: *Emily Garner*

Cartoonist: *Steve Barr*
Cover Designer: *Bill Thomas*
Book Designer: *Trina Wurst*
Indexer: *Brad Herriman*
Layout: *Ayanna Lacey*
Proofreader: *Laura Caddell*

Contents at a Glance

Contents

Foreword

A book is a good book, even a great book, if you keep saying to yourself as you go through it: "Now, how did they learn *that*?"

A continual sense of wonder in you, the reader. That's the key. That's how you measure whether a book is really helpful, or not. And what I've learned over the years is that such wonder is not produced simply by a writer's experience. It's produced by experience plus one other ingredient, harder to find: wisdom. If you're puzzled about what I mean by "wisdom," I mean learning to separate the important from the unimportant. I mean learning to separate the wheat from the chaff. I mean learning, as Susan Ireland herself says in this most helpful book of hers: What is the least you need to know? Ah, there is wisdom, right there!

Books about resumes—of which there are hundreds, if not thousands—often are "yawners," I regret to report—after reading them for 35 years. On and on and on, they go. While visions of sugarplums, or at least of soft pillows, dance in their readers' wee little heads.

The authors of books about resumes commonly seem to feel there is so much to tell, and so little time. *You must remember this, you must remember that, and oh yes, you must remember this also.* They believe we live in the Information Age, as is commonly said. Well, that's not exactly true. We live in the Too-Much-Information Age. Most of us wander, as David Shenk first pointed out back in 1998, in a kind of overwhelming *Data Smog*.

Hence, "what is the least you need to know?" is the true place, the wise place, where a book on resumes needs to start.

There is a lot of wonder and wisdom in this book. When I came across Susan's words—like "If your resume generates job interviews for work you're not interested in, something is wrong with your resume"—I found myself thinking, "Now, how did she learn *that*?" And, in fact, I found myself thinking this continually, throughout the book.

But the point of a book, of course, is not "how did *she* learn that?" but "how can *I* learn that?" That's easy. Put yourself in Susan's hands. Trust her. Trust this book. I recommend it highly, for the obvious reasons: its wisdom and your wonder.

—Richard Bolles

Richard Bolles is the most widely read and respected leader in the whole career development world. His book, *What Color Is Your Parachute? A Practical Guide for Job-Hunters & Career-Changers*, is now in its 35th annual revision, and has sold more copies (8 million) than any other career book in the world.

Introduction

You're looking for a job, and for that, you need a great resume.

I don't have to tell you the job market's tighter than a sailor's knot. Headlines tell us daily that we're in one of the toughest employment situations in decades. So many resumes are in circulation, it's a wonder online databases can hold them all. And with so many applicants going for each job, you really—I mean *really*—need a top-notch resume to compete. It has to contain all the right keywords, accomplishments, and skill sets for your job objective.

Your resume is the primary marketing piece for your job hunt. Once you've created it, you need to be savvy about how to send it to recruiters and hiring managers, post it online, and repurpose it in other online formats—all so it can work as hard as possible for you.

With this book, you're going to spend about three hours creating the perfect resume. Then, you'll learn how to get it into the hands of hiring managers. You'll also get the hang of how to build your online professional network, where your resume will play a key role as your online profile.

As a professional resume writer who has helped thousands of job seekers, I've seen how well-written resumes lead to promising interviews and job offers. Now, as the proud owner of *The Complete Idiot's Guide to the Perfect Resume, Fifth Edition*, you have me as your personal resume coach. Imagine that I'm sitting right at your elbow as you work at your desk or kitchen table. My job is to guide you through the entire process as you ...

- Develop a winning resume strategy.

- Choose the right format for your resume.

- Write each line to make the most of your qualifications.

- Compose a compelling e-mail or letter to accompany your resume.

- Send thank you notes that keep a prospective employer interested in you.

- E-mail your new resume to recruiters and employers.

- Post your resume online for more exposure.

- Take advantage of online social networking and blogging to further your job hunt.

To illustrate my points, I've included lots of sample resumes that reflect goals and challenges similar to what you might be facing. These samples may spark some ideas that you can use in your own resume.

The secret to success in using this book is to relax and take one step at a time. You'll be surprised how painless the process of writing a resume is!

Between the Covers

Because helping you craft a winning resume is the goal of *The Complete Idiot's Guide to the Perfect Resume, Fifth Edition*, let's talk about what's inside:

Part 1, "Resumes That Work in Today's Job Market," explains how your resume can market you in today's quickly changing job climate. You'll learn why keywords are more important than ever before. You'll also find "The Resume Commandments," which are my secrets to creating a compelling resume.

Part 2, "Putting Together a Resume That Wins," is where you find my straightforward, six-step process for writing an effective resume. Before you know it, you'll be finished with your resume.

Part 3, "The Correspondence Connection," shows you when to send a job search e-mail or hardcopy letter: along with your resume, as a follow-up to a recruiter's request, after an interview, and to thank those in your network who helped with your successful job hunt.

Part 4, "Your Job Search on the Web," turns you into a pro at preparing resumes that can be e-mailed and posted on websites. You'll discover how to retool your resume for your social network profile and blog resume.

As if all that wasn't enough, I've also included a Portfolio of Sample Resumes at the end of the book, jam-packed with resumes that focus on industries and professions for today's job market.

Advice Along the Way

Whether you read this book from cover to cover or open it to specific points to get help with your job search, you'll notice the following sidebars throughout:

Job Hunt Hint

With the job search tips you'll find in these sidebars, you'll get your new job in no time!

def•i•ni•tion

These sidebars will keep you informed about buzz-words in the job hunt business.

Bonus Check

For that extra kick in your job hunt, check out these sidebars. They're filled with juicy tidbits you probably didn't think of.

Career Casualty

Don't miss these important warnings. They'll save you lots of work, angst, and time.

Acknowledgements

I'd like to thank Beth Brown, Catherine Sutton, and Nancy Rosenberg (professional resume writers on my team) for the resumes they contributed to this book. I also want to thank the following colleagues, friends, and family for their resume samples and career insights: Roberta Rosen, Maureen Nelson, Jan Johnston-Tyler, David Snyder, Susan Joyce, Bryan Zembrowski, Geoffrey Welchman, Marc Korchin, Dana Klyver, Jed Parsons, Kathleen Lyon, Grace Ireland, Kara Ireland, Christopher D'Ambrosio, Laura Stark, Jon Stark, and Robert Withers. Special gratitude and remembrance goes to my mentor and friend, Yana Parker (author of *The Damn Good Resume Guide*). My thanks to Andreé Abecassis (my agent at Ann Elmo Agency), Randy Ladenheim-Gil (my senior acquisitions editor), Lynn Northrup (my development editor), Kayla Dugger (my production editor), Emily Garner (my copy editor), and, of course, Mom and my husband, Charlie.

Trademarks

All terms mentioned in this book that are known to be or are suspected of being trademarks or service marks have been appropriately capitalized. Alpha Books and Penguin Group (USA) Inc. cannot attest to the accuracy of this information. Use of a term in this book should not be regarded as affecting the validity of any trademark or service mark.

Part

Resumes That Work in Today's Job Market

There's no question we're experiencing hard economic times. Unemployment is high and jobs in many fields are scarce. You may be feeling uncertain or even desperate about your job search, wondering which way to turn for employment opportunities and how to approach them. If so, you're not alone. Many job seekers, even highly qualified professionals, are feeling tossed around like a rowboat at sea in a hurricane.

Don't despair! In Part 1, we look at the situations many job seekers are facing in today's job market and suggest some viable resume solutions. We're also going to look at how recruiters are searching for top-notch applicants—like you—and how your resume can rise to the top of the pile on a recruiter's desk. That's right, we're going to get your resume in shape for some promising career options that will give you a new start and carry you into a bright future.

So turn the page, and let's get sailing!

Tough Times Call for Seriously Great Resumes

In This Chapter

- ◆ The economic slowdown and your job search
- ◆ Resume pointers to help you fit into emerging industries
- ◆ How to highlight a new degree or retraining on your resume
- ◆ Time to change careers?

With the constant change in today's job market, you need to be ready to move on a dime in almost any direction to get a job. That means staying current on what employers are looking for in job candidates and keeping your resume loaded with those qualifications.

This chapter looks at how to use your resume to reposition yourself for a jump into a new and promising industry or find a job in one of the old standbys that's likely to hold steady through thick and thin.

A Resume for All Reasons

You're looking for a job. No matter what the reason, the slow economy probably isn't making your job hunt easy. With so many applicants per job, you need to have a really great resume to compete, and you need to get that great resume out where recruiters and employers can easily find it.

First, let's look at what brings you to the point of looking for a job. Then we'll figure out what sort of job you want and how to create a resume that will impress employers, even in these tough times.

Pink Slip Blues

Getting laid off or fired feels awful! Whether you see a pink slip coming your way or it lands on your desk with no forewarning, it can feel like a wrecking ball fell on your head. With the number of layoffs happening today, you may have already been a victim of job termination, or suspect you could be next in line.

If you're dealing with job termination, get right on the case:

1. Figure out what job you want next.

2. Create a resume that targets your job objective.

3. Get your resume in front of recruiters and employers who are trying to fill job openings for your desired type of work.

If you're scared or just feeling down because the job market is so tough, read on to see how others have refocused their resumes to get into growing and stable industries such as biotech, green products manufacturing, or website technology. Before you know it, you'll be back on your feet with a new job!

Time for a Change

You may not be in job termination crisis. Maybe you're simply looking for a job that's better than the one you currently hold. Or maybe you see opportunities in new fields that interest you. If so, you're ready to ...

1. Define your next career move.

2. Learn as much as possible about your new profession or industry.

3. Create a resume using a format that markets you for your career transition.

4. Get that resume out there!

Whether you're currently employed or unemployed, you have some very exciting career possibilities before you: healthcare, education, renewable energy, and telecommunications, to name just a few. Let's look at examples of how others have made successful transitions, and how their resumes helped them.

Going Green

The environmental movement is at the forefront of the emerging new economy, and it needs a strong workforce to make it succeed. Green ventures are springing up in virtually all industries, so if you have a hankerin' to earn a paycheck saving the planet, get a *green collar* job.

Kathryn Dobson had an administrative job at a magazine publishing company. She'd always wanted a well-paying job doing something positive for the environment but never saw an opportunity she was qualified for. A few years ago,

---

Career Casualty

Don't use the words *laid off* on your resume. Usually there's no need to explain on your resume why you left a job. If, however, you've been laid off more than three times in two years, simply put the reason for your lay-off, such as "plant closed" or "company merger," so the employer won't think it's your fault your jobs were short-lived.

---

def•i•ni•tion

Blue- and white-collar jobs are turning green—that is, any job that helps and doesn't harm the environment can be defined as **green collar**.

she decided to redirect her career toward management in a green company. Realizing she needed some education in the field, she enrolled in a Green Master's in Business Administration (GMBA) program at a local university.

When it came time to apply for a job as Program Manager in an environmentally conscious organization, she updated her resume to include the following:

- Green university coursework

- Volunteer position at an environmental organization

- Solid business experience

- Achievement statements that fully support her job objective

Check out Kathryn's resume at the end of this chapter. Not surprisingly, she won her dream green job!

The good news about green industries? Applicants for many jobs in this field are not expected to have much experience because the field is relatively new. This means it's a more level playing field among the competition. Conveying your enthusiasm for preserving and improving the environment, and participating in local community projects, will take you further than offering simply a laundry list of marginally relevant jobs. That being the case, go through your paid and unpaid work experience with a fine-tooth comb and make a list of those things that support your job objective, including:

- Projects (paid or unpaid)

- Activities (personal or professional)

- Classes, workshops, seminars, certifications, and degrees

With this list in hand, incorporate relevant items into a chronological or combination resume format (see Chapter 4). If neither the chronological nor combination format works for your situation, use the functional format. To see more green resumes, look under "Environmental" in the Portfolio of Sample Resumes at the back of this book.

You Got a Degree in *What?*

We all hear stories of people who found success by following their passions. But what if your passion—and college degree—is in a noncommercial field such as Latin? In the following scenario, see how Jed pursued his passion for Latin and then landed a job as a software engineer.

Jed got his Master's degree and Ph.D. in Latin, with the idea of going for a career in research/teaching ancient languages. Near the completion of his Ph.D. program, he changed his mind—he decided to apply for a job in software development.

On his resume, Jed pointed to his nonacademic experience, to which he had devoted a fair bit of time writing collaborative textbook software, educational software for the blind, and his own research tools for searching the corpus of Greek and Latin texts on digital media. His resume stood out among others because of the level of his intellectual curiosity and diversity of experience.

Jed was interviewed and accepted for a job as Production Software Engineer at a company that provides visual effects for the entertainment industry. He believes he won the job because in his resume, correspondence, and job interview he was frank about why he changed his career path. In doing so, he showed he's smart, intellectually flexible, and passionate about whatever he takes on.

> **Bonus Check**
>
> A slowdown in your industry or profession could be a blessing in disguise. It may open a door to a new and exciting line of work for you!

Techie Heads for Medical Field

Healthcare is predicted to be one of the most stable industries as time goes on, because no matter how the economy performs, there will always be a need for medical attention and supplies. Healthcare, of course, employs a number of occupations from janitors to surgeons, IT professionals to social workers. In this next story you'll meet Robert Silverstein, who had no medical training but found his way into the healthcare arena after being laid off from his job in high-tech.

As a test engineer for a large electronics firm, Robert thought his job was secure. But when funding for his project dried up, he was laid off. Unemployed for the first time in his adult life, Robert created a bare-bones resume (found at the end of this chapter) that said nothing but the essentials of where he'd been and what his marketable skills were. Then he added a special Technical Skills section near the top in which he listed all his technical keywords.

He got a few short-term jobs but no steady work. He often had long stretches of unemployment between assignments. During one particularly long span of unemployment, he worked for no pay at his son's alarm company. As he updated his resume, here's how Robert made these short-term job stints look more stable:

◆ He placed all his contracting assignments under one job title: 2006–pres., Contract Test Engineer.

◆ He beefed up his experience by listing his work for his son.

Eventually Robert landed a contractual job with a medical equipment manufacturer. To his delight, his short-term contract in the R&D department turned into a permanent job as part of a team doing groundbreaking work with difibulators. He couldn't have been happier.

Selling the Case for Healthcare

If your industry has slowed down and you're lucky enough to have a *transferrable occupation*, maybe you can head for another industry where you can wear the same professional hat. That's exactly what Raj did when he saw a roadblock ahead.

When the U.S. auto industry took a turn for the worse, Raj decided it was time to get out of car sales. Sales was all Raj knew; the idea of doing anything else wasn't even a consideration.

Opportunity knocked when he visited his doctor's office for his annual bend-over-and-cough exam. In the waiting room, he sat next to a woman who had a sales case in hand. Recognizing a fellow salesperson, he struck up a conversation and soon learned she was about to get her foot in the door with Raj's doctor to promote a new electronic stethoscope. Raj asked the woman lots of questions while they were waiting, and by the time he left his appointment he had decided to investigate transferring his sales talent from the sickly auto industry to the healthy healthcare industry.

Here's how Raj tailored his resume for his career move:

> ◆ Near the top of his resume, he put "Sales Manager" to announce that he is clearly established in his profession.

> ◆ In the body of his resume, he wrote strong achievement statements without mentioning cars, trucks, or SUVs. Rather, he used non-industry-specific language (such as quotas, items, merchandise, or units) when showing off his transferable sales skills. For example: "Achieved 110 percent of personal quota early in the fourth quarter, enabling the entire sales team to attain 125 percent by year's end."

> ◆ At the end of his resume, he briefly mentioned that he's bilingual in Hindi and English, because he realized there are numerous doctors from India who would be his customers.

With his resume in hand (and online), Raj networked his way into a job selling pharmaceuticals to medical facilities. His sales career now feels far more secure.

Stepping into the Classroom

You may need to push the career refresh button by changing professions without leaving the industry you're established in. That's what our next job seeker did when he could no longer work in construction.

Greg was the manager of a construction company that went belly up when the housing market took a dive. It became evident that his career on rooftops was over and he needed to find a new means of support.

---

def•i•ni•tion

A **transferrable occupation** is a job function that exists across industries, allowing a job seeker in that line of work to move easily from one industry to another. Such a minor career change can usually be achieved using a chronological or combination resume format (see Chapter 4).

He met with a counselor with whom he had many discussions about possible career options. Not surprisingly, the conversation always came back to construction. Building was what he knew best, so Greg easily put together a resume for a teaching position at a local vocational college. His resume ...

- Highlighted his extensive knowledge in construction.
- Spoke about his training and supervision of his crew.
- Featured his Master's degree in mechanical engineering, which qualified him to teach in the classroom.
- Listed his ability to speak Spanish.

Greg's resume won him an interview, and he now derives great satisfaction helping high school graduates gain skills in construction and mechanical fields, which many will find employable in the emerging green building industry.

Going Digital

Sometimes a little retraining in your current field can open up new possibilities. As industries change, you may need to keep up with new technology so you remain marketable to employers. Or, you may simply need to tweak your dream career to get your sails lined up with the financial winds.

Fred is a professional singer-songwriter whose gigs alone didn't pay the bills. Realizing he needed a "day job," he started looking for something—anything—just to get by. Everything he found online sounded either boring or didn't match his skill set. Then he got the bright idea of retooling his musical career to include a new dimension.

He was naturally interested in sound engineering and had dabbled in it when he recorded his own songs. He decided to get some training in digital arts at a nearby college. Using all unpaid activities, Fred was able to build a functional resume—the bulk of his relevant experience came from his coursework and hours of personal recording.

His resume won him a "real" job as a digital sound engineer for a web-based multimedia company. He still plays gigs in his spare time and hasn't given up the dream of being a full-time professional musician someday.

It's Your Move

The job market is a little shaky right now, but with some courage, flexibility, and a great resume, you will land a job. Don't wait for a pink slip to land on your desk before you start examining your career options. Start the process right now by updating your resume for a new job possibility!

Job Hunt Hint

If the job market is tight in your specialized line of work, consider going back to school for a new degree or certification to realign your specialty with current market trends. Then highlight that new degree or certificate on your resume.

The Least You Need to Know

◆ Whether you're currently employed or unemployed, there are exciting job possibilities for you in this changing economy.

◆ Use paid and unpaid experience on your resume to show you have what it takes to work in a different industry or occupation.

◆ Place your new degree or retraining prominently on your resume to show you qualify for your career shift.

◆ On your resume, demonstrate qualifications that are relevant to ethnic diversity and the global economy.

◆ Consider going back to school to gain new skills in a different field.

Kathryn Dobson

105 Blake Street   New York, NY 12345   123-555-1234   kathryndobson@bamboo.com

OBJECTIVE: Program Manager in an environmentally conscious company

SUMMARY

- A systems thinker and ideas generator with a passion for sustainable lifestyle and technologies, and four years' experience developing and/or running programs and marketing initiatives.
- Creative and resourceful, a practiced writer and editor with a talent for communicating green values. A highly organized budget manager and team player with an entrepreneurial streak.
- A quick study; proficient in Microsoft Office, Dreamweaver, and Filemaker Pro on Macs or PCs.

EDUCATION

Critical Thinking; Human Relations & Organizational Behavior; Systems Thinking Lab 2007-08
Green M.B.A. Course, Boston University, Boston, MA
B.A., English Literature, Nazareth College, Rochester, NY   2003

RELEVANT ACHIEVEMENTS

- Managed the two largest programs at Bella's, Inc., a $95M natural and organic foods company, while co-coordinating marketing booths at green tradeshows throughout the U.S.
  - Oversaw a donation program with an annual budget of $45K; delegated financial and food grants to classrooms, non-profits, environmental groups, and women's organizations.
  - Increased impact of Bella's $50K Environmental Studies Scholarship program by refining its focus.
- Redefined Bella's 2008 marketing plan to reflect total brand redesign and evolution of community outreach programs and to establish a fresh identity for a brand-new team.
  - Conceived and wrote copy for e-newsletter with 20,000 readers, a consumer blog, website content, and environmental education on packaging, as "Voice of Bella's."
  - Initiated and ran the Social Club, a team of five that enhanced office culture on a tight budget by introducing fun, plants and organic BBQs; planned and coordinated parties for up to 75 staff.
- Remotely coordinated travel logistics, catering, agenda, and $70K budget for two multi-day workshops on research for groups of up to 100, including special populations, academics, and NGO representatives.
  - Edited grants and publications for program director, maintained websites, and managed day-to-day office functions. Learned Dreamweaver software to design and build a workshop website within one week. Acted as liaison between vendors and NYU accounting department.
- Assisted in construction of a sustainable campsite for 30 people and a 20-square-foot booth on carbon footprint education, as only student representative along with GMBA alumni and co-founder. Co-designed survey and acted as point person for the project throughout the event.
- Co-conceived an experiential, action-based learning facility for students at GMBA to practice systemic thinking tools and for alumni to consult with local businesses.

WORK HISTORY

BUSINESS WORLD, New York, NY   2008-present
Professional Organizer & Personal Assistant
COLLEGE OF NATURE AND SCIENCE, New York University, New York, NY   2008
Program Assistant, Environmental & Forestry Outreach (EFO)
GREEN MBA PROGRAM (GMBA), Boston University, Boston, MA   2007-08
Co-Founder, IdeaWorks, 2008; **Project Co-Manager,** Natural Life, 2007
BELLA'S, INC., New York, NY   2004-07
Project Manager, Website Redesign & Content Revision, 2007
Assistant Brand Manager & Copywriter, 2006-07
Cause Marketing Coordinator, 2004-06

ROBERT SILVERSTEIN
P.O. Box 123, Bangor, ME 12345
123-555-1234, robertsilverstein@bamboo.com

TEST ENGINEER
Focusing on healthcare technology

QUALIFICATIONS

- Over 15 years of team leadership, designing digital logic and microprocessor systems.
- Recent contractual experience in test engineering in the medical field.
- Available for project management assignments throughout the U.S.

TECHNICAL SKILLS

PCA functional test stations   ATM switch
Cable modem switch test station   VXI/LabView systems
In-circuit test development   HP 3065 – Cheap Boundary Scan

EXPERIENCE

2006-pres.   **Contract Test Engineer**
Clients include:

Alliance Medical Group, Bangor, ME
- Led team to develop three PCA functional test stations.

Elektra Interactive, Greenville, ME
- Developed cable modem switch test station.

Quinn Banking Systems, Stratton, VT
- Developed functional test for ATM switch.

Tulsar Alarm, Weston, VT
- Designed central station management, CCTV, computer network, alarm and access control systems.

2003-06   **Frazier Recording Company, Allentown, PA**
Lead Test Engineer
- Developed product line manufacturing test strategies.
- Team leader for seven test engineers.
- Integrated functional test into Teradyne in-circuit test development.

1990-03   **Mayflower Electronics, Seattle, WA**
Principal Test / Project Engineer
- Developed test specifications and testability enhancements in designs.
- Project leader and cost account manager for VXI/LabView systems.
- In-circuit tests for HP 3065 – Cheap Boundary Scan.

EDUCATION

BSEE, University of Tucson, Tucson, Arizona
Graduate coursework: Northwestern University

Chapter 2

Keywords That Get You Noticed

In This Chapter

- ◆ How recruiters use keywords to find job seekers like you
- ◆ Targeting your resume to your job objective
- ◆ Making a list of your keywords
- ◆ How to incorporate keywords into your resume

Search engines are key to getting a job in today's job market. Every minute of every day, recruiters and employers are entering keywords into search engines to find job candidates. To get your next job, you need to play the keyword game.

In this chapter, I'll discuss ways to find what keywords an employer will look for on your resume and how to weave those words into your resume's content.

What Are Keywords?

We commonly type *keywords* into search engines such as Google or Yahoo! in hopes of pulling up information we seek. In much the same way, a recruiter trying to fill a job enters keywords into a search engine online or in a resume database to find ideal candidates' resumes.

def•i•ni•tion

Keywords are terms (one word or a few strung together) that capture the essence of a topic. When looking for a job online, use as many keywords in your search as necessary (such as job title, skills, zip code) to pull up job posts that match your qualifications.

This explains why it's so important for your resume to contain all the keywords for the job you're going for. You want your resume to pop up in the recruiter's search results window—and you want your resume to be at or near the top of that list of results. How will you manage that? By making sure your resume has every single keyword and its acronym (for example, "Project Management Office" and "PMO") that a recruiter might possibly key into the search engine.

Here's how you can make that happen:

1. Create a list of keywords for the job you seek.

2. Incorporate them into your resume.

Sounds easy enough, doesn't it? With a computer at your fingertips, it's a quick process.

The Job Title

Before you sit down to write your resume, you need to figure out what job you're going for. Why? Because that job title (your job objective) is one of the most important keywords on your resume.

Think of your resume as a marketing piece that you'll post on the Internet. Like any good online marketing piece, it should be filled with all the terms a recruiter's search engine uses to find someone like you. You may ask, "Can't I make a generic resume, and *then* decide what job I want?" I highly recommend you *not* use a generic resume. Instead, take the following steps:

1. Research job possibilities in the industry and occupation you've chosen.

2. Find job postings for specific jobs in that line of work that you can and want to do.

3. Print out (or save to your computer) job posts that you want to respond to.

4. If you find more than one job (and you likely will), prioritize those posts so your first choice is on top.

5. Create a *targeted resume* for job choice number one that includes all the keywords from that job post.

6. Make a copy of your resume for job choice number one, and adjust it so it's targeted for job choice number two.

7. For each job post that you respond to, tailor your resume for that specific job, paying attention to appropriate keywords for each post.

In later chapters, I talk about how to tailor each section of your resume for the job objective on the resume. For now, though, let's look at how one job seeker adjusted his resume to include the right keywords as he applied for three different jobs. All three resumes are at the end of this chapter.

Drumming Up the Right Keywords

An easy way to use the right keywords for a particular job is to ...

1. Print out the job post.

2. Highlight or underline the keywords in the job post.

3. Write statements or create lists that contain those keywords on your resume.

> ## def•i•ni•tion
>
> A **targeted resume** is created for a very specific job or line of work. It contains keywords and qualifications that unmistakably define its job objective. Don't be lazy about customizing your resume. Your investment of time and energy to make a targeted resume for each application will pay off.

Eduardo was applying for a customer service representative position. He found the following job post on Monster.com, printed it out, and underlined the keywords for the job.

CUSTOMER SERVICE REPRESENTATIVE

<u>Bilingual</u> professionals are encouraged to apply.

◆ This is an entry-level position in a <u>fast-paced</u> Customer Service <u>Call Center</u> environment. On an average day, our experienced customer service representatives take approximately 15 <u>calls</u> per hour and perform a variety of <u>forms processing</u>.

◆ <u>Attendance</u>, <u>dependability</u>, and <u>attention to detail</u> are key characteristics that will make you successful in this position.

◆ To begin learning the necessary information and <u>computer screens</u>, we provide a 6–8 week classroom training program which is a combination of lecture and practice on live <u>customer accounts</u>.

After looking at the job post, notice how Eduardo managed to get all of the underlined keywords into his first resume.

Highlighting Terms for Your Resume

After Eduardo created his first resume, he decided to apply for a job in marketing. Here's the job post for his second application.

Regional Marketing Representative

Industry: <u>Education</u>

Education Level: <u>Bachelor's Degree</u>

Career Level: Experienced (Non-Manager)

About the Job

Responsible for growing business in the company's <u>tutoring and test preparation programs</u> in assigned territory. Includes calling on <u>schools</u> (and other organizations) and implementing <u>grassroots</u> <u>sales</u> and <u>marketing campaigns</u> to generate <u>enrollment</u>, <u>word-of-mouth</u>, and a <u>positive reputation</u>. The part-time position will report to and work closely with the company's regional director.

Specific responsibilities include growing student enrollment through both private-paid tutoring and test preparation as well as contract <u>instructional services</u> to schools and other agencies in assigned markets. For example:

- Expand the company's delivery of private-paid tutoring by building <u>relationships</u> that will lead to providing effective services through private tutoring and tutoring classes.

- Expand the company's number of <u>contract programs</u> with schools.

- Develop and nurture relationships with schools (including <u>principals</u>, <u>counselors</u>, <u>PTA presidents</u>, etc.), <u>districts</u>, and other <u>community organizations</u>, including local <u>employers</u> and <u>referral sources</u>.

- Implement grassroots marketing tactics to maximize word-of-mouth, including <u>community events</u> that educate the potential customer.

- <u>Schedule</u> program start dates and <u>implement</u> campaigns several times per year to fill them.

- Develop and implement <u>strategies</u> and <u>tactics</u> to provide high levels of <u>customer service</u> to our clients.

Ideal Candidate

- Experience and a documented record of success in <u>marketing</u> and <u>sales</u>, preferably with complex professional services organizations (education experience helpful but not required)

- Exceptional <u>communication skills</u>, both <u>oral</u> and <u>written</u>, including <u>presentations</u>

- Strong <u>computer</u> skills

- Ability to consistently make <u>calls</u> every day to achieve <u>quota</u>

- A positive attitude and strong work ethic

- A self-starter

Now look at Eduardo's second resume for this job objective. Can you spot all the keywords in this version of his resume?

And the Top Two Keywords Are ...

For his third resume, Eduardo decided to place the topmost defining keywords in his Job Objective statement, as well as incorporating the other keywords into the body of his resume. Identifying the top two keywords can help you focus your resume, cover letter, and even your job interview answers. By narrowing down your qualifications to simply a few essentials, you can make your documents and responses focused and relevant.

Read the following job post for his third application; then check out his matching resume.

Sales Representative

Employer is currently looking for a <u>Sales Representative</u> to focus on new, <u>business-to-business account development</u> in our Facility Services business. Responsibilities include <u>prospecting</u>, <u>cold calling</u>, setting <u>appointments</u> with <u>prospects</u>, <u>presenting programs</u>, and delivering a <u>sales quota</u>. Sales Representatives may also transport samples of products for presentations. Employer provides a thorough training program, including product knowledge and development of our company sales process.

- ◆ Valid driver's license

- ◆ High school diploma required; Bachelor's degree preferred

- ◆ New business-to-business experience preferred

- ◆ Minimum of 1 year outside sales experience required; 2 or more years preferred

- ◆ Knowledgeable in Microsoft Office applications (including Outlook, Word, Excel, PowerPoint), Internet/Intranet, and Contact Management System preferred

---

Trolling for Your Ideal Job

What if you're not applying for a specific job, but rather simply putting your resume up on one of the huge job boards for a recruiter to find? How can you tailor that resume? Easy! Write a resume for your ideal job. Here's how:

1. Write a job description for your ideal job, using your imagination to picture exactly what the job would entail and what sort of company culture you want that job to be in (for example, young and hip, or traditional and conservative).

2. Make a list of keywords that define all the things you want in that job (for instance, working with "teens" or doing "outside sales").

3. Write your resume for the ideal job you've just described, being sure to include all the keywords from your list.

If you follow these steps to the T, your marketing piece has a strong chance of drawing your ideal job to you. Wouldn't that be cool?

Let's follow a few job seekers to see how they created their lists of keywords, then sliced and diced them into their resumes.

Mr. Green Goes Searching

Peter Dubro is a solar energy engineer who knows exactly what kind of job he wants. He made the following list of keywords that are required in his line of work:

Master's (degree)	Environmental management
Energy engineering	Project management
Renewable energy	Installation
Solar	Performance metrics
Wind	Shade characteristics
Photovoltaic (PV)	ArchiCAD
Battery	AutoCAD

> **Bonus Check**
>
> Technical job seekers often create a Technical Skills section on their resumes where they can make lists of their technical languages, hardware, and software. Other professionals who might find this technique useful are healthcare practitioners and anyone else with many items they want a search engine to find.

Check out Peter's resume in the Green section of the Portfolio of Sample Resumes at the back of the book to see how he wove most of the keywords into the text of his resume. For his many computer skills, he created a special Skills section where he could list dozens of technical terms.

Healthy Keywords

When Amy Moore wrote her resume for a program management position within a healthcare setting (found in the Healthcare section in the Portfolio of Sample Resumes), she was sure to include the following list of keywords. She found most of these keywords in a job post on a hospital website, for which she was tailoring this version of her resume. Here is Amy's list of keywords:

Project management	Training
Program management	Leadership
Healthcare	Contract negotiations
Medical	Marketing strategies
Budget	Strategic partnerships

Publicity	Education
Patient satisfaction	Community
Quality of care	Assess
Physicians	B.A.
Supervise	

Amy managed to squeeze all of these keywords into her resume so she would meet the search engine requirements for the job.

Online Expert Knows Her Keywords

As a User Interface Architect, Paula White knows a lot about how people use search engines to find what they want on the Internet. You can see from her resume (found in the High-Tech section of the Portfolio of Sample Resumes) that she thought through the keyword issue when creating it. Here are the most important keywords she included:

> **Job Hunt Hint**
>
> The search engine will find a keyword even if it's part of a larger word. For instance, if the keyword is "leader," the engine will pick up "leadership" in your resume because it contains the word "leader."

Interface architect	Analyst
User experience	Statistics
Interaction	Navigation
Design	Data
Development	Wireframes
Usability	System
UI	Visio
Testing	Dreamweaver
IT	MS Office Suite
Technology	HTML
Website	CSS
Architecture	XML
Analysis	JavaScript

These keywords are incorporated so naturally into Paula's resume, the human reader may not realize she consciously put them there. However, the recruiter's search engine quickly picks them out as if they were neon lights in the dark.

The Least You Need to Know

◆ Before writing your resume, figure out what job you want next.

◆ Scrutinize job posts to identify keywords that need to be in your resume.

◆ Each time you apply for a job, adjust your resume so it contains all the keywords for that specific job.

◆ One easy way to insert keywords is to create a Skills or Technical Skills section on your resume.

Eduardo Ortiz

123 Blake Circle • Anaheim, CA 12345 • (123) 555-5555 • edortiz@bamboo.com

JOB OBJECTIVE

Customer Service Representative

HIGHLIGHTS OF QUALIFICATIONS

- ❑ History of representing organizations with professionalism, poise, and integrity.
- ❑ Adept at handling a high quota of phone calls in a fast-paced environment with calm and grace.
- ❑ A hard-working team member who gets along well with everyone.
- ❑ Bilingual: Spanish and English.

PROFESSIONAL ACCOMPLISHMENTS

2006-pres.   Henderson Motor Club, Anaheim, CA
Customer Care Representative

- ❑ Managed numerous customer accounts through the Customer Service Call Center, consistently following up to ensure resolution.
- ❑ Trained new customer service reps to appreciate and clearly communicate membership benefits and promotions.
- ❑ Cultivated excellent long-term relationships with members using a friendly approach to questions and problems.
- ❑ Recognized by management for good attendance, dependability, and attention to detail.

2003-06   Main Street Library, Santa Barbara, CA
Assistant Librarian

- ❑ Assisted patrons with various levels of technical ability to use the library's computer screens to navigate the library system.
- ❑ Showed extreme patience and interest when answering questions and helping patrons with forms processing.
- ❑ Received regular, outstanding feedback from Head Librarian.

2001-03   Pro Pet Products, Los Angeles, CA
Marketing Assistant

- ❑ Presented products and addressed questions from prospective customers at trade shows.
- ❑ Interacted daily with team members to synchronize completion of projects.

EDUCATION

Ongoing coursework in Intercultural Studies
Anaheim University, Anaheim, CA

COMMUNITY SERVICE

2004-pres.   KidPride, Teen Mentor
2003-05   Disaster Relief and Prevention, Neighborhood Coordinator

Eduardo Ortiz

123 Blake Circle • Anaheim, CA 12345 • (123) 555-5555 • edortiz@bamboo.com

JOB OBJECTIVE

Marketing Representative in the field of Education

HIGHLIGHTS OF QUALIFICATIONS

- ❑ History of representing organizations with professionalism and integrity.
- ❑ Creative and enthusiastic about participating in community educational programs.
- ❑ Demonstrated communication skills, both written and oral.
- ❑ A hard-working team member who gets along well with everyone.

PROFESSIONAL ACCOMPLISHMENTS

2006-pres. Henderson Motor Club, Anaheim, CA
Customer Care Representative

- ❑ Handle numerous calls, promoting enrollment and contract programs, often exceeding daily call quotas.
- ❑ Schedule and implement presentations for new representatives, to teach the strategies and tactics for excellent customer service.
- ❑ Maintain positive reputation and cultivate excellent long-term relationships with members, using a friendly approach to questions and problems.
- ❑ Recognized by management for superior service to the company.

2003-06 Main Street Library, Santa Barbara, CA
Assistant Librarian

- ❑ Assisted in tutoring and test preparation programs as part of the library's instructional services.
- ❑ Coordinated with local schools, principals, counselors, PTA presidents, school districts, and community organizations to generate grassroots marketing campaigns that involved word-of-mouth sales, community events, referral sources, and support of local employers.
- ❑ Received regular, outstanding feedback for positive attitude and strong work ethic from Head Librarian. Known as a self-starter.

2001-03 Pro Pet Products, Los Angeles, CA
Marketing Assistant

- ❑ Presented products and addressed questions from prospective customers at trade shows.
- ❑ Interacted daily with team members via computer to synchronize completion of projects.

EDUCATION

Ongoing coursework toward Bachelor's Degree in Intercultural Studies
Anaheim University, Anaheim, CA

COMMUNITY SERVICE

2004-pres. KidPride, Teen Mentor
2003-05 Disaster Relief and Prevention, Neighborhood Coordinator

Eduardo Ortiz
123 Blake Circle • Anaheim, CA 12345 • (123) 555-5555 • edortiz@bamboo.com

JOB OBJECTIVE
Sales Representative focusing on business-to-business account development

HIGHLIGHTS OF QUALIFICATIONS
- ❑ History of representing organizations with professionalism and enthusiasm.
- ❑ Experience with business-to-business account development and outside sales, including prospecting, cold calling, and presenting sales programs.
- ❑ Adept at maintaining a positive atmosphere in the workplace and resolving problems with calm and grace.
- ❑ A hard-working team member who gets along well with everyone.

PROFESSIONAL ACCOMPLISHMENTS
2006-pres. Henderson Motor Club, Anaheim, CA
Customer Care Representative (a membership sales position)
- ❑ Recognized by management for often meeting the weekly sales quota and for superior service to the company.
- ❑ Trained new customer care reps to sell-up by clearly communicating membership benefits and promotions.
- ❑ Generated new prospects and cultivated excellent long-term relationships with members, using a friendly approach to questions and problems.
- ❑ Handled member concerns with diplomacy, and followed through by setting up appointments to ensure resolution.

2003-06 Main Street Library, Santa Barbara, CA
Assistant Librarian
- ❑ Assisted patrons with various levels of technical ability to use the library's public computers.
- ❑ Showed extreme patience and interest when answering questions and helping patrons from diverse backgrounds.
- ❑ Received regular, outstanding feedback from Head Librarian.

2001-03 Pro Pet Products, Los Angeles, CA
Marketing Assistant
- ❑ Presented products and addressed questions from prospective customers at trade shows.
- ❑ Interacted daily with team members to synchronize completion of projects.

EDUCATION / LICENSE
Ongoing coursework toward Bachelor's Degree in Intercultural Studies
Anaheim University, Anaheim, CA

High School Diploma, Anaheim, CA

Valid California State Driver's License

COMPUTER SKILLS
Microsoft Office (Outlook, Work, Excel, PowerPoint), Internet / Intranet, and ACT (similar to Contact Management System)

Chapter 3

Insider Tips for a Great Resume

In This Chapter

◆ Designing a resume that creates the future you want

◆ Using past successes for future rewards

◆ Keeping secrets from the employer

◆ Making your resume quick and inviting to read

◆ To lie or not to lie?

Writing the perfect resume takes a little time and concentration, but when you finish, you'll feel like a million bucks—or as if you could *make* a million bucks!

Trust me, time spent working on a resume is time well spent. I've seen lots of people walk away with finished resumes, saying they never knew they could look so good on paper (or onscreen); they never thought their work history could appear so impressive; or they never thought they could look qualified for something they'd never done in the past.

A few principles lie behind the kind of job-winning resume I'm talking about. This chapter discusses key concepts that will not only provide you with resume wisdom, they'll also solve every resume problem you'll encounter. At the end of this chapter you'll find sample resumes that demonstrate these principles.

The Commandments

Before you boot up your computer (or get your ballpoint pen and paper if you're sitting at your kitchen table), I want to impart a few tricks that even some professional resume writers don't know. These concepts can make the difference between a boring resume that just sits on a manager's desk (or, even worse, gets thrown away) and one that demands, "Read me, read me! Call me, call me!" These resume tips are so important I've dubbed them "The Resume Commandments."

The Resume Commandments

    I. Thou shalt not write about your past; thou shalt write about your future!

    II. Thou shalt not confess.

    III. Thou shalt not write job descriptions; thou shalt write achievement statements.

    IV. Thou shalt not write about stuff you don't want to do again.

    V. Thou shalt say less rather than more.

    VI. Thou shalt not write in long paragraphs; thou shalt use bullet points.

    VII. Thou shalt not lie.

Now let's look at each of these commandments to understand why they are so important.

Thou Shalt Not Write About Your Past

> **Career Casualty**
>
> Some folks think a list of statements should end with the best one. Not on a resume! What if an impatient or busy reader never gets to the end of the list? Always start a list with your best item.

Because your resume is a marketing piece for your next job, it concerns your future, not your past. If you're writing a chronological resume (explained in Chapter 4), don't write your resume as if it were a historical document. Even though the body of your chronological format is structured around your work history (your past), the achievement statements should support your Job Objective statement (your future).

"My resume is about my future?" you ask. "But it talks about my work history and what I did at my previous jobs. Doesn't that mean it's about my past?" That's exactly what most people think, but the secret to getting a new and exciting job is to build your resume around the job you're striving for, not the ones you've previously held. So before you even start writing your resume, you need to plan what kind of work you want to do next.

Create a resume that's about your future by imagining that you're an artist with an empty canvas (such as your computer screen) in front of you. Your assignment is to paint a picture of yourself at your next job, using any of the following four tools:

◆ Your experience, such as previous job titles, volunteer work, or school projects.

◆ Your skill areas, such as management, computer knowledge, or sales.

◆ Your concerns, such as the environment, homelessness, or human rights.

◆ Your personality, such as dependability, sense of humor, or ability to communicate.

When you're finished, you should have a word-picture of you working for your next employer.

What will the employer think of your future-oriented resume? At first glance, she may assume she's reading about your past, but as she gets drawn into it, she'll find herself imagining that you're working for her. And that's what will make her want to call you for an interview.

Thou Shalt Not Confess

"Forgive me, Father, it's been a year since I last updated my resume," you cry. Have no fear, my friend; I'm here to fill you in on all the tips, including this one: don't let one trace of that confessional tone leak onto your resume!

Why? Because your resume is not a confessional—you don't have to tell all. Don't waste space or distract the reader by putting anything on your resume that doesn't support your job objective or cast you in the best light possible with regard to experience, ability, age, and personality. (In Part 2, I talk about how to work with these issues specifically.)

Be selective. Pick through all your information and choose only what's relevant to your job objective. The resumes later in this chapter show you how to apply this commandment.

Shooting Yourself in the Foot

Teresa Smith was having trouble finding a position as a marketing director. She needed a job desperately and decided to go for a position as an administrative assistant. If she listed her M.B.A. degree under her Education heading, she knew she would look overqualified for a clerical job. Take a look at her resume at the end of this chapter. Notice that she decided not to include her degree in order to improve her chances of getting an interview.

If you're applying for a job for which you might appear overqualified, consider leaving the heavyweight qualifications off your resume. Remember, your resume is not a confessional; you aren't obligated to disclose all.

Get Your Priorities Straight

Trudy Caldwell had been a secretary and receptionist for a number of years and wanted to move into the field of human resources. In preparing for her career change, she had gone back to college and earned a degree in human resources while continuing her occupation as a secretary.

Notice how Trudy prioritized information on her resume (at the end of this chapter) to make the most marketable items pop out at the reader. Because her degree was more marketable than her work history, she decided to show it off by positioning her Education section near the top of her resume. This helps the reader quickly see that she's a new graduate in human resources who worked her

Job Hunt Hint

Don't be afraid to leave things off your resume if you're worried those items might make you look like the wrong candidate for the job. It's acceptable to delete information that isn't relevant to your job objective, as long as you don't create gaps in your work history.

way through school. Trudy then de-emphasized her former job titles by placing Work History at the bottom of the page and listing the job titles after the company names.

When a busy manager receives your resume, she'll skim it very quickly to see whether she's interested in reading it word for word. For that reason, it's vital that you place your material according to how relevant it is to your job objective. Prioritizing correctly will make your resume declare, "I'm the one you're looking for!" (You'll read more about this concept in Part 2.)

By prioritizing the sections of your resume, you can highlight aspects that are most relevant to your job objective. For instance, you might wish to move your volunteer experience near the top of your resume if it's particularly meaningful to the job you're applying for.

Bonus Check

If your resume generates job interviews for work you're not interested in, something is wrong with it! Before sending your resume to another employer, revise it according to the following points to ensure that it markets you for the type of work you want to pursue:

- ◆ Use a resume format that highlights the appropriate skills and experience.
- ◆ Don't mention responsibilities you don't want to hold at your next job.

Drop Irrelevant Info

For the past two years, Christopher Bond spent most of his time managing a family crisis, a situation he decided was not appropriate to put on his resume. During that time span, he did some freelance catalog production for a former colleague.

Notice how Christopher constructed the Work History section on his resume (at the end of this chapter) without mentioning his personal situation, even though it consumed about 80 percent of his time and energy.

Like Christopher, you may have a situation in your work history that you don't want to mention on your resume. As long as you don't create a void in your work history, it's perfectly fine not to bring up the sticky matter on your resume. To find creative ways to deal with tricky issues in your work history, turn to Chapter 7.

It's Okay to Understate Experience

When applying for a specific position, use the job posting as a checklist for what should appear on your resume. Without copying the ad's exact wording, try to match each of the qualifications (and keywords) the employer is seeking in his candidate.

Sara Cartwright had 15 years of experience as an auditor and accountant. Because jobs were scarce in her field, she was compelled to take a lower position than she would have liked. In creating her resume, she thought that if she put "15 years as an accounting professional" in her Summary of Qualifications section, she might seem too high-powered because the job announcement asked for 5 to 7 years of experience.

As you can see from her resume (at the end of this chapter), Sara decided to write, "More than seven years as an accounting professional." Sara's revised statement is true (because 15 years is certainly more than 7 years) and makes her look more suitable for the job she's seeking.

You may choose to generalize your qualifications on your resume to downplay them. This is perfectly acceptable as long as your statements are honest.

The second commandment is going to come in handy when you are trying to figure out …

- How far back to go in your work history.

- What to say about gaps in your employment.

- Whether to present your volunteer work.

- How to list sensitive issues.

Your resume should serve as a teaser. It should contain statements that say enough to spark the manager's interest without giving away all the details, especially when those details are about a sensitive issue that would be better addressed in the job interview, if at all.

As you set out to write your resume, let this commandment give you peace of mind, knowing you don't have to write a complete autobiography.

Thou Shalt Not Write Job Descriptions

If you were an employer, what three questions would you ask a job candidate? You would probably ask …

- Do you have any experience?

- Are you good at what you do?

- Do you like this kind of work?

Don't be shy—answer "yes" to all of these questions by writing about achievements instead of job duties on your resume. Achievement statements are the most powerful way to say, "I'm good at what I do!"

Make sure your achievements are stated appropriately for the type of work you're interested in. For example, a salesperson's achievement statements will probably be much more dramatic (for example: exceeded sales quotas by 300 percent) than the ones that appear on an accountant or technician's resume (for example: used spreadsheet applications to analyze reports for upper management).

Examine the two resumes for Diane Short at the end of this chapter. The first is a job-description resume (blah!); the second is an achievement-oriented resume (yes!). See how much more enticing the second one is? Diane's achievement statements provide the following information:

◆ She has particular experiences.

◆ She's good at what she does.

◆ She believes in and likes her work.

She's given the employer three good reasons to call her for an interview.

I expand on this commandment in Chapter 8 when you write your achievement statements. At this point, I want you to understand the concept of using your resume to brag a little (or a lot) about your successes.

Thou Shalt Not Write About Stuff You Don't Want to Do

def•i•ni•tion

Nondisclosure (not mentioning something) is not the same as lying (telling something that isn't true). Nondisclosure is acceptable on a resume. Lying is not!

Writing your resume is like writing your next job description, because everything you put in your resume suggests what you're eager to do in your new job. Never write about duties you don't want to do again, no matter how good you are at them! *Nondisclosure* on your resume could be the ticket to landing a job you really love.

For example, when George was applying for a database programming position at a high-tech firm, he specifically did not want to supervise any staff. Even though in his previous job he had been in charge of a department and had been commended for his ability to build team spirit under adverse conditions, he was determined not to acquire that kind of responsibility in his next job. In his resume, he spoke about his many programming projects, but never once mentioned that he had managed anyone. Consequently, he attracted a programming job he loves with no supervisory responsibilities.

I'll remind you about this commandment as you go through the steps to create your resume. For now, just keep in mind that you are in the seat of power: you get to create your future by choosing what to put in and what to leave out of your resume!

Thou Shalt Say Less Rather Than More

Ah, the oxymoron that works so well in marketing: less is more. Let's consider why it has withstood the test of time.

When it comes to things we all value, time sits near the top of the list, along with wealth and health. We say things such as "time is money" and "it's not worth my time." Because time is at a premium in today's hectic world, it stands to reason that a promotional piece that takes less time to read is more likely to succeed than a lengthy one. Therefore, less text is more effective at grabbing the reader's attention.

Following the "less is more" theory has another advantage. By distilling all of your skills and experience into a minimum of words on one or two sheets of paper, you automatically put down only the very best stuff. So less is more in the sense that even though you provide less information, it's all high-quality information, which makes the resume more impressive.

The Eight-Second Test

In today's job market, your resume has only about eight seconds to catch an employer's attention. In eight seconds, an employer scans your resume and decides whether she will invest more time to consider you as a job candidate. The secret to passing the eight-second test is to make your resume look inviting and quick to read. That's why I recommend having a one-page resume if possible. Having a one-pager says, "I'm organized, and I'm not a motor-mouth."

Goody Two-Pages

For those who have a beefy career history or lengthy list of must-read accomplishments, one page may not be enough. If you're one of those people, go for it—just don't exceed two pages unless you're sure the reader is expecting more. For instance, if you're applying for an academic or scientific position, you'd probably have a seven- or eight-pager called a curriculum vitae, which I discuss in Chapter 4.

If your resume is just a little more than a page, do your best to get it down to one page by using your editing and computer graphics skills. Then ask yourself, "Is it easy to read?" If the print is too small or dense, you're better off with a two-page resume.

Thou Shalt Not Write in Paragraphs

Many resumes have long paragraphs filled with juicy information. The problem is that a busy manager is unlikely to read a resume made up of long paragraphs. A paragraph demands too much time to read.

Do the reader (and yourself) a favor by using bullet points to break your material into bite-sized pieces. A bullet at the beginning of a statement effectively says, "Here's an independent thought that's quick and easy to read," whereas a paragraph implies that one has to read the whole thing to get the full meaning.

For the best effect, start each achievement statement on a new line so that all the bullet points line up on the left, like the following:

- Made classroom presentations to students K–8, demonstrating the importance of art to man's physical and mental survival.

- Tutored high school students of Project Read, integrating reading and writing to offer new perspectives and respect for their own life stories.

- Conducted cultural field trips to sites including businesses, performing arts centers, and museums.

In case you're not convinced that bullet statements are a good idea, take a look at the two versions of Marty Ramirez's resume, at the end of this chapter. You'll see the same resume in two graphic layouts: the first uses paragraphs; the second uses bullet points to break up the blocks of print. Which do you think looks quicker to read?

There is an exception to the "no paragraph" commandment. In the Summary of Qualifications section it's acceptable to use two paragraphs, each of which is no longer than three lines and begins with an introductory word or phrase in bold text (more about this technique in Chapter 6).

Thou Shalt Not Lie

I'm starting to sound like your mother, aren't I? I have to say it anyway: never tell a lie on your resume. If you're wondering what kinds of lies I'm talking about, here are some that frequently appear on resumes and are apt to catch an employer's attention:

- Stating experience at a particular place of employment where you never worked

- Misrepresenting the level of responsibility you held (for example, listing "Art Director" when you were really a graphic designer)

- Listing a school you didn't attend

- Claiming to have a degree you didn't obtain

- Taking credit for someone else's achievement

- Overstating skill levels in a technical field

Lying on your resume can cause more damage to your career than you may realize. Here are some good reasons to create a resume that contains only the truth:

- A lie on your resume can undermine your self-confidence during a job interview. If you're anything like me, just knowing that the interviewer might ask a question about your fib will make you nervous. To make matters worse, noticeable anxiety will most likely make a bad impression on your potential employer.

- After you're hired, a falsehood on your resume can be grounds for termination. If your resume is examined as part of your promotion review, you could lose your job if someone discovers a lie.

- A lie on your resume might indicate that you don't believe you're qualified for the job. Maybe you need to rethink your job objective or perhaps you need counseling to build your self-esteem.

As you can see, it's in your short- and long-term interest not to lie on your resume.

The Least You Need to Know

- Write about your future on your resume, not about your past.

- You don't have to tell everything in your resume—stick to what's relevant and marketable.

- Use your resume to talk about your achievements, not monotonous job descriptions.

- Don't write about anything that you don't want to do again.

- Grab the reader's attention by being concise and using bullet point statements.

- Be creative but honest in your resume.

Teresa Smith

123 Serendipity Lane
Pierre, SD 12345
(123) 555-1234
teresasmith@bamboo.com

JOB OBJECTIVE

Administrative Assistant

HIGHLIGHTS OF QUALIFICATIONS

- Seven years combined administrative and research experience.
- Adept at handling sensitive business issues with discretion and professionalism.
- Cited as one of the top administrative assistants at Kramer Associates, Inc.

PROFESSIONAL EXPERIENCE

2004-pres. **Kramer Associates, Inc.,** Pierre, SD
ADMINISTRATIVE ASSISTANT

- Charged with organizing and generating correspondence for major clients involved in confidential government activities.
- Re-designed the office computer system, enabling 125% more work to be processed.
- Commended for creating weekly "Casual Day," which brought a friendlier and more cooperative atmosphere to the workplace.
- Prepared legal and business documents using word processing and spreadsheet applications.

2002-2004 **University of South Dakota,** Pierre, SD
RESEARCH ASSISTANT

- Conducted bibliographic research that contributed to paper delivered at the National Psychology Symposium in Washington, D.C.
- Word-processed voluminous notes and provided accurate transcriptions of university and professional lectures.
- Translated German scientific text and compiled readers for undergraduate and graduate classes.

EDUCATION

B.A., Business Administration & German
University of South Dakota, Pierre, SD, 2002

Trudy Caldwell

123 Fremont Avenue • San Francisco, CA 12345
(123) 555-1234 • tcaldwell@bamboo.com

Human Resources Professional

SUMMARY OF QUALIFICATIONS

- More than five years of experience in business office work with recent assignments in personnel administration.
- Competent project manager with an eye for added results.
- Eager to pursue a career in human resources.

EDUCATION

M.S., Human Resources, University of California, San Francisco, CA, 2007

RELEVANT ACCOMPLISHMENTS

PERSONNEL ADMINISTRATION

- Processed a minimum of 100 applications per week, using a database to file and sort data accessed by 12 managers. (Barstow & Bigelow, Inc.)
- Conducted orientations for new hires: explained company policies and gave employee tours of company. (Goodman Lumber)
- Coordinated payroll data by compiling information from time card machine and tallying employee vacation calendars. (Barstow & Bigelow, Inc.)

PROJECT MANAGEMENT

- Redesigned the mail system to expedite sorting and delivery. (Williams Sonoma Co.)
- Managed a 4,000-piece direct mail effort that met seasonal marketing deadlines despite heavy in-house workloads. (Barstow & Bigelow, Inc.)
- Initiated a company-wide recycling program that resulted in excellent publicity for the firm. (Goodman Lumber)

WORK HISTORY

2006-present	Executive Assistant, Barstow & Bigelow, Inc., San Francisco, CA
2003-2006	Administrative Assistant, Williams Sonoma Co., San Francisco, CA
1997-2003	Receptionist, Goodman Lumber, Daly City, CA

Christopher Bond

123 Piedmont Avenue
Atlanta, GA 12345
123-555-1234
chrisbond@bamboo.com

Catalog Production Coordinator

SUMMARY OF QUALIFICATIONS

- Seven years as a print production professional, working in corporate and independent settings.
- Degree in journalism with additional training at daily news publication.
- Noted for accelerating production through strong managerial skills.

PROFESSIONAL EXPERIENCE

2008-pres.   **Thomas Govington** (independent artist), Atlanta, GA
BROCHURE PRODUCTION SPECIALIST
- Designed and coordinated production of a four-color brochure that portrayed the artist's talent in three media: paint on canvas, ceramics, and bronze.

2003-08   **Johnson Paper, Incorporated,** Atlanta, GA
CATALOG PRODUCTION COORDINATOR
- Managed full production of a 400-page catalog distributed to more than 4,000 retailers and 80 distributors.
- Coordinated deadlines among six departments that sprinted from creative to shipping in less than two months per run.
- Supervised 35 artists and technicians; handled relations with more than 15 vendors.
- Represented the Production Department at management meetings.
- Instructed local college interns in print production techniques and systems.

2000-02   **Emory University Press,** Atlanta, GA
PRINT PRODUCTION INTERN
- Gained hands-on experience in every aspect of print production, working under the press's most senior printer.
- Frequently assisted in technically demanding assignments for major clients.

EDUCATION AND AFFILIATIONS

B.A., Journalism, Emory University, Atlanta, GA, 1994
Junior year abroad in Madrid for work-study program at prominent newspaper

American Printers Association
International Paper and Print Production Institute

SARA CARTWRIGHT, CPA
123 Turandot Street • Oakland, CA 12345
(123) 555-1234 • scartwright@bamboo.com

OBJECTIVE

A position in Audit Management

SUMMARY OF QUALIFICATIONS

- More than seven years as an accounting professional with particular strength in conducting audits.
- Skilled at gaining cooperation from internal and external professionals.
- Experienced consultant to executive management on sensitive financial issues.

PROFESSIONAL EXPERIENCE

2008-pres.   Auditing Operations Manager, Anderson Electronics, San Leandro, CA
- Realized $40,000 in six months for the company by discovering several major unnoticed past-due collections.
- Audited expense reports to verify compliance with company and governmental policies.
- Implemented CEO- and CFO-directed projects to restructure accounting procedures.

2002-08   Senior Auditor, Internal Accounting, Dartmouth Enterprises, Oakland, CA
- Conducted quarterly and annual audits for headquarters and 15 branch offices.
- Guided management through setup of accounting departments in four new business units located in separate Western states.
- Facilitated external audits that showed 100% compliance with professional standards.
- Authored analysis sections of SEC annual 10K and quarterly 10Q corporate reports.
- Designated Senior Auditor after four months with company as Internal Auditor.

1994-02   Accountant, Brokaw, Farnsworth & Associates, CPAs, San Francisco, CA
- Provided auditing services to corporate clients engaged in international manufacturing.
- Served as financial consultant to one of the nation's largest banking institutions.
- Prepared federal and state tax forms for a wide range of corporate structures.

EDUCATION AND CERTIFICATION

B.S., Accounting, California State University, Hayward, CA
CPA since 2001

(Job-Description Resume)

DIANE SHORT
Marketing Communications Director

123 Walnut Avenue, #2, Berkeley, CA 12345, d_short@bamboo.com (123) 555-1234

SUMMARY OF QUALIFICATIONS

- More than 10 years in marketing with recent experience as Director, Marketing Communications for the largest manufacturer in its classification.
- Creative thinker whose ideas have directly increased profitability.
- Manage multiple projects at once, with strict adherence to time and budget constraints.

PROFESSIONAL EXPERIENCE

2004-pres.   Macy's, San Francisco
Director, Marketing Communications, 2008-pres.
Director, Public Relations & Licensing, 2005-2008
Marketing Consultant, 2004-2005

- Created sales collateral and ran creative aspects for advertising campaign.
- Developed and managed a national publicity program.
- Authored and designed press kits.
- Developed GWPs (gift with purchase).
- Collaborated with University of San Francisco Medical Center to design a promotion.
- Currently developing a merchandise strategy for a TV program.
- Analyzed competition, oversaw product development, approved prototypes, and managed business relations with licensees.
- Designed merchandise packaging and displays; negotiated with licensees to use visuals.

2000-2004   Delaney Advertising, Inc., New York City
Director, Marketing Communications Services
- Directed the New York office.
- Supervised staff and managed photographic production and budgets.

1996-2000   Gap, Inc., San Francisco
Media Coordinator
- Developed and implemented advertising campaigns. Managed creative development and execution. Monitored media budget.

EDUCATION

B.A., Communication Studies, with a minor in Business Administration
San Francisco State University, San Francisco, CA

Multimedia Program, University of California, San Francisco, currently enrolled

(Achievement-Oriented Resume)

DIANE SHORT
Marketing Communications Director
123 Walnut Avenue, #2, Berkeley, CA 12345, d_short@bamboo.com (123) 555-1234

SUMMARY OF QUALIFICATIONS

- More than 10 years in marketing with recent experience as Director, Marketing Communications for the largest manufacturer in its classification.
- Creative thinker whose ideas have directly increased profitability.
- Manage multiple projects at once, with strict adherence to time and budget constraints.

PROFESSIONAL EXPERIENCE

2004-pres. MACY'S, San Francisco **Director, Marketing Communications,** 2008-pres.
Director, Public Relations & Licensing, 2005-2008
Marketing Consultant, 2004-2005

- Created sales collateral (including videos) and ran the creative efforts for national advertising campaign that established Macy's as the manufacturer of quality products.
- Developed and managed a national publicity program that increased retail sales more than 5% and dramatically enhanced brand recognition.
- Authored and designed the first press kit that clearly defined the company's image and product range.
- Enhanced product value and increased sales by developing GWPs (gift with purchase).
- To position company as an advocate for women's health, collaborated with University of San Francisco Medical Center to design a promotion that shared proceeds.
- Currently developing a merchandise strategy for an hour-long cable television program to air Christmas of next year.
- Analyzed competition, oversaw product development, approved prototypes, and managed business relations with national and international licensees.
- Designed merchandise packaging and displays, and successfully negotiated with licensees and retailers to utilize these visuals to maintain consistent image.

2000-2004 DELANEY ADVERTISING, INC., New York City, **Director, Marketing Communications**

- Directed the New York office for this national full-service advertising company.
- Supervised staff and managed high-volume photographic production and budgets.

1996-2000 GAP, INC., San Francisco, **Media Coordinator**

- Developed and implemented advertising campaigns. Managed all phases of creative development and execution. Monitored media budget.

EDUCATION

B.A., Communication Studies, with a minor in Business Administration
San Francisco State University, San Francisco, CA
Multimedia Program, University of California, San Francisco, currently enrolled

(Resume with Paragraph Formatting)

Marty Ramirez
123 Antelope Avenue
Boston, MA 12345
(123) 555-1234
mramirez@bamboo.com

OBJECTIVE

Field Representative for Local 510

DEMONSTRATED EFFECTIVENESS

Effectively negotiated and arbitrated grievances and contracts. Served on three contract negotiating committees, each strengthening the union shop. Co-developed first steward training classes for Local 510. Enforced collective bargaining agreements, health and safety standards, and grievance procedures as Rotating Floor Steward or Permanent Shop Steward since 1990. Chaired strike committees in 2003 and 2006, developing picketing plans, choosing picket captains, and informing membership of legal behavior on the picket line. Co-developed and led Local 510 affirmative action workshops, using bilingual and bicultural skills to stress commonalties among people. Conducted training and strategy sessions for U.N.H. labor and academic professionals, resulting in Partnership Programs.

WORK HISTORY

1987-pres.   **Journeyman Installer**
SIGN, DISPLAY, AND ALLIED CRAFTS, LOCAL 510, I.B.P.A.T.

2004   **Primary Campaign Manager**
WILSON RILES, JR., MAYORAL CANDIDATE, BOSTON, MA

2001-04   **Teacher, World Cultures/Spanish/Bilingual**
OAKLAND UNIFIED SCHOOL DISTRICT

EDUCATION

B.A., Comparative Culture, University of New Hampshire, 1987
Graduate Studies, Latin American Culture, Harvard University

MEMBERSHIPS

West County Central Labor Council
Local 510 Political Action Committee
Boston Direct Action Committee
Former Member, A.P.R.I. & C.B. T.U.

(Resume with Bullet-Point Statements)

Marty Ramirez
123 Antelope Avenue, Boston, MA 12345
(123) 555-1234, mramirez@bamboo.com

OBJECTIVE

Field Representative for Local 510

DEMONSTRATED EFFECTIVENESS

- Effectively negotiated and arbitrated grievances and contracts.
    - Served on three contract negotiating committees, each strengthening the union shop.
    - Co-developed first steward training classes for Local 510.
    - Enforced collective bargaining agreements, health and safety standards, and grievance procedures as Rotating Floor Steward or Permanent Shop Steward since 1990.
- Chaired strike committees in 2003 and 2006, developing picketing plans, choosing picket captains, and informing membership of legal behavior on the picket line.
- Co-developed and led Local 510 affirmative action workshops, using bilingual and bicultural skills to stress commonalties among people.
- Conducted training and strategy sessions for U.N.H. labor and academic professionals, resulting in Partnership Programs.

WORK HISTORY

1987-pres.   **Journeyman Installer**
Sign, Display, and Allied Crafts, Local 510, I.B.P.A.T.

2004   **Primary Campaign Manager**
Wilson Riles, Jr., mayoral candidate, Boston, MA

2001-04   **Teacher, World Cultures/Spanish/Bilingual**
Boston Unified School District

EDUCATION

B.A., Comparative Culture, University of New Hampshire, 1987
Graduate Studies, Latin American Culture, Harvard University

MEMBERSHIPS

West County Central Labor Council
Local 510 Political Action Committee
Boston Direct Action Committee
Former Member, A.P.R.I. & C.B. T.U.

Part **2**

Putting Together a Resume That Wins

Picture Christopher Columbus standing at the bow of his ship looking out at the horizon, about to embark upon his famous voyage of 1492. Not knowing how vast the Atlantic Ocean was or exactly what he was getting into, he probably had a major anxiety attack, which is a normal response to a seemingly impossible task. To keep his sanity, he must have taken this monumental trip one knot at a time until he finally spotted land some 34 days after setting sail.

Like Columbus, you're probably feeling a little overwhelmed as you set out to put your life on paper. Most job seekers feel this way. To keep your stress level down and help you reach your destination (getting a perfect job) as quickly as possible, I've divided the process into manageable pieces, which I talk about in this part of the book.

Turn the page and read about the first of six steps for writing your resume. Set aside about three hours (that's an average length of time to write a resume if all goes smoothly). Follow each step, and, like Columbus, you'll reach land. If you get stuck on one step, don't worry about it—just go on to the next step and come back to the hard one later.

Chapter 4

Step One: Choose the Right Resume Format

In This Chapter

- ◆ Why choose a chronological format?
- ◆ When to use a functional resume
- ◆ How to create a combination resume
- ◆ How a curriculum vitae differs from a resume

You've probably heard the real estate adage: "location, location, location." In resume writing, the adage is "format, format, format." The format of your resume is so crucial that it can make or break your chances for a job interview. The right format will immediately tell the reader you're a top-notch candidate for the job.

The three basic resume formats are chronological, functional, and combination. This chapter covers the guidelines and shows you templates for these three formats. It also discusses resume formats for academic and scientific applications. In a very short time, you'll make one of the most important decisions in the resume writing process: choosing the best format.

Highlighting Your Chronology

The chronological resume is the most traditional resume format. It's been around for years and has done well for millions of job seekers.

The template on the following page for a chronological resume outlines the content of a resume in this format. Notice this format highlights a job seeker's dates of employment, places of employment, and job titles (the chronology of the person's work history) by using them as headings. Achievements are then listed under these headings.

(Chronological Resume Template)

Name
Street
City, State Zip
Phone, E-mail

JOB OBJECTIVE

The job you want next

SUMMARY OF QUALIFICATIONS

- How much experience you have in the field of your job objective, in a related field, or using the skills required for your new position.
- An overall career accomplishment that shows you'd be good at this job.
- What someone would say about you as a recommendation.

PROFESSIONAL EXPERIENCE

20xx-pres.   **Company Name, City, State**
Job Title
- An accomplishment you are proud of that shows you're good at this profession.
- A problem you solved and the results.
- A time when you positively affected the organization, the bottom line, your boss, your co-workers, your clients.
- Awards, commendations, publications, etc., you achieved that relate to your job objective.

20xx-xx   **Company Name, City, State**
Job Title
- A project you are proud of that supports your job objective.
- Another accomplishment that shows you're good at this line of work.
- Quantifiable results that point out your skill.

20xx-xx   **Company Name, City, State**
Job Title
- An accomplishment you are proud of that shows you will be valued by your next employer.
- An occasion when someone "sat up and took notice" of your skill.

EDUCATION

Degree, Major (if relevant), 20xx (optional)
University, City, State

Most employers (especially those in conservative fields such as law and finance) like chronological resumes for the following reasons:

◆ They're used to reading chronological resumes and, therefore, feel comfortable with an applicant who uses this conventional approach.

◆ They can see a job seeker's work history in a flash because it's highlighted in the body of the resume.

Use the chronological format if you want to emphasize your work history for any of the following reasons:

◆ You want to make a horizontal career move within your current field.

◆ You'd like to make a vertical career move within your current field.

◆ Your most recent (or current) position is one you are proud of.

◆ If you have one or more major gaps in your work history, you can fill that gap with an activity that's relevant to your job objective, or at least shows that you have good character.

Keep in mind that the templates in this book are not boilerplates! The bullet point statements are ideas that I might suggest if I were with you as you create your resume. Because not all of these statements will apply to your situation, use only the ones that give you the opportunity to support your job objective. If these prodders aren't enough, check out the brainstorming exercises in Chapters 6 and 8.

> **Career Casualty**
>
> There is a mistaken impression among job seekers that the chronological format is old-fashioned and should not be used. Don't fall for this faulty thinking! The chronological format is still the most widely accepted type of resume and should be used if its criteria fit your career goals.

Get Functional

Work trends have changed dramatically in the past 50 years. It used to be that someone got a job shortly after graduating and kept it for the rest of his life. If things went well, he might move up the ladder within the company, but he usually felt sentenced to the same boss for 20 years to life. Loyalty to the company equaled stability, something greatly valued by employers (and by mothers-in-law, too, for that matter). An applicant who had job-hopped—not to mention changed careers—was considered unstable and therefore a risk for a would-be employer.

But since the early 1980s, the rate of job and career change has increased to such a point that it's now typical for a professional to shift careers three or four times during his adult life and to move to a new job once every two years. In this new climate, job-hopping is now called diversity, and many employers consider diversity an asset as long as the job seeker's rate of change is in line with the average for the industry.

How did this employment trend affect resume writing? It brought about the need for a new format: the functional resume (also referred to as the skills resume). If you want to be defined by your skills instead of your work history, the functional format is effective. As an alternative to the chronological format, the functional format works wonders for adventurous professionals such as the following:

♦ Extreme career changer who is leaving behind her previous industry and occupation for a new occupation in a new field.

♦ Parent re-entering the workforce who has little or no relevant experience.

♦ Adventurer who took long spans of time off to travel or pursue a personal project.

♦ Survivor of one or more long bouts of unemployment with nothing relevant to say for that time.

♦ Person who has had the same responsibilities for years and years at multiple job sites.

♦ Volunteer with relevant experience, which wouldn't get highlighted if he used a chronological resume.

♦ Older job seeker who needs to emphasize skills or experience from an early part of his work history.

The functional format presents your accomplishments under skill headings (instead of under job title headings, as in the chronological format), giving you the freedom to prioritize your accomplishments by significance rather than by chronology.

By placing your achievement statements front and center, this format enables you to define yourself by your skills instead of your work history—a great relief if you have a checkered past.

As you can see from the functional template, Work History is a very concise section at the bottom of the resume, and achievement statements are placed in the body of the resume according to skill headings.

(Functional Resume Template)

Name
Street
City, State Zip
Phone, E-mail

JOB OBJECTIVE

The job you want next

SUMMARY OF QUALIFICATIONS

- How much experience you have in the field of your job objective, in a related field, or using the skills required for your new position.
- An overall career accomplishment that shows you'd be good at this job.
- What someone would say about you as a recommendation.

RELEVANT EXPERIENCE

MAJOR SKILL

- An accomplishment you are proud of that shows you have this skill.
- A problem you solved using this skill, and the results.
- A time when you used your skill to positively affect the organization, the bottom line, your boss, your clients.
- Awards, commendations, publications, etc., you achieved that relate to your job objective.

MAJOR SKILL

- A project you are proud of that supports your job objective.
- Another accomplishment that shows you're good at this line of work.
- Quantifiable results that point out your skill.
- An occasion when someone "sat up and took notice" of your skill.

WORK HISTORY

20xx-present	Job Title	COMPANY NAME and city
20xx-xx	Job Title	COMPANY NAME and city
20xx-xx	Job Title	COMPANY NAME and city
20xx-xx	Job Title	COMPANY NAME and city

EDUCATION

Degree, Major (if relevant), 20xx (optional)
University, City, State

The Best of Both: The Combination Format

You've considered the chronological and functional resume formats, but neither one is quite right for your situation. Here's an idea: bring together the benefits of both to develop a combination format. Creating a *combination resume* is kind of like borrowing from two recipes to come up with a wonderful new entrée.

Let's say your career transition fits the criteria for using a chronological resume, but you want to highlight your transferable skills the way a functional resume would. You could start with the chronological structure and then add skill subheadings under the job titles in your Professional Experience section. To see this concept in action, take a look at the following template, which represents a combination resume.

At first glance, the combination format looks like the traditional chronological format because the job seeker's achievements are presented as part of the work history in the body of the resume. The difference is that the achievement statements under each job heading are listed under skill subheadings.

Take a look at the following sample Professional Experience section of a resume. The applicant has created two skill subheadings, Management and Marketing, under which she placed relevant achievement statements.

After you've created two or three skill subheadings under a job title on your combination resume, prioritize those subheadings according to how relevant they are to your Job Objective statement.

When should you consider using a combination format instead of the chronological format? If you fit into one of the following circumstances, a combination format might be the way to go:

◆ You're making a career change, and you want to highlight the transferrable skills you used in your recent job(s).

◆ You're looking for a promotion.

◆ You're switching industries.

◆ Your job titles are nondescript.

◆ Your work history looks stagnant; that is, you've been in the same position for many years.

With the current changes in the job market, more job seekers are using the combination resume to demonstrate how flexible their qualifications are.

(Combination Resume Template)

Name
Street
City, State Zip
Phone, E-mail

JOB OBJECTIVE

The job you want next

SUMMARY OF QUALIFICATIONS

- How much experience you have in the field of your job objective, in a related field, or using the skills required for your new position.
- An overall career accomplishment that shows you'd be good at this job.
- What someone would say about you as a recommendation.

PROFESSIONAL EXPERIENCE

20xx-pres.   **Company Name, City, State**
Job Title

MAJOR SKILL

- An accomplishment you are proud of that shows you have this skill.
- A problem you solved using this skill, and the results.
- A time when you used your skill to positively affect the organization, the bottom line, your boss, your clients.
- Awards, commendations, publications, etc., you achieved that relate to your job objective.

MAJOR SKILL

- A project you are proud of that supports your job objective.
- Another accomplishment that shows you're good at this line of work.
- Quantifiable results that point out your skill.

20xx-xx   **Company Name, City, State**
Job Title
- An accomplishment you are proud of that shows you will be valued by your next employer.
- An occasion when someone "sat up and took notice" of your skill.

EDUCATION

Degree, Major (if relevant), 20xx (optional)
University, City, State

def•i•ni•tion

Curriculum vitae is Latin for "life's course." In the academic and scientific worlds, it's a detailed document used as a resume. A curriculum vitae is also referred to as **vita** or **CV**.

When You Really *Are* a Brain Surgeon: The Curriculum Vitae

Curricula vitae (*vita* or *CV* for short) have been called the brainy resumes because they're used by scholars, scientists, and, yes, brain surgeons. But you don't have to have a degree in brain surgery to write one. In fact, now that you understand the principles behind good resume writing, you're almost ready to write your own curriculum vitae.

When seeking a faculty, research, or leadership position at an academic or scientific organization, you need a curriculum vitae. If you think a curriculum vitae sounds like a formal document, you can relax; there's no need to put on your evening gown or tuxedo to write your CV! Writing one will be a casual event for you because you've already learned the principles behind an effective resume. (Take another look at The Resume Commandments in Chapter 3.)

Four things make a CV different from a resume:

- Most CVs are more than two pages long.

- The information on a CV tends to be detailed, providing extensive data about your publications, presentations, and other academic activities.

- A CV doesn't necessarily contain a Job Objective statement (see Chapter 5), although it's perfectly okay to include one.

- Most CVs don't have Summary of Qualifications sections (see Chapter 6); however, if you have a special need for one (perhaps you're making a career change and a Summary of Qualifications section would introduce that change), it's acceptable to have one on your CV.

Let's look at each of these points more closely.

When More Is More

The length of a CV may vary. A CV for a recent Ph.D. graduate would normally range from three to eight pages. For someone with extensive professional experience, a CV could run as long as 20 pages. That's a lot of paper, but in the academic world, that's a good thing. The people reading CVs seem to live by the slogan, "more is more." (That's the CV twist on the "less is more" theme I've been espousing all along for resumes.)

Just the Facts

Your CV audience is more interested in the facts and details of your career than it is in hype (that is, language that sounds exaggerated in order to impress). Data such as reference information, dates, and exact titles are important, because they give a means for verifying information. Providing technical descriptions also gives you a chance to show that you know what you're talking about without sounding like a braggart.

Here's an example of what I mean. Instead of saying:

> Prominent scientist who has been honored at universities around the world for groundbreaking discoveries.

Use a more modest tone:

> Organic chemist who has presented discoveries and research at universities in Russia, Mexico, Canada, and the United States.

No Objectives

Many CVs don't include Job Objective statements, especially if the applicant intends to stay in the same field. Between the college degree and the work history, it's usually obvious what type of position is being sought. However, if you're planning to change careers (for example, from research to teaching), a Job Objective statement at the top of your CV would be helpful to the potential employer.

No Need to Summarize

Most CVs target employers who are more interested in facts (found in the Professional Experience, Publications, and other laundry list sections) than in the interpretation of facts (typically found in a Summary of Qualifications section). For this reason, the Summary of Qualifications section is not necessary on most CVs. If your job objective is in line with your education and career achievements, you can omit this section on your CV. However, if you're making a career change, it's fine to create a Summary of Qualifications section that helps the reader understand how your education and background will apply to your new job objective.

Freedom of Format

Because the CV usually addresses a conservative reader, many people assume that it needs to follow a standard, rigid format. Not so! You can be creative in presenting your strengths while respecting the expectations of the academic, scientific, or institutional employer. That means you can use any one of the three formats I've suggested so far: chronological, functional, or combination. Use the guidelines mentioned earlier in this chapter to determine which format is best for your CV.

If a heading isn't applicable to you, disregard it. If you have only one or two items to list in a section, combine two similar sections. Then create a heading to reflect your combination, such as Publications and Presentations.

Career Casualty

Some employers will want to see that you know how to follow strict guidelines for academic writing. Be sure to list your published work properly on your CV. To learn the appropriate style for your industry, consult the bibliography section of a style guide that's commonly used in your field, or look at how bibliographies are presented in your trade publications.

Good Schooling

The Education section of a CV almost always appears near the top of the first page. It should provide information about each degree you have acquired:

◆ Your area of study

◆ The date you received your degree

◆ The institution where you received it

◆ The city and state of the institution

◆ Titles of your thesis and dissertation

Job Hunt Hint

To indicate that a laundry list on your CV does not include every single item in that category, add *Selected* or *Relevant* in the heading—for instance, Selected Presentations or Relevant Presentations.

You might also list course titles if they demonstrate relevant knowledge and aren't obvious from the major you declared. You can place internships under the Education heading, in a section of their own (called Internships), or under Experience, depending on which strategy makes the most sense for your situation.

Are You Published?

You need a Publications section if you've authored or co-authored material such as articles, books, or chapters in books. When listing publications, mention the following:

◆ The author (that's you!) or co-authors (you and your colleague)

◆ The title of your article or chapter (if one of these applies)

◆ The title of your book or the publication in which your article or chapter appeared

◆ The date of publication

◆ The publisher

◆ The ISBN (if it applies)

This information appears in sentence format with commas placed between each element. There are a few standards for order in which you place the elements within the sentences, so check a style manual such as *The Chicago Manual of Style* or *The Gregg Reference Manual* to find one that's right for you.

Putting on a Show

You may have presented papers at conferences. If so, you could have a section called Presentations, Lectures, Symposia, Conferences, or Seminars. In this section, state the following information:

◆ Titles of papers you presented

◆ Names of conferences

- Locations
- Dates

It's a good idea to elaborate on other roles you played at the conferences (such as serving on panels) if doing so will add to your qualifications.

Joining the Team

If you've been selected to serve on one or more committees, consider creating a section entitled Committees, Appointments, Boards, or the like. Under your heading, list the following:

- Your titles
- Names of committees
- The city and state of each committee
- Dates you served on the committees

If appropriate, you could include bullet point statements that say what results were achieved during your tenure. For instance:

President, University of Colorado Alumni Association, 2000–02

- Designed the organization's first website, which enabled online member giving.
- Collaborated with Board to develop the Annual Alumni Scholarship Award.

Hangin' with the Right Folks

The associations that you belong to can be listed alphabetically, chronologically, or in order of relevance to your profession. You could call this section something like Professional Affiliations, Professional Associations, or Professional Memberships. If you held or currently hold an office, also note that in this section.

Forget Anything?

Here are some other headings that might appear on your CV:

- Exhibitions
- Awards and Honors
- Research
- Studies
- Grants

- Lectures
- Teaching
- Licenses
- Media Appearances

Remember, "more is more" when it comes to your CV, so think hard about all you can include.

Create Your CV

Now that you have your feet wet, it's time to jump in. Create strong sections in your CV by using the concepts presented in Chapter 3. With the additional sections mentioned in this chapter, your CV is likely to run several pages, all of which should have the following information:

- Your name at the top of each page
- The page number (placed on either the top or bottom of each page)
- *Continued* at the bottom of each page (except the last one)

When you've finished writing your CV, sit back, read through it, and admire how accomplished you are!

The Least You Need to Know

- The chronological resume is the most traditional resume format. Use this format if you are making either a vertical or horizontal career move.
- A functional resume frames your experience according to skills rather than job titles. It allows you to prioritize your achievements according to impact rather than chronology.
- The combination format emphasizes your career history while highlighting skills that are particularly relevant.
- The curriculum vitae is used in academic and scientific communities. It is usually longer than 2 pages (and may be as long as 20 pages).

Chapter 5

Step Two: Start Off Strong

In This Chapter

- ◆ Designing a heading that makes your name stand out
- ◆ Listing contact information and a website address
- ◆ Why include a job objective?
- ◆ Crafting a clear and concise Job Objective statement

Who you are and what you want are two critical pieces in any job search conversation. When you introduce yourself to a recruiter, hiring manager, or networking associate, you wouldn't mumble your name so softly your new acquaintance doesn't hear it. When he asks what line of work you're interested in, you wouldn't ignore his question or reply in such a meek manner he assumes you don't know how you fit into the work world. Of course not! You want to say your name clearly and explain your career goal concisely, so he'll be able to connect you with your dream job.

Likewise, on paper, you want to make a confident impression when you present your name and job objective. Whether you're writing a chronological, functional, or combination resume, the guidelines in this chapter for creating the Heading and Job Objective sections apply.

The Heading Section: Heading the Right Way

The Heading section of a resume appears at the top of the page, as highlighted in the template found later in the chapter. The heading includes your name and contact information.

You've been putting your name at the tops of papers since you learned how to write in first grade. It's so automatic you probably just plop it there without thinking. Before you do that on your resume, read the tips on the following page on how to make your name and other contact information stand out.

♦ Your name and contact information should appear at the top of your resume, not at the bottom of the page. This information is traditionally placed at the top, and that's where an employer will expect to find it.

♦ Consider incorporating a horizontal line or shaded bar into the design of your heading to set it apart from the rest of your resume. To get ideas, browse through the sample resumes throughout this book, in the Portfolio of Sample Resumes at the back of this book, and on my website, SusanIreland.com. All of the resumes in these sources were created in MS Word, using techniques you can learn from the program's Help menu.

What's in a Name?

If you have a non-gender-specific first name (such as Chris, Pat, or Robin), you can use some tricks to indicate whether you're male or female. But before you let your secret out, be sure that you want the employer to know. The following two scenarios may help you decide whether you want to keep your gender a mystery.

Robin Harris (a man) knew that even though sex discrimination is illegal in the job placement process, the company for whom he wanted to work gave its most productive sales territories to men. Therefore, he wanted the employer to know right off that he was a man, because that would put him ahead of all the female candidates in the stack of resumes.

Here are a few ways you can clarify your gender on paper:

♦ Use a gender-specific nickname instead of your given name (for example, Rob Harris instead of Robin Harris).

♦ Include a middle name if it's clearly male or female (for example, Robin Frank Harris).

♦ Start your name with Mr. or Ms. (for example, Mr. Robin Harris).

If you're considering this last option, think twice. This technique is seldom used and looks somewhat awkward. However, if you're applying within the United States and have an unusual or non-American name that probably won't be recognized as male or female no matter what you do to it, the Mr. or Ms. technique would work.

Now let's look at a situation where it might not be to the job hunter's advantage for his or her gender to be known. Terry Hoover (a woman) was after the same job that Robin (in the last scenario) wanted. In order to be considered for the job, she chose not to add anything to her name—she simply put Terry Hoover on her resume, knowing the employer would have to guess whether she was a man or a woman until Terry met the employer in person. At that point, she'd be at the interview and able to sell herself as a fully qualified candidate.

Bonus Check

Contrary to what you might think, your resume is not a formal document—it's a marketing piece that introduces you. So refer to yourself the way you would like to be addressed. If your first name is Elizabeth, but you want to be called Beth, use Beth in your Heading section. Middle initials are optional.

(Resume Heading)

Name
Street
City, State Zip
Phone, E-mail

JOB OBJECTIVE

The job you want next

SUMMARY OF QUALIFICATIONS

- How much experience you have in the field of your job objective, in a related field, or using the skills required for your new position.
- An overall career accomplishment that shows you'd be good at this job.
- What someone would say about you as a recommendation.

PROFESSIONAL EXPERIENCE

20xx-pres. **Company Name, City, State**
Job Title
- An accomplishment you are proud of that shows you're good at this profession.
- A problem you solved and the results.
- A time when you positively affected the organization, the bottom line, your boss, your co-workers, your clients.
- Awards, commendations, publications, etc., you achieved that relate to your job objective.

20xx-xx **Company Name, City, State**
Job Title
- A project you are proud of that supports your job objective.
- Another accomplishment that shows you're good at this line of work.
- Quantifiable results that point out your skill.

20xx-xx **Company Name, City, State**
Job Title
- An accomplishment you are proud of that shows you will be valued by your next employer.
- An occasion when someone "sat up and took notice" of your skill.

EDUCATION

Degree, Major (if relevant), 20xx (optional)
University, City, State

Showing Off Credentials

If you have a degree or credential that indicates your profession, you could put the initials of your degree or credential next to your name in the Heading section. For example, Francine Wilks was going for a position as a CPA in an accounting firm where her credential was extremely important to the job. She showed it off nicely by placing it in her heading.

Warren Samuels wanted the reader of his resume to immediately see that he's a physician. He got the message across quickly by placing his degree next to his name in the Heading section of his resume.

Francine Wilks, CPA

123 Linden Place • Tempe, AZ 12345 • (123) 555-1234 • fwilks@bamboo.com

Warren Samuels, M.D.

123 Franklin Avenue, #2, St. Paul, MN 12345   (123) 555-1234   w_samuels@bamboo.com

Job seekers respond differently to seeing their credential or degree letters next to their names. Some folks like the look of it; others aren't at all comfortable having them there. It's entirely up to you—do what feels appropriate for your field and personality.

 Job Hunt Hint

Make the font size of the letters of your credentials one or two point sizes smaller if you place them immediately after your name. In this way, they maintain importance without graphically overpowering your name.

Home Sweet Home

Putting your street address in your heading is preferable to listing a PO Box number, because a home address conjures up a more stable image. If you have a specific reason not to give out your street address, however, it's acceptable to use a post office address.

Following are some examples of addresses in headings. Patricia Ferrari used her home address in her Heading section. Juanita Cuellar didn't feel comfortable giving out her street address, so she chose to use her PO Box number in her heading. Both headings are permissible, but Patricia's address made her look a little more stable than Juanita.

Patricia Ferrari

123 Rippling Rock Avenue
Memphis, TN 12345
(123) 555-1234
pferrari@bamboo.com

Juanita Cuellar

P.O. Box 123, Charlotte, NC 12345-1234
(123) 555-1234
jcuellar@bamboo.com

I've Got Your Number

Your phone number is critical in your resume's Heading section because your first contact from an employer may very well be by phone. Depending on your situation, you may want to list one or two phone numbers—but don't go overboard by listing every contact number you have (home, office, cell, and pager). Give only the one or two needed to reach you or to leave a message.

By putting a phone number on your resume, you automatically give your potential employer permission to …

- ◆ Call that number.

- ◆ Leave a message about your job search.

- ◆ Expect you to speak freely if you pick up the phone.

Be sure you're okay with all three of these assumptions for each phone number in your heading. Following are a few cases in point.

Gretchin Hendley didn't want any job search phone calls at her place of work, so in her heading, she listed only her cell number, which she could check for messages during her work breaks. Larry Picasso, on the other hand, was being laid off, and everyone in his department was aware that he was looking for a new job. Therefore, it made perfect sense for him to list his office phone number in his heading, because he could receive messages and speak freely about his job search during business hours.

If you list only one phone number in your heading (as Gretchin does in her heading), it will be assumed that it's your home or personal line. If you give more than one phone number, you need to indicate the difference between them (as Larry does in his heading).

Employers hardly ever fax a response to a job applicant, so putting a fax number on a resume is a waste of valuable space.

Gretchin Hendley
123 Green Lane • Harristown, VA 12345 • (123) 555-1234 • ghendley@bamboo.com

Larry Picasso
123 Fountine Blvd. • Denver, CO 12345
Office: (123) 555-1234 • Home: (123) 555-5678
lpicasso@bamboo.com

E-Mail Giveaway

Listing your e-mail address (if you have one) in the Heading section is beneficial, because it can greatly expedite the employer's response. Don't list your work e-mail address on your resume, because doing so would send your prospective employer the message that you use company resources for personal pursuits—in this case, your job hunt. Instead, get a personal e-mail account (if you don't already have one) and put that address in the Heading section. Yahoo!, Google, and other online services offer free e-mail accounts with access from almost everywhere around the world.

Don't clutter up your heading with unnecessary stuff. When writing your e-mail address in your heading, there's no need to prefix the address with *e-mail:* because most readers know that an e-mail address contains an @ sign.

Alice Friend put her e-mail address on her resume, showing that she's easy to reach and comfortable online.

Alice Friend
123 Fruit Tree Blvd.
Omaha, NE 12345
(123) 555-1234
alice_friend@bamboo.com

Job Hunt Hint

If you have a professional website, blog, or social network profile that speaks to your career, be sure to include your site's URL in your resume heading. You don't need to prefix the address with *Website address:* as most readers recognize a website address.

The Job Objective Section: It's All About Marketing

Whether you're a world traveler or a job seeker, it's important to know where you're going in order to get there. And when asking for help in getting there, you need to tell the guide where you're headed. On your resume, this destination is shown through the Job Objective statement that appears just below your Heading section.

Your resume is effectively your career brochure because it markets you for your next career move. Just like any other marketing piece, your resume needs to be created with an objective in mind.

A marketing professional for an event production company would never create a poster for a concert until she knew what type of music was going to be performed, where it was being held, and who the target audience was. It's the same with your job search. Before you can produce your powerful marketing piece, you need to know what job you're going after, what skills are required for the job, and, if possible, who the reader of your resume is. After you have that information, you can put together a resume that'll get your foot in the door.

If you aren't sure what your job objective is, turn back to Chapter 1 for help figuring out what role (for example: outside sales or marketing communications) you want to play for an employer. Then write your resume with a Job Objective statement on it.

Multiple Choice

If you find yourself with a list of two or more job objectives, don't make the mistake so many job seekers do by trying to create a generic resume to cover all possible job objectives. A generic resume is likely to fall flat on its face because it will make you look like a jack of too many trades—a weak contender against other candidates who are specialized in their fields.

Instead of developing a generic resume, follow the guidelines in Chapter 2 to create more than one targeted resume.

In this way, you can create multiple resumes, each of which can stand strong against specialized competition in today's job market.

Job Hunt Hint

The Job Objective section of your resume could also be titled any one of the following:

- ◆ Objective
- ◆ Career Objective
- ◆ Goal
- ◆ Career Goal

The Weight of a Job Objective

By starting your resume with a Job Objective statement, you immediately tell your potential employer …

- ◆ What position you're looking for.
- ◆ Who needs to get your resume. A human resources clerk will probably be the first person to see your resume. Your Job Objective statement will indicate to that clerk which hiring person should receive your resume.

◆ How to interpret your resume. Your Job Objective statement tells the reader, "Everything that follows is relevant to this position." That's an important point to make, because this is a marketing piece, not your life history!

In short, a Job Objective statement makes it easier for a potential employer to understand what you have to say in your resume. A resume without a Job Objective statement effectively says, "This is what I've done. Could you figure out what I should do next?" That's a weak approach! A job objective gives your resume focus and strength, and makes a powerful first move toward title and salary negotiations.

The highlighted section of the resume template on the next page shows where your Job Objective statement should be placed. (To learn about alternatives to having a Job Objective section on your resume, see "Breaking the Rules" later in this chapter.)

Wording with an Objective

I've said it before, and I'll say it again: less is more! You need to say everything as concisely as possible, starting with your Job Objective statement.

Putting your Job Objective statement near the top of your resume is the clearest way to tell the reader what you want for your immediate future.

Some resumes have flowery opening statements with job objectives buried deep inside them. They use phrases such as "challenging position," "room for advancement," and "opportunity to grow." Give the reader of your resume a break—cut out all the fluff because it doesn't say much anyway. Stick to what's important:

◆ The job title you'd like next, if you know it (for example, Manager or Sales Representative).

◆ The area of work you want to be in (for example, Marketing or Sales). On rare occasions, this might include an area of specialization (for example, "with an emphasis on new business development" or "focusing on graphic design").

 Career Casualty

Don't include "entry-level" in your Job Objective statement. Why tell the reader you want the lowest-level job, with pay to match? Leave it out, and you may be given a position that's a little higher up the food chain.

Challenge yourself to write your job objective in 10 or fewer words. (Of course, the employer won't count them, so it's okay to exceed 10 words if you have to.) Give yourself a bonus check if you can narrow it down to just a few words.

(Job Objective Section)

Name
Street
City, State Zip
Phone, E-mail

JOB OBJECTIVE
The job you want next

SUMMARY OF QUALIFICATIONS
- How much experience you have in the field of your job objective, in a related field, or using the skills required for your new position.
- An overall career accomplishment that shows you'd be good at this job.
- What someone would say about you as a recommendation.

PROFESSIONAL EXPERIENCE

20xx-pres.   **Company Name, City, State**
Job Title
- An accomplishment you are proud of that shows you're good at this profession.
- A problem you solved and the results.
- A time when you positively affected the organization, the bottom line, your boss, your co-workers, your clients.
- Awards, commendations, publications, etc., you achieved that relate to your job objective.

20xx-xx   **Company Name, City, State**
Job Title
- A project you are proud of that supports your job objective.
- Another accomplishment that shows you're good at this line of work.
- Quantifiable results that point out your skill.

20xx-xx   **Company Name, City, State**
Job Title
- An accomplishment you are proud of that shows you will be valued by your next employer.
- An occasion when someone "sat up and took notice" of your skill.

EDUCATION
Degree, Major (if relevant), 20xx (optional)
University, City, State

Take a look at the following examples of Job Objective statements:

> **Not so good:** A challenging position that will utilize my skills and experience as Director of Marketing
>
> (Yawn! Everyone wants to be challenged, and of course you'll be using your skills and experience.)
>
> **Much better:** Director of Marketing
>
> **Not so good:** An administrative position in a growth-oriented company where I can use my background in finance to promote the firm
>
> (This statement sounds like you're judging the company's ability to provide for your future.)
>
> **Much better:** Administrative position with a focus on finance
>
> **Not so good:** A position as Associate Field Producer in TV Programming that offers room for advancement and high rewards
>
> (Bad idea! It sounds like you want the job of the person reading the resume!)
>
> **Much better:** Associate Field Producer, TV Programming

Want to see this concept at work? Review the Job Objective statements in the Portfolio of Sample Resumes at the end of this book.

Straight as an Arrow

Jack Kraus knew exactly what position he was going after at the university, so he listed the precise title from the job posting he was responding to in the Job Objective section on his resume (at the end of this chapter). His concise statement had no frills—it went straight to the point and didn't waste the reader's time.

If you know the exact title of the job you're applying for, by all means use that as your job objective. Doing this leaves no doubt as to what position you want. If you later apply for a job with a slightly different job title, you can always change your job objective to match.

Spreading Your Umbrella

Like an umbrella, David Goldstein's job objective covered a number of things: his prospective job title and his three areas of expertise. By creating a column with eye-catching bullet points, he suggested to the employer several ways he could fit into the organization. Smart guy! (See his resume at the end of this chapter.)

The approach David used is a good one for professionals such as the following:

- Consultants who offer several services

- Generalists who want to show off their special skills

- Administrators who need to say they can wear several hats

- Technical folks who have expertise in a number of areas

Do you fall into one of these categories? If so, you might benefit from the umbrella technique David used.

Breaking the Rules

Now that you've learned the rule of having a Job Objective statement, I'm going to tell you about a technique that breaks, or at least bends, that rule.

If you're continuing in a profession in which you have substantial experience, consider putting your *professional title* next to your name or near the top of your resume. This can be a stronger approach than using a Job Objective statement. A title effectively says, "This is what my profession is." A Job Objective statement says, "This is what I want to be." If you have enough experience to give yourself a title, it can be a more forceful introduction.

def•i•ni•tion

Your **professional title** could be an official job title you've held or simply the professional role you're qualified to fill. For instance, a resume writer (such as myself) could use any of the following professional titles at the top of her resume:

- Resume Writer

- Resume Consultant

- Job Counselor

- Career Development Professional

She would choose her professional title based on what type of work she was looking for.

Using your professional title instead of a Job Objective statement can do the following:

- Give you an edge on your competition by presenting you as an established professional in your field

- Set a strong foundation for title and salary negotiations

Robert McFarland had been a construction dispute consultant for a number of years and was using his resume (at the end of this chapter) to move to another consulting firm. By placing his professional title immediately under his heading, he established himself as someone grounded in his field. This assertive approach not only won him an interview, it also paid off big when he negotiated his salary.

Do you have a professional title that would tell the employer which role you want to play in his organization? If so, consider using it on your resume instead of a Job Objective statement.

The Least You Need to Know

◆ Your Heading section is at the top of your resume, and contains your name, phone number, and other contact information.

◆ List a personal e-mail address (not your work e-mail), professional website, and social network profile if appropriate.

◆ To have a perfect resume, you must make it targeted to a job objective.

◆ Your Job Objective statement should be concise, and placed immediately below the Heading section of your resume.

◆ Instead of using a Job Objective statement, you can use a professional title.

Jack Kraus

123 Godfrey Avenue, #2, Philadelphia, PA 12345   **(123) 555-1234**   **jkraus@bamboo.com**

JOB OBJECTIVE

Student Affairs Officer II, Housing & Dining Services: Residential Programs

SUMMARY OF QUALIFICATIONS

- 19 years as a professional educator with strengths in program development and administration.
- Enthusiastic team leader and outstanding communicator, both one-to-one and before groups.
- Creative in solving problems and maximizing resources. Computer literate.

EDUCATION

M.A., Educational Administration, Temple University, Philadelphia, PA, 1999

B.A., History, St. John's College, Santa Fe, NM, 1989

RELEVANT ACCOMPLISHMENTS

PROGRAM ADMINISTRATION

Philadelphia Unified School District
- Developed new educational programs, including:
    - Tutoring program for ESL students that achieved highest recommendations.
    - "Future System" curricula, a hands-on approach that included a computer lab.
    - $12,000 ham radio station project for high-achieving students.

- As Teacher-in-Charge, supervised 45 teachers in principal's absence and assisted in administrative decision-making and program development.

- Chaired ESL Advisory Committee comprised of parents, administrators, and teachers, which served as a forum for student issues.

TEACHING

Church Street School
- Currently teach basic college courses (English, history, and writing) to students, ages 18-50 and from diverse educational and cultural backgrounds.

- Tutor and advise students regarding study skills and career development.

Philadelphia Unified School District
- Instructed adults in basic education skills, GED preparation, and ESL, in addition to holding a full-time elementary teaching position.

TXN Newsroom Guest Speaker
- Delivered presentations to school groups and cable companies on new technologies in the classroom.

WORK HISTORY

2007-present	Instructor	Church Street School, Philadelphia, CA
2005-2007	Guest Speaker	TXN Newsroom, Philadelphia, PA
1989-2007	Educator	Philadelphia Unified School District, Philadelphia, PA

David Goldstein

123 Lincoln Avenue • West Hollywood, CA 12345 • **(123) 555-1234** • daveg@bamboo.com

OBJECTIVE: Sales Trainer in the areas of: Interpersonal Communication
Sales Techniques
Product Knowledge

SUMMARY OF QUALIFICATIONS

- 15 years as a successful sales professional.
- Experienced at teaching others how to improve interpersonal communication.
- Skilled at training sales associates in proven sales techniques.
- Ability to develop presentation and training materials.

PROFESSIONAL ACCOMPLISHMENTS
TRAINING

Jewel Junction
- Trained 24+ franchisees regarding: Product knowledge Projected trends
                                                      Merchandising   Proven selling techniques
- Trained City Center sales staff including 23 associates and one assistant manager.
- Led staff meetings to introduce lines and instill respect and enthusiasm for products.
- Served on the product development committee charged with determining seasonal merchandise and promotions.
- Diffused numerous conflicts among sales staff through group and individual counseling.
- Designed employee incentive program that rewarded improved performance.

Clearwater, Inc.
- Trained sales staff in numerous department stores nationwide for short-term promotional sales of Clearwater accessories.

SALES

- Consistently ranked among the highest in sales at Jewel Junction, using strong presentation skills to sell luxury items in a slow economy.
- Commended for achieving above-average sales and for developing strong rapport with customers at Grove Jewelry Distributors.
- Exceeded sales record 20% in a 10-state, 20-store region of Clearwater, Inc.

WORK HISTORY
2006-present   Merchandising Manager, Jewel Junction, Inglewood, CA
2004-2005   Customer Service/Sales Associate, Grove Jewelry Distributors, Long Beach, CA
2001-2003   Sales Associate, Beemans (department store), Miami Beach, FL
2000   Promotional Representative, Clearwater, Inc., Santa Monica, CA
1994-1999   Sales Representative, Frost's Fifth Avenue, Hollywood, CA

EDUCATION
Liberal Arts, Quincy College, Key West, FL
Professional development courses: Interpersonal Communications, Sales Training, Product Knowledge and Presentation

Robert McFarland
123 Middlesex Street • Wethersfield, CT 12345 • (123) 555-1234 • rmcfarland@bamboo.com

Construction Dispute Consultant

HIGHLIGHTS OF QUALIFICATIONS

- 16 years as construction consultant and owner of mid-sized construction firm.
- Extensive experience in woodframe construction.
- Skilled at resolving contract disputes.

RELEVANT EXPERIENCE

CONSTRUCTION BUSINESS MANAGEMENT

- Built a prominent construction business that grew from 0 to 250 employees and from annual gross of $25K to $9M in six years.
- Managed approximately 300 construction projects, including:
  New commercial buildings
  Commercial tenant improvement
  New and remodel residential work
  Structural rehabs
- Oversaw 500,000 sq. ft. per year wood framing operation.

PROBLEM RESOLUTION

- Successfully negotiated numerous contract and labor disputes, initiating compromises that led to resolutions of up to $125K.
- Collaborated with architects and owners to create most cost-effective designs on projects up to $2.5M in value, frequently requiring resolution of competing interests.
- Continually generated technical and interpersonal solutions that met tight budget and time constraints.

PRESENTATIONS

- Wrote hundreds of analyses for construction projects, focusing on financial, safety, and time issues.
- As guest lecturer at local community college, spoke on resource-efficient construction.

WORK HISTORY

2006-present	Construction Consultant/Contractor, Cosgrove Contractors, Hartford, CT
1996-2006	President/Operations Manager, Golly Co., West Hartford, CT
1990-1996	General Contractor, Ruby Construction, Hartford, CT

EDUCATION

B.A., Religious Studies, Springfield College, Springfield, MA

Chapter 6

Step Three: Knock 'Em Off Their Feet

In This Chapter

◆ Kicking off your resume with a strong Summary of Qualifications section

◆ Exceptions to the no-paragraph rule

◆ Figuring out what to say and how to say it

◆ Avoiding resume clichés that put the employer to sleep

◆ Facilitating a smooth career change with effective phrases

Experienced players in the marketing game know it's important to create a splash right away in a promotional piece. The way to do that on your resume is to give top billing to qualifications that will knock your potential employer off her feet. In this chapter, you'll learn how to choose and compose opening statements that will draw in employers and make them start itching to call you.

Right from the Start

Kick off your resume with a Summary of Qualifications section. This section is a list of the top three or four reasons you're qualified for the job you're seeking. The resume template found later shows where the Summary of Qualifications section appears on the resume.

For example, the opening section of Christopher Columbus's resume might have read as follows:

Summary of Qualifications

◆ First European to make verified contact with Americans since the Vikings five centuries before.

◆ Christened six Caribbean islands (whose names now signify choice vacation spots).

◆ Noted captain and navigator of four Atlantic crossings who set contemporary world sailing records.

Wouldn't you want this guy to captain your next transoceanic sailing trip?

You may not be able to tout mind-blowing achievements like Columbus, but you can look pretty terrific with three or four smashing statements that set you apart from the crowd. Talk about anything that makes you stand out in your field. That could be any of the following:

◆ Your experience

◆ Your credentials

◆ Your expertise

◆ Your personal values

◆ Your work ethics

◆ Your background

◆ Your personality

In the *Summary of Qualifications* section, you're free to make claims, drop names, and do your best to entice the employer to call you for an interview. Remember, all claims must be substantiated later when you write the body of your resume, so be honest while giving yourself full credit.

def•i•ni•tion

The **Summary of Qualifications** section is a brief set of points that say you're qualified for your job objective. This section can also be called:

◆ Highlights of Qualifications

◆ Qualifications

◆ Highlights

◆ Summary

◆ Profile

There's room to be creative in naming this section, so go for it!

(Summary of Qualifications Section)

Name
Street
City, State Zip
Phone, E-mail

JOB OBJECTIVE

The job you want next

SUMMARY OF QUALIFICATIONS

- How much experience you have in the field of your job objective, in a related field, or using the skills required for your new position.
- An overall career accomplishment that shows you'd be good at this job.
- What someone would say about you as a recommendation.

PROFESSIONAL EXPERIENCE

20xx-pres.   **Company Name, City, State**
Job Title
- An accomplishment you are proud of that shows you're good at this profession.
- A problem you solved and the results.
- A time when you positively affected the organization, the bottom line, your boss, your co-workers, your clients.
- Awards, commendations, publications, etc., you achieved that relate to your job objective.

20xx-xx   **Company Name, City, State**
Job Title
- A project you are proud of that supports your job objective.
- Another accomplishment that shows you're good at this line of work.
- Quantifiable results that point out your skill.

20xx-xx   **Company Name, City, State**
Job Title
- An accomplishment you are proud of that shows you will be valued by your next employer.
- An occasion when someone "sat up and took notice" of your skill.

EDUCATION

Degree, Major (if relevant), 20xx (optional)
University, City, State

Exceptions to the No-Paragraph Commandment

Remember Commandment VI from Chapter 3, "Thou shalt not write in long paragraphs; thou shalt use bullet points"? The Summary of Qualifications section is one place where you can break that rule. In this section, there are two options for formatting your statements:

◆ Three or four bullet point statements (as used in the sample resumes at the end of this chapter).

◆ Two short paragraphs, each introduced with a term (such as "Experience" or "Leadership") and followed by statements that support that introductory term. Each paragraph should be no longer than three lines, so that it's quick and easy to read. (To see an example of this short-paragraph technique, see Maureen Nelson's resume in the Portfolio of Sample Resumes at the back of this book.)

Most job seekers use the first option because bullet points are a conventional technique for business presentations such as resumes. However, some executives and seasoned professionals prefer the second option, because they think paragraphs look more serious and therefore more appropriate for their field or level of responsibility. It's purely a personal choice. As long as the paragraphs or bullet point statements are kept to the three-line limit, they will grab the employer's attention.

Say It with Style

Whatever you do in your Summary of Qualifications, don't use hackneyed phrases such as "excellent written and oral communication skills," "outstanding organizational abilities," "goal-oriented individual," or other overused, vague lines.

Columbus's resume would have gotten lost in the pack if it had read as follows:

Summary of Qualifications

◆ Exceptional organizational and people skills

◆ Goal-oriented, self-motivated individual

◆ Excellent communication skills

Don't get me wrong—the meanings behind most of those phrases are wonderful and may be perfectly true for you. But because these clichés appear on almost everyone's resume, they don't pack much of a punch and, frankly, are not taken seriously.

Before you put a statement in your Summary of Qualifications, ask yourself: Is it a grabber? Is it news to the reader? If it's what everyone else says, it's not news, and it won't grab the reader. It has to be said in a way that's remarkable and memorable.

Always make your point as concretely as possible. Use facts to create credibility and to instill a sense that you are unlike any other candidate applying for the job. Ask yourself the following questions:

◆ What specifically have I done that demonstrates that I have the desired quality?

◆ How will my skills translate into success at my next job?

Here are some examples of what I mean:

◆ Fred was applying for a pizza delivery position. Because this type of employment has a high no-show rate, he felt his reliability was a marketable asset. So instead of writing, "Excellent record of attendance," he wrote, "Never missed a day of work in 11 months."

◆ When Sandy was going for a customer service position, she knew the potential employer was looking for someone with excellent communication skills. She wrote, "Deemed Customer Service Rep of the Month for resolving problems diplomatically."

◆ Instead of "Goal-oriented professional," Frank wrote, "Exceeded quotas for four consecutive years" on his resume for a sales position.

For more ideas on Summary of Qualifications statements, see what the following two job seekers wrote on their resumes (found at the end of this chapter).

> **Bonus Check**
>
> Throughout your resume, write in the first person without using pronouns. In other words, phrase your statements as though you were talking about yourself without saying "I." For example, write, "Understand the art of conflict resolution" instead of "I understand the art of conflict resolution."

Keeping Up with the Fast Trackers

Jamie Choi designed a Summary of Qualifications section in his resume that told his potential employer that he's experienced in his field and valued by those who work with him. Notice his clever technique of getting someone else to say he was a good employee relations specialist: he quoted one of his former clients. His summary statements alone made the employer want to read his entire resume.

Look through your evaluation forms and letters of recommendation from former employers to see if you have a quotable quote for your resume.

On the Lines of a Career Changer

The Summary of Qualifications is one of the most important sections on a career changer's resume because it becomes a bridge between the job seeker's past and future. In his resume, Charles Humphries used just three statements to provide the following information:

◆ He had experience in the field he was moving into (even though he'd never held the job title he was going after).

◆ He had the required skills and motivation for the position.

◆ He had a technical background, which was something his competition might not have.

His Summary of Qualifications section packaged Charles as a low-risk, high-value candidate.

Your Summary of Qualifications statements should so strongly paint a picture of you at your next job that there appears to be little or no transition into your new job, even if you're making a big career change.

Go Figure

Now it's time to write your Summary of Qualifications statements. To help you come up with three or four strong statements, answer the following questions and convert your answers to summary statements. If one doesn't apply to your situation, skip it and move on to the next.

How much experience do you have in this profession, in this field, or using the required skills?

Example: Someone staying in the field of financial management might answer, "I've worked as a financial manager for a mid-size company for the last 14 years."

Summary statement: Fourteen years as the financial manager of a company with current sales of $75 million.

Example: A job seeker making the transition from teaching to corporate training might answer, "I spent the last seven years teaching things to all kinds of kids."

Summary statement: Seven years of professional experience using strong communication skills to enhance learning of children from diverse backgrounds.

Imagine that your best friend is talking to the hiring person about the job you want. What would your best friend say about you that would make the employer want to call you for an interview?

Example: The best friend of a job hunter desiring an editorial position with a newspaper might say, "She even won the Pulitzer Prize! I don't think anyone from the *Examiner* has ever done that before."

Summary statement: First syndicated journalist from the *Examiner* to receive the Pulitzer Prize.

Example: The colleague of a CEO seeking a membership on the Board of Directors of a crisis-prevention nonprofit organization might say, "He led a group that helped the community recover from hurricane Katrina."

Summary statement: Known for leading a committee that took the first step toward community rehabilitation after hurricane Katrina.

How is success measured in the position mentioned in your Job Objective statement? How do you measure up?

Example: A salesperson reaching for a sales management job might answer, "I have always sold more than my quota and tried to motivate other salespeople so my team could meet group goals."

Summary statement: Consistently exceeded personal quotas and inspired sales team members to meet group goals.

Example: A software developer wishing to make a move into technical writing might answer, "Many different users have told me that my explanations are easy to understand."

Summary statement: Reputation for writing clear and concise explanations for technical and nontechnical users.

What credentials do you have that are important for this job?

Example: A fashion buyer looking for a position as a graphic designer might say, "My college degree was in design."

Summary statement: Bachelor of Fine Arts with an emphasis on design.

Example: A geology teacher seeking a position at a community college in California might answer, "I have a Lifetime California Community College Teaching Credential in Earth Science."

Summary statement: California Community College Teaching Credential, Earth Science, Lifetime.

What is it about your personality that makes this job a good fit for you?

Example: A customer-service representative staying in the same field might answer, "I am very diplomatic, so I get good results."

Summary statement: Outstanding diplomacy that consistently produces win-win results for customers and the company.

Example: An architect applying for a post in a professional organization could say, "I have natural problem-solving skills that lead to good solutions."

Summary statement: Natural problem-solving skills that create both practical and agreeable solutions.

What personal commitments or passions do you have that would be valued by the employer?

Example: Someone wanting to lead an environmental organization could say, "I am committed to educating people about industrial waste hazards that are endangering the environment."

Summary statement: Strong commitment to preserving nature through education about hazards to the environment.

Career Casualty

Be careful not to list tasks you don't like to perform. Mentioning them is a sure way of finding them in your next job description.

Example: A psychologist going for a job in human resources might answer, "I like to help others achieve their potential through evaluation of their personal skills."

Summary statement: Dedicated to maximizing others' potential through careful assessment and acknowledgment of their personal skills.

What other experience do you have that will be a bonus to the employer?

Example: A new graduate seeking her first job as a nurse could answer, "I volunteered in a medium-size clinic."

Summary statement: Volunteer experience in a clinic with an interdisciplinary staff of 12.

Example: Someone trying for a position on the mayor's administrative staff might mention, "My family includes three generations of political professionals, so I'm used to debating controversial issues."

Summary statement: Developed talent for debating controversial issues as a member of a family with three generations of political professionals.

Do you have any technical, linguistic, or artistic talents that would be useful on the job?

Example: Someone applying to be a teacher in a multilingual school might answer, "I can speak Spanish, Italian, and Russian."

Summary statement: Fluent in Spanish, Italian, and Russian.

Example: An artist seeking a commission from the city's museum could say, "I have worked in just about every kind of medium."

Summary statement: Adept at working in a range of mediums, including paint, pen and ink, clay, metal, collage, and wood.

Not all of these questions will work for your situation. Just answer the ones that do, and you're bound to come up with three or four good statements for your resume.

The Least You Need to Know

◆ A strong Summary of Qualifications section will grab an employer's attention and make him or her think, "Here's the person for the job."

◆ Your Summary of Qualifications highlights skills for your next job (your future); it doesn't summarize your past.

◆ Don't write overused phrases such as "excellent communication skills."

◆ Prioritize your Summary of Qualifications statements so that the strongest one comes first.

Jamie Choi

123 Montecito Street, #1 • Santa Cruz, CA 12345 • (123) 555-1234 • jchoi@bamboo.com

OBJECTIVE: Employee Relations Specialist

SUMMARY OF QUALIFICATIONS

- More than 10 years as an expert in: Wholeness in the Workplace
  The Psychology of Work

- Skilled at assisting people from all levels of employment and cultural backgrounds.

- "You've changed my understanding of work. I now find it a dynamic and energizing principle." — Manufacturing Manager

TRAINING AND DEVELOPMENT ACCOMPLISHMENTS

2007-pres.   Chrysalis, Santa Cruz, CA   **Instructor,** Wholeness in the Workplace
- Taught professionals, managers, office workers, and tradespeople from multicultural backgrounds. Topics include:

Dealing with Stress	Concentration
Responsibility and Commitment	Organizational Skills
Dynamics of Teamwork	Dealing with Difficult People

- Turned around a failing institutional library and, with no previous professional librarian experience, produced an efficient system within four weeks.
  - Trained volunteers.
  - Organized holdings and standardized procedures.

- Managed building renovation project, training and supervising a crew of student volunteers with no experience in construction. Finished project within time constraints.

1999-2006   MacMillan Institute, Albuquerque, NM   **Trainer/Manager**
- Trained professionals, artists, tradespeople, and students in productive work habits that increased proficiency, work satisfaction, and income.

- Created a "work laboratory" that provided hands-on experience in development of:

Teamwork	Self-Esteem
Conflict Management Skills	Client Relations
Dynamic Work Style	Time Management Skills

1997-1999   Center for Humanistic Studies, Santa Fe, NM   **Full-Time Student,** Human Development

1992-1994   Los Alamos Properties, Los Alamos, NM   **Co-Manager**
- Trained and supervised renovation staff working on residential projects.

EDUCATION

M.A., Human Resources, University of California, Santa Cruz, CA

Charles E. Humphries

123 Baytown Avenue • Jacinto, TX 12345 • (123) 555-1234 • c_humphries@bamboo.com

JOB OBJECTIVE: Technical Sales Account Manager

SUMMARY OF QUALIFICATIONS

- 13 years as an engineer collaborating on key marketing/sales strategies for one of the nation's largest corporations.
- Enjoy making sales presentations that motivate audiences to "buy into" new products.
- Technical versatility: construction, computer systems, telecommunications, and safety.

PROFESSIONAL ACCOMPLISHMENTS

SALES / MARKETING

- Increased premium product sales 15% ($4.1 million) by designing a $2.7 million advertising and point-of-sale strategy. Led team of sales experts, merchandising specialists, market researchers, P.O.S. vendors, and product engineers.
- Made winning "sales" presentation regarding a $37 million retail automation project. Built consensus among company divisions with competing interests by facilitating needs assessment, goal setting, and cooperative strategy planning.
- Increased revenue $12 million annually by convincing 8,300 retailers to use electronic funds transfer system.
- Led several testimonial and training presentations that "sold" new technologies to audiences with resistance to change.

TECHNICAL PROJECT MANAGEMENT

- Led technical development of customer-activated credit/debit card payment system implemented at AP stations nationwide. Increased corporate annual sales $154 million.
- Led development of computerized maintenance dispatch system for 8,250 retail outlets and 60 bulk facilities that eliminated down time, increasing sales $8.4 million per year.
- Directed the $49 million construction of 40 service stations, designing architectural plans that met environmental regulations and local government demands.

WORK HISTORY

1996-present American Petroleum Inc., Houston, TX

Environmental Safety Fire and Health Specialist, 2008-present
Trading Analyst, 2006-2008
Project Manager, Market Place Development, 2005-2006
Project Manager, Electronics Systems - Service Stations, 2002-2005
Analyst for Product Order and Delivery, 2001-2002
Project Manager, Service Station Construction, 1998-2001
Staff Engineer, 1996-1998

EDUCATION

B.E., Chemical Engineering, Massachusetts Institute of Technology, Cambridge, MA, 1996
Professional Development: American Demographics Annual Marketing Conference
Sales and negotiations seminars

Chapter 7

Step Four: Make History

In This Chapter

- ◆ Creating a Work History section that shows off your strengths
- ◆ Using dates on your resume to fight age discrimination
- ◆ Disguising gaps in your employment history
- ◆ Adding volunteer experience to your Work History section
- ◆ Making your promotions noticeable at a glance

Employers give a lot of attention to the Work History section of a resume. It's one of the first things they look for after they see your job objective. They want to know about your track record, where you've been and how long you stayed there. What they're trying to figure out is: Are you a stable person? What are your demonstrated talents? And most important, would you be a good fit for the job opening they have?

A well-presented Work History section is clearly important. Building one that maximizes your experience is what this chapter is all about.

Location, Location, Location

Where you list your previous positions depends on what type of resume format you're using. If you're a chronological or combination resume writer (remember that lesson in Chapter 4?), your work history will be distributed throughout the midsection of your resume. The following chronological and combination templates show you exactly where it would appear in each.

If you're a functional resume writer (see Chapter 4), Work History will be listed as one section at the bottom of your resume. This chapter's functional resume template highlights the area I'm talking about.

Writing History

Of all the sections of your resume, your Work History is the most likely to be verified by a potential employer. Be sure your entries in this section coincide exactly with the information your former employers will give.

As you read through this chapter, remember Resume Commandment II from Chapter 3: thou shalt not confess. In other words, you don't have to tell everything. Stick to what's relevant and marketable. Rely on this commandment when resolving issues in your Work History section.

The next step is to put the Work History section in your resume. Sounds easy enough, doesn't it? But what if you have a situation that's tricky to present in your employment history? This situation could be any of the following:

♦ Dates that go back so far that they trigger age discrimination

♦ So little employment history that you appear too young for the job

♦ Gaps in your work history

♦ Multiple positions at the same company

Let's take a closer look at some work history issues and figure out ways you can resolve them. Be sure to reference the sample resumes at the end of this chapter.

Fight Age Discrimination

"How far back should I go in my work history?" is a good question to ask yourself as you set out to document your work experience. In general, you're not expected to go back more than 10 years, but you can if it's to your benefit. To help you figure out how far back to go in your work history, consider the following:

♦ How relevant your earliest positions are to your job objective

♦ How old you want to appear on your resume

 Job Hunt Hint _____

Dates in your Education section are optional. List them if they make you look the right age for the job you are going for. Delete them if they lead the reader to deduce that you are older or younger than you want to appear.

(Work History in Chronological Resume)

Name
Street
City, State Zip
Phone, E-mail

JOB OBJECTIVE

The job you want next

SUMMARY OF QUALIFICATIONS

- How much experience you have in the field of your job objective, in a related field, or using the skills required for your new position.
- An overall career accomplishment that shows you'd be good at this job.
- What someone would say about you as a recommendation.

PROFESSIONAL EXPERIENCE

20xx-pres.   **Company Name, City, State**
Job Title

- An accomplishment you are proud of that shows you're good at this profession.
- A problem you solved and the results.
- A time when you positively affected the organization, the bottom line, your boss, your co-workers, your clients.
- Awards, commendations, publications, etc., you achieved that relate to your job objective.

20xx-xx   **Company Name, City, State**
Job Title

- A project you are proud of that supports your job objective.
- Another accomplishment that shows you're good at this line of work.
- Quantifiable results that point out your skill.

20xx-xx   **Company Name, City, State**
Job Title

- An accomplishment you are proud of that shows you will be valued by your next employer.
- An occasion when someone "sat up and took notice" of your skill.

EDUCATION

Degree, Major (if relevant), 20xx (optional)
University, City, State

(Work History in Combination Resume)

Name
Street
City, State Zip
Phone, E-mail

JOB OBJECTIVE

The job you want next

SUMMARY OF QUALIFICATIONS

- How much experience you have in the field of your job objective, in a related field, or using the skills required for your new position.
- An overall career accomplishment that shows you'd be good at this job.
- What someone would say about you as a recommendation.

PROFESSIONAL EXPERIENCE

20xx-pres.   **Company Name, City, State**
Job Title

MAJOR SKILL
- An accomplishment you are proud of that shows you have this skill.
- A problem you solved using this skill, and the results.
- A time when you used your skill to positively affect the organization, the bottom line, your boss, your clients.
- Awards, commendations, publications, etc., you achieved that relate to your job objective.

MAJOR SKILL
- A project you are proud of that supports your job objective.
- Another accomplishment that shows you're good at this line of work.
- Quantifiable results that point out your skill.

20xx-xx   **Company Name, City, State**
Job Title
- An accomplishment you are proud of that shows you will be valued by your next employer.
- An occasion when someone "sat up and took notice" of your skill.

EDUCATION

Degree, Major (if relevant), 20xx (optional)
University, City, State

(Work History in Functional Resume)

Name
Street
City, State Zip
Phone, E-mail

JOB OBJECTIVE
The job you want next

SUMMARY OF QUALIFICATIONS
- How much experience you have in the field of your job objective, in a related field, or using the skills required for your new position.
- An overall career accomplishment that shows you'd be good at this job.
- What someone would say about you as a recommendation.

RELEVANT EXPERIENCE

MAJOR SKILL
- An accomplishment you are proud of that shows you have this skill.
- A problem you solved using this skill, and the results.
- A time when you used your skill to positively affect the organization, the bottom line, your boss, your clients.
- Awards, commendations, publications, etc., you achieved that relate to your job objective.

MAJOR SKILL
- A project you are proud of that supports your job objective.
- Another accomplishment that shows you're good at this line of work.
- Quantifiable results that point out your skill.
- An occasion when someone "sat up and took notice" of your skill.

WORK HISTORY

20xx-present	Job Title	COMPANY NAME and city
20xx-xx	Job Title	COMPANY NAME and city
20xx-xx	Job Title	COMPANY NAME and city
20xx-xx	Job Title	COMPANY NAME and city

EDUCATION
Degree, Major (if relevant), 20xx (optional)
University, City, State

Age discrimination works in two ways. An employer may disqualify a job candidate because he is either too old or too young. Age discrimination is illegal, but like it or not, employers usually try to figure out your age using the dates you give. Most employers have an age range they consider to be ideal for a particular job, based on the following factors:

- Salary expectations

- Skill level

- Ability to supervise or be supervised

- Amount of life experience needed

- Company or industry image

A well-written resume uses dates to lead the employer to deduce that you are the ideal age for the job you're after, regardless of your actual age. The following two sections show you how to work with dates on your resume to create the ideal image.

Putting Your Younger Foot Forward

Sally, 35 years old, was applying for a job as a sales clerk in a clothing store that catered to teenagers and young adults. She thought the employer was probably looking for a woman in her mid-20s because the employer wanted someone who fit the image of the store and who wouldn't expect wages as high as someone who had been in the field for many years.

To present herself as the ideal candidate, Sally decided to go back only five years in the Work History section on her resume, because the employer was most likely to …

1. Take 20 years of age as a starting point.

2. Add the five years of work experience shown in her Work History section.

3. Conclude that Sally was at least 25 years old.

Likewise, in her Education section, she stated her degree but did not give her graduation date because doing so would give away her age.

The dates on Sally's resume were all honest, they just didn't tell all. In the interview, she would have the opportunity to sell herself with her enthusiasm, professional manner, and appropriate salary request, thereby fulfilling the employer's expectations of the ideal candidate.

If you feel at all uncomfortable about abbreviating your Work History section in order to avoid age discrimination, you may want to call that section Relevant Work History or Recent Work History.

Career Casualty _____

If you've owned a business, don't say so on your resume. In the hiring world, it's often thought that once people have worked for themselves, they'll never make good employees again, because self-employed people like being the boss and are driven by the profit motive. A way around revealing your self-employment is to give yourself a job title in your business, choosing a title that supports your current job objective, if possible.

Older Is Better

Sam was a new graduate who worked in his dad's business all through high school and college. He was a remarkable achiever and was ready for more responsibility in the workforce than most people his age. He applied for a position as a store manager, knowing that if he could just get his foot in the door he could convince the owner he could handle the job.

He thought that the employer was probably expecting to hire someone in his late 20s. So on his resume, Sam went back in his Work History section eight years to when he started working for his dad in low-level positions, and showed his progression over the following years. He stated that he had a degree, but he did not give the date of completion, because it might indicate that he was only 22. Everything on Sam's resume honestly painted the picture of someone who had the experience and maturity of a 30-year-old without ever revealing his age.

Down and Dirty Formula

Here's a quick and easy method for understanding how dates on your resume make an impression about your age. I call it my EPT (Experience Plus Twenty) formula. Subtract the earliest date on your resume from today's date (using years only, no months). Add that number of years to 20 (as a ballpark figure for how old you might have been when your experience started). Your perceived age is equal to or greater than this total. For example, a resume written in 2010 with a Work History that starts in 1994 tells the employer that the job applicant is at least 36 years old (16 years of experience + 20 = 36).

> **Bonus Check**
>
> If your potential employer isn't likely to recognize a company you list in your Work History section, you may want to give some explanation as to what industry it is in or what product it sells. You can do that by writing a short overview statement immediately beside or under the company name.

Unsightly Unemployment Blemishes

"What's wrong with a few gaps in my work history?" you might ask. "Isn't everyone entitled to a little time off?" Many responsible professionals have taken breaks in their careers to travel, take care of ill parents, recover from personal illnesses, or for other legitimate reasons. But for some reason, employers don't like to see gaps in your work history. Unexplained gaps may cause an employer to think that you're hiding something or that you might have a past or current problem (such as substance abuse, incarceration, laziness, or instability) that would affect your ability to work. They would rather see the unemployed time explained, especially if the explanation is somehow connected to your job objective or at least shows strength of character. To gain the employer's trust, it's important to justify your employment gaps. If you have a period of unemployment in your history, the following sections explain some ways of dealing with it.

Years Go Solo

Use only years, not months, when referring to spans of time in your Work History section. Using years makes it quicker for the potential employer to grasp the length of time and can eliminate the need to explain gaps of less than one year.

Notice the gap in this presentation:

12/05–3/09	Manager	Friendly's Ice Cream Parlor, Trenton, NJ
2/02–12/04	Manager	Lyon's Restaurant, Milbrae, CA

Without the months, there is no apparent gap:

2005–2009	Manager	Friendly's Ice Cream Parlor, Trenton, NJ
2002–2004	Manager	Lyon's Restaurant, Milbrae, CA

Months complicate the presentation and make it harder (and therefore longer) for someone to figure out. Remember the eight-second scan I talked about in Chapter 3? Providing just the years will help you pass that eight-second test.

Filling In the Gaps

If your unemployment covers two calendar years or more, you need to explain the void. Consider all the things you were doing during that time (volunteer work, school activities, internships, schooling, travel, and so on) and present it in a way that's relevant to your job objective, if possible. You may have two or three "job titles" that could fill an employment gap on your resume. If so, choose the title that is most relevant to your job objective.

Someone looking for a medical sales position who took care of an ill parent for two years might list the following:

2005–07	Home Care Provider for terminally ill relative

An applicant for a travel agent position could refer to a vacation:

2007–09	Independent travel: Europe, Asia, and South America

A mother wanting to re-enter the job market as a teacher's aide might say:

2004–09   Full-Time Parent and PTA Volunteer,
                       St. John's Academy

Character That Counts

Even if your activities during your unemployment have no apparent relevancy to your job objective, you need to account for the gap. Explain what you were doing in a way that is honest and feels comfortable to you. If your main activity was something you don't want to talk about, think of something else you were doing during that time, even if it doesn't relate to your job objective, and refer to that activity instead of using a job title in your Work History. Don't refer to personal illness, unemployment, or rehabilitation. These topics usually raise red flags, so avoid mentioning them at all cost.

Some suggested substitutes for a job title include the following:

Full-Time Parent

Home Management

Family Management

Family Financial Management

Independent Study

Personal Travel

Adventure Travel

Travels to (fill in the place you traveled to)

Professional Development

Freelance Work (replace *Work* with the type of work you did, such as writer, artist, or plumber)

Student

Consultant

Contractual Work (replace *Work* with the type of work you did, such as administrator, accountant, or hair stylist)

Relocation from Abroad

Volunteer

Civic Leader

There's no need to elaborate on your filler job title, unless doing so will support your job objective. For instance, if your Job Objective statement reads "Fund-raiser," you might say, "Volunteer (emphasis on fundraising)" in your Work History section.

The Gapless Resume

Janet Bennett had a long period of recent unemployment. For that reason, she chose to use the functional format for her resume (found at the end of this chapter) and filled in her gap with two job titles:

- Childcare Teacher (which was a volunteer position at her church)
- Full-Time Parent (for her two children)

These two titles not only demonstrate that she's a stable citizen, they also qualify her for her job objective. Can you see how she used both experiences in the achievement statements in the body of the resume?

If you include unpaid experience in your Work History section as Janet did, be sure that you call this section either Work History or History, not Employment History, because the word *employment* implies that you were paid.

Promoting Your Promotions

You can be especially proud of your work history if you've been promoted within a company. So go ahead, this is your chance to brag!

Potential employers will be impressed by your promotions because they indicate employment stability and high performance. Let's look at ways to show off your promotions in your Work History section.

Imagine that you have been promoted three times within a company called Harrison Productions. Notice what kind of impression you might make if you used this format:

2007–present	President, Harrison Productions, Chicago, IL
2006–2007	Vice President, Harrison Productions, Chicago, IL
2003–2006	Producer, Harrison Productions, Chicago, IL

At first glance, the employer is likely to think you are a job-hopper who had three jobs in four years. (Ouch!) Only upon closer examination might she understand that your three jobs were at the same company. But what if the employer doesn't take the time to figure that out? You will have made a negative impression when you had an excellent opportunity to make a positive one.

I suggest organizing the same information in this way:

2003–present	HARRISON PRODUCTIONS, Chicago, IL
	President, 2007–present
	Vice President, 2006–2007
	Producer, 2003–2006

Bonus Check

Employers must be very careful about what questions they ask in a job interview, because they can be sued for asking questions that suggest illegal hiring practices. Therefore, an employer might choose not to interview you rather than risk a lawsuit by asking about unexplained employment gaps on your resume.

Notice how this second version makes it immediately clear that you were a loyal employee who had multiple promotions.

The good news is that this concept applies to both the chronological and functional formats, as demonstrated by the following three job seekers, whose resumes are at the end of this chapter.

Grass Underfoot

Dianne Woo was concerned that a potential employer would view her as stagnant because she'd worked at General Electric for so many years. To avoid creating such a negative image, she separated her job titles under the company heading and inserted achievements for each one, as you can see in her resume. Doing so made it obvious the grass hasn't been growing under her feet!

If you have many years at the same organization, emphasize your promotions by placing bullet point achievement statements under each job title. Doing so will give your Work History a sense of dynamism and diversity, thereby countering the image of being a stick-in-the-mud that sometimes comes from exceptional longevity at one company.

Straight Up

Barry Rizkallah presented his comprehensive career at Chevron in a concise list in the Work History section of his functional resume. At a glance, the reader could see that Barry was an accomplished marketing professional—why else would he have been promoted through such a healthy tenure?

When listing your promotions at one place of employment, organize the dates of your job titles so the reader understands at a glance that they are a subset of the overall dates at the company.

Zipping Along

When Shane Mathews wrote his resume in 2009, he wanted to show off his promotions at his last two companies. By grouping his job titles as subsets under each company heading, he achieved two things:

- He made it easy for employers to see that he'd been promoted.
- He avoided having to go into detail about each job title.

The employer surely appreciated this smart move.

The Happy Job-Hopper

Temporary employment or short-term assignments can make your Work History look complicated and sometimes create gaps in employment. If that's the case for you, don't worry. You have two solutions to choose from.

The first solution is to list the name of the employment agency you worked for, followed by a subset of impressive clients, as in the following example:

Creative Employment Agency, Graphic Designer, 2004–pres.

Clients included: Xerox Corp.
                                         IBM
                                         First Bank

The second option is to justify the span of time with a professional title preceded or followed by a term such as *contractor*, *freelance*, or *consultant*, whichever is appropriate for your field. The following examples show this strategy:

Creative Employment Agency, Freelance Graphic Designer, 2004–pres.

Clients included: Xerox Corp.
                                         IBM
                                         First Bank

Marketing Consultant, 2003–present
                                         McMillan Financial Services
                                         Lewiston National Bank
                                         Prosperity Trust

By bundling your short-term assignments under a professional title in your Work History, you'll no longer look like a job-hopper.

Formatting Tricks

In addition to the tips mentioned so far in this chapter, here are a few you might need to know about:

- Because there is no prescribed order in which to list your Work History components (date, job title, employer's name, city), you are free to prioritize the elements according to relevance. For instance, the President of Universal Studios might present his work history in any one of these ways:

  2008–pres., President, Universal Studios, Los Angeles

  President, Universal Studios, Los Angeles, 2008–pres.

  Universal Studios, Los Angeles, President, 2008–pres.

  Universal Studios, Los Angeles, 2008–pres., President

- You may state your date ranges either with the century digits in both years (for example: 2005–2006) or with the century digits in the first year and not in the second (for example: 2004–06). The key is to be consistent throughout your resume.

◆ If your list of job titles at one company is so long you think it might overwhelm the employer, you can list only the ones that support your job objective. In that case, preface your list with something such as "Relevant Positions" or "Positions Included," and don't list dates for each job. The following example shows this strategy:

2003–present	TransAmerica State Insurance, Wilmington
Relevant Positions:	Marketing Manager
	Business Analyst
	Marketing Specialist

◆ Depending on what you list in the Work History section of your functional resume, consider naming this section one of the following:

Work History	History
Employment History	Experience
Relevant History	Career History

The Least You Need to Know

◆ Use only years, not months, when presenting your work history.

◆ Avoid age discrimination by using the EPT formula.

◆ Disguise gaps in your work history by giving yourself a job title that explains the unemployed span.

◆ Arrange your Work History section to show off your promotions within a company.

Janet Bennett

123 Amboy Street • Little Rock, AR 12345 • **(123) 555-1234** • jbennett@bamboo.com

JOB OBJECTIVE: A position teaching preschool and elementary-age children.

SUMMARY OF QUALIFICATIONS

- More than 20 years teaching preschool and elementary-age children.
- Good communication skills with children and adults.
- Capable of leading projects. Supportive team worker.
- Experience working in low-economic settings.

EXPERIENCE

WORK WITH CHILDREN

- Taught children of low-income families at State of Arkansas Preschool Program, a parent participation program.
- Incorporated parents into the preschool program, being sensitive to the parents' needs for shared responsibility.
- Planned the preschool's parent education programs and trained them in effective communications with children.
- Collaborated with fellow preschool teacher to share ideas and solutions, as well as to train teacher aide in classroom management style and curriculum.

SCHOOL-COMMUNITY RELATIONS

- Served on PTA Board as president (four years) and coordinator of parent services in the classroom (four years) of Briarcliff Elementary (my children's school).
- Taught Parent Educator Program (five years) at Briarcliff. Co-planned curriculum, and facilitated discussions on prevention of drug/alcohol abuse and self-esteem.
- Volunteered extensively for classroom activities, field trips, etc. at Booker Baptist Church.
- As member of School Site Council, planned use of state funds for school.
    - Identified the area of need; built a consensus of how to address it.
    - Applied for funding.

WORK HISTORY

Childcare Teacher	Booker Baptist Church, North Little Rock, AR,	2009
Full-Time Parent	Little Rock, AR	1993-09
Classroom Teacher	State of Arkansas Preschool Program, Sherwood, AR	1986-93
Classroom Kindergarten Teacher	Pine Bluff Public Schools, Pine Bluff, AR	1984-86

EDUCATION AND CREDENTIALS

B.S., Elementary Education, University of Arkansas, Little Rock, AR, 1983
State of Arkansas Teaching Credential, K-9 and Early Childhood, lifetime

DIANNE WOO

123 Hollister Place, St. Louis, MO 12345   (123) 555-1234   diannewoo@bamboo.com

OBJECTIVE

Office Manager

SUMMARY OF QUALIFICATIONS

- 12 years office management experience in one of the nation's leading corporations.
- Consistent record of increasing productivity by maintaining effective interdepartmental relations and office systems.
- Excellent IBM and Macintosh skills.
- International background. Bilingual: Mandarin/English.

PROFESSIONAL EXPERIENCE

1997-present   GENERAL ELECTRIC, INC., St. Louis, MO
Administrative Secretary to Director, Corporate Communications, 2002-present
- Independently streamlined this fast-paced department that generates annual, quarterly, and monthly publications with individual circulation of up to 120,000.
- Devised electronic network that facilitates immediate written communications with over 200 remote locations.
- Managed budgets totaling $1 million. Prepared estimates and proposals for new publications.

Secretary to Vice President, Merchandising, Office Products, 2000-2002
- Set up and managed office procedures for the Merchandising Department, which produced a national wholesale office products catalog.
- Provided office support for 13 managers.

Secretary/Assistant to Manager, Office Services, 1997-2000
- Increased quality of office services for the 750-person headquarters building by improving customer service and inventory systems.

Assistant to Managing Director, Missouri Training Academy, 1997
- Assisted Director in setting up training program for technical and media professionals.

1989-1997   FOREIGN OFFICE, REPUBLIC OF CHINA
Administrative Secretary to Consul General, St. Louis, MO, 1992-1997
Secretary to Ambassador, Beijing, China, 1989-91
- Represented Republic of China to foreign diplomats and maintained strict confidentiality as "right-hand" to the Consul General and the Ambassador.
- Served as translator to Chinese officials during state visits.

EDUCATION

B.S. equivalent, University of Beijing, China, 1989
Certificates, Foreign Language Correspondent, Beijing, China

Barry M. Rizkallah
123 Banana Drive • Wheeling, WV 12345 • (123) 555-1234 • rizkallah@bamboo.com

Marketing Professional

Summary of Qualifications
- 13 years as a marketing professional for one of the nation's leading corporations.
- Expertise in project management, marketing, and vendor relations.
- Computer proficient: Excel, PowerPoint, MS Word, Vizio, Lotus Notes, Microsoft Project.

Selected Accomplishments
at Chevron U.S.A. Products, Inc.

PROJECT MANAGEMENT
- Led a team of operations, advertising, and product development managers for the $200,000 launch of a new product.
- Coordinated analytical team efforts to standardize quality of service in 8,500 retail sites.
- Increased sales and improved customer relations by developing Chevron International's first co-op advertising program.
- Organized sales retreats in U.S. and overseas resorts for 50 agents from around world.
- Trained regional coordinators and outside consultants in new computer programs.

MARKETING
- Created "Who's Who," a 12-page, four-color brochure distributed world-wide that promoted Chevron as a valuable international player.
- Designed a $15,000 booth for international trade shows for Chevron's cultural diversity.
- Produced "Technical Tables and Charts," a detailed 50-page publication used in the shipping industry. Updated content and image, dramatically increasing demand.

Work History
1996-present	**Chevron U.S.A. Products, Inc., Wheeling, West Virginia**
	Business Analyst, 2009-present
	Marketing Specialist, 2005-2009
	Senior Marketing Assistant, 2002-2005
	Marketing Help Desk Representative, 2001-2002
	Collections Representative, 2000-2001
	Customer Representative, 1996-2000
	Administrative Assistant, 1996
1995-1996	**Saudi Research & Marketing, Inc., Houston, TX**
	Publication Subscription Manager

Education
B.A., Public Relations, minor: Business, West Virginia State College, Wheeling, WV, 1994

Shane Mathews

123 Bay Court • Columbus, OH 12345 • (123) 555-1234 • shanem@bamboo.com

JOB OBJECTIVE: Collections Administrator

SUMMARY OF QUALIFICATIONS

- Ten years of business experience, including eight years in the financial services industry.
- Proficient at utilizing computer systems to produce analytical reports.
- Enhance operations through strong organizational and problem-solving skills.

EXPERIENCE

THE BANK OF OHIO, Columbus, OH, 2005-pres.
Corporate Operations Manager
Banking Officer
Banking Assistant

- Retrieved data, analyzed information, and spread financial reports for management, using mainframe and PC systems. LAN Administrator for two years.
- Bank-certified to respond to credit inquiries using Robert Morris Associates criteria.
- Administered operational systems that satisfied auditors for four consecutive years.
- Reduced liability and standardized corporate banking operations by instituting risk management policies.
- Served as liaison to account officers, clients, and bank departments, ensuring quality customer service through problem resolution.
- Supervised personnel; handled salary reviews, performance counseling, and training.

GREAT MID-WESTERN BANK, Cleveland, OH, 2001-2004
Management Trainee
Administrative Assistant

- Compiled and calculated statistics for weekly and quarterly reports.
- Prepared human resources reports that included salary and turnover analyses.

UNIVERSITY OF CLEVELAND, Cleveland, OH, 1999-2000
Full-time MBA Student

WHITE MEADOWS CENTER, INC., Cleveland, OH, 1998-1999
Assistant Marketing Manager

- Assisted in development of annual calendar and budget for this large shopping center.
- Collaborated with merchants and management to produce joint promotions.

EDUCATION

MBA, Marketing, 2003, University of Cleveland, Cleveland, OH
BA, Administration and Legal Processes, 1998, Kent State, Kent, OH

Chapter 8

Step Five: Show 'Em You're an Achiever

In This Chapter

- ◆ Why achievement statements are a smart use of your resume real estate
- ◆ How to present major headings in your functional resume
- ◆ How to make the value of your experience obvious to an employer
- ◆ Add power to your sentences with action verbs

Most resumes are dry (so dry you need to drink a couple glasses of water just to get through them) because they focus on boring job duties. Although your potential employer wants to know what you've done, she is even more concerned with whether you've achieved the desired results on the job. In this chapter, you determine what your relevant achievements are and learn how to put them on your resume, so you can get the most out of every word.

Chronologically Clear

The achievement statements in your chronological or combination resume appear under the company name where you performed the achievements. To understand what section I'm referring to, look at the highlighted areas in the following chronological and combination templates.

By the way, Professional Experience is the name of the midsection in the templates shown in this chapter (which contains your work history and achievement statements). That section may also be called the following:

- ◆ Professional Accomplishments
- ◆ Career Achievements
- ◆ Achievements
- ◆ Selected Accomplishments
- ◆ Experience

(Achievement Statements in Chronological Resume)

Name
Street
City, State Zip
Phone, E-mail

JOB OBJECTIVE

The job you want next

SUMMARY OF QUALIFICATIONS

- How much experience you have in the field of your job objective, in a related field, or using the skills required for your new position.
- An overall career accomplishment that shows you'd be good at this job.
- What someone would say about you as a recommendation.

PROFESSIONAL EXPERIENCE

20xx-pres.   **Company Name, City, State**
Job Title
- An accomplishment you are proud of that shows you're good at this profession.
- A problem you solved and the results.
- A time when you positively affected the organization, the bottom line, your boss, your co-workers, your clients.
- Awards, commendations, publications, etc., you achieved that relate to your job objective.

20xx-xx   **Company Name, City, State**
Job Title
- A project you are proud of that supports your job objective.
- Another accomplishment that shows you're good at this line of work.
- Quantifiable results that point out your skill.

20xx-xx   **Company Name, City, State**
Job Title
- An accomplishment you are proud of that shows you will be valued by your next employer.
- An occasion when someone "sat up and took notice" of your skill.

EDUCATION

Degree, Major (if relevant), 20xx (optional)
University, City, State

(Achievement Statements in Combination Resume)

Name
Street
City, State Zip
Phone, E-mail

JOB OBJECTIVE

The job you want next

SUMMARY OF QUALIFICATIONS

- How much experience you have in the field of your job objective, in a related field, or using the skills required for your new position.
- An overall career accomplishment that shows you'd be good at this job.
- What someone would say about you as a recommendation.

PROFESSIONAL EXPERIENCE

20xx-pres.   **Company Name, City, State**
Job Title

MAJOR SKILL
- An accomplishment you are proud of that shows you have this skill.
- A problem you solved using this skill, and the results.
- A time when you used your skill to positively affect the organization, the bottom line, your boss, your clients.
- Awards, commendations, publications, etc., you achieved that relate to your job objective.

MAJOR SKILL
- A project you are proud of that supports your job objective.
- Another accomplishment that shows you're good at this line of work.
- Quantifiable results that point out your skill.

20xx-xx   **Company Name, City, State**
Job Title
- An accomplishment you are proud of that shows you will be valued by your next employer.
- An occasion when someone "sat up and took notice" of your skill.

EDUCATION

Degree, Major (if relevant), 20xx (optional)
University, City, State

If you're a chronological or combination resume writer, skip past the next few sections about the functional resume and jump into "Dynamite Achievements" later in this chapter.

Functionally Sound

You're still reading, so you must be a functional resume writer. Your achievement statements should appear under the appropriate skill headings in the body of your resume. Check out the following functional resume template to see what I mean.

Do you have a feel for where your achievements are going to be listed? Good. Now read on to learn some important things about creating the skill headings for your functional resume.

Bonus Check

Be sure that the print of your skill headings appears smaller than your major section headings. You can accomplish this by doing one of the following:

- Make the skill heading type one or two font sizes smaller than the major section headings.
- Use all uppercase letters in the major heading, and use uppercase and lowercase in the skill headings (see Michael Wong's resume at the end of this chapter).

Functional Help

One of the key advantages to using a functional resume is that you define yourself by your skills, rather than by your former job titles. That's why it's an especially good format for career changers and those with tricky employment histories.

The way to put the spotlight on your skills in the functional resume is to create skill headings, which appear in the body of the resume. The purpose of using the skill headings is to help the potential employer quickly identify you as someone with the talents needed to do the job. (Don't forget you have to make a good impression during an initial eight-second scan!) If you keep your skill headings brief and put them in bold or large print, the employer will quickly define you by your skills, rather than by your previous job titles.

One Plus One Is Enough

To figure out what skill headings to put on your functional resume, imagine that you are an employer who is writing an ad for the job mentioned in your Job Objective statement. What skills would you list as requirements?

(Achievement Statements in Functional Resume)

Name
Street
City, State Zip
Phone, E-mail

JOB OBJECTIVE
The job you want next

SUMMARY OF QUALIFICATIONS
- How much experience you have in the field of your job objective, in a related field, or using the skills required for your new position.
- An overall career accomplishment that shows you'd be good at this job.
- What someone would say about you as a recommendation.

RELEVANT EXPERIENCE

MAJOR SKILL
- An accomplishment you are proud of that shows you have this skill.
- A problem you solved using this skill, and the results.
- A time when you used your skill to positively affect the organization, the bottom line, your boss, your clients.
- Awards, commendations, publications, etc., you achieved that relate to your job objective.

MAJOR SKILL
- A project you are proud of that supports your job objective.
- Another accomplishment that shows you're good at this line of work.
- Quantifiable results that point out your skill.
- An occasion when someone "sat up and took notice" of your skill.

WORK HISTORY

20xx-present	Job Title	COMPANY NAME and city
20xx-xx	Job Title	COMPANY NAME and city
20xx-xx	Job Title	COMPANY NAME and city
20xx-xx	Job Title	COMPANY NAME and city

EDUCATION
Degree, Major (if relevant), 20xx (optional)
University, City, State

Let's say you're the manager of a retail store, and you're looking for a Director of Customer Service. Your help wanted ad might read: "Applicant must be skilled in supervision and customer service." Now step back into the shoes of the job seeker. *Supervision* and *Customer Service* would be the two skill headings you should use on your resume.

Don't overwhelm your reader by having too many skill headings. Two (at most three) headings are usually plenty to make a good first impression. Also, don't write lengthy skill headings in your resume. Limit them to no more than three words each. Otherwise they become too difficult to read in the employer's typical initial eight-second scan.

Let's role-play again: as a supervisor in a software development firm looking for a technical supervisor, you might write, "Applicant must be proficient in computer programming and team leadership." As a job seeker, you understand that *Programming* and *Leadership* would be good skill headings to use on your resume for this job.

Take a look at the resume for Michael Wong, found at the end of this chapter. Notice how his skill headings define his job objective, which differed from his work history. This resume is an excellent example of how a resume should be about a job seeker's future, not his past.

Skills for Sale

Some functional resume writers have trouble coming up with skill headings. When selecting the skill headings for your functional resume, be sure to choose ones that define your future (your job objective), not your past (your work history). If you feel stuck, take a look at the following list of skills. It's also a good idea to visit your industry's websites to learn what skill sets are sought after in your field. Notice that I've categorized this list according to four general occupational areas: business management, education, engineering/ technical, and nonprofit management. Although you may want to focus on an area that's close to your job objective, I suggest you read through the entire list. Maybe a word in another category will inspire you to define your skill set in a way that is uniquely yours.

Job Hunt Hint

"Responsible for" is a slippery phrase that doesn't clearly describe your level of involvement. Did you think of an idea that others carried qut, or did you work overtime to implement every detail of a project? Either way, be sure to give yourself full credit by using action verbs (instead of "responsible for") to indicate exactly what your role was.

Business Management

Accounting	International Relations	Presentations
Accounts Payable	Inventory Control	Product Development
Accounts Receivable	Inventory Management	Production
Administration	Investor Relations	Project Management
Advertising	Leadership	Promotions
Benefits	Legal	Public Relations
Budget Management	Management Consulting	Purchasing
Business Development	Marketing	Quality Assurance
Client Relations	Media Relations	Re-engineering
Community Relations	Mediation	Recruitment
Conflict Resolution	Meeting Planning	Retail Management
Consulting	Negotiations	Sales
Copy Writing	Office Management	Shipping
Corporate Giving	Operations	Speech Writing
Customer Service	Order Fulfillment	Strategic Planning
Executive Management	Organizational	Supervision
Financial Management	Development	Training
Human Resources	Personnel	Vendor Relations
Insurance	Presentation Coaching	Writing

Education

Administration	Curriculum	Program Development
Admissions Evaluation	Development	Research
Classroom Management	Interdisciplinary	Teaching
Committee Leadership	Teamwork	Tutoring
Counseling	Parent Relations	

Engineering/Technical

Analysis	Engineering	System Evaluation
Computer	MIS	Systems Analysis
Customer Support	Planning	Team Leadership
Data Collection	Presentations	Teamwork
Database Management	Programming	Technical Support
Design	Research	Technical Writing
Development	Survey Coordination	
Documentation	System Design	

Nonprofit Management

Advocacy	Counseling	Grant Proposal Writing
Board Relations	Development	Leadership
Calendar Management	Event Planning	Major Donor Giving
Community Outreach	Financial Management	Media Relations
Consensus Building	Fundraising	Needs Assessment

continues

Nonprofit Management   (continued)

Program Coordination	Public Speaking	Staff Management
Program Development	Recruiting	Volunteer Management
Project Coordination	Service Delivery	Volunteer Recruitment
Public Relations	Solicitations	Writing

Dynamite Achievements

Nab the employer's interest right away with an achievement-oriented resume. By writing about your experience in terms of achievements, not job descriptions, you'll convey three things:

◆ You have the experience and skills to do the job.

◆ You're good at this work and at using these skills.

◆ You like your work. (You must! There's pride in your statements.)

Achievements will impress the reader, make your resume far more interesting to read, and stimulate productive conversation during the interview. Powerful achievement statements that speak to the employer's bottom line also build a strong foundation for your salary negotiations. When you create your achievement statements, be careful not to emphasize any aspect of the experience that you don't enjoy doing. Only stress the parts of the achievement that you would like to repeat. Also, when listing items within an achievement statement, prioritize those items so that the most relevant one comes first. When listing them in a column, list them either according to relevance or alphabetically.

Who's Your Audience?

Keep in mind while you write your resume that your audience is the hiring manager for the position mentioned in your Job Objective statement. To sell yourself to this potential employer, talk about yourself in ways that are meaningful to her. In some cases, you may need to do one or more of the following:

◆ Translate terminology to downplay differences between your past experience and your job objective.

◆ Select only aspects of your achievements that paint a picture of you at your next job.

◆ Prioritize your points so that your most relevant achievements are emphasized.

Downplay Differences

Avoid job-specific jargon in order to downplay the differences and emphasize the similarities between your previous position and your job objective. For example, Elizabeth was a nurse who was applying for a customer service position at a department store. She used general terms when referring to her hospital work so the employer would see that her customer service skills were just what was needed in the department store.

> **Instead of writing:** Explained medical procedures and equipment to Hamilton Medical Center patients and their families to enable them to make wise decisions regarding surgery, care, and discharge.

> **Elizabeth wrote:** Educated clients about new products and procedures at the medical center and assisted them in making personal decisions based on financial, lifestyle, and timeline concerns.

When Charles's military service ended, he wanted a job in corporate public relations, so he phrased his statements using civilian terminology to de-emphasize his career transition.

> **Instead of writing:** Managed public relations for the U.S. Navy's Fleet Week, a $1.5 million celebration that drew 50,000 civilians.

> **Charles wrote:** Managed public relations for a $1.5 million celebration sponsored by the Bay Area's largest employer and attended by some 50,000 people.

Always make it simple for an employer to understand how you fit into her organization. If necessary, translate your experience into terminology that she will identify with easily.

Keep It Relevant

Your achievements consist of several ingredients, some of which may have nothing to do with what you will offer your next employer. Make an impression that you're a good fit by presenting only the aspects of your achievements that relate to your job objective.

For example, Henry was an excellent event planner who wanted to use his organizational skills in a new field—graphic layout for a daily newspaper. He knew he could not assume the employer would conclude that Henry was capable of laying out newspaper copy just because he knew how to plan events, so Henry took extra care to draw parallels between the two occupations.

> **Instead of writing:** Produced social and business events for up to 2,000 people, managing budgets, catering, entertainment, and logistics.

> **Henry wrote:** Maintained a perfect record of on-time delivery of at least 20 projects a month, involving time, budget, and space constraints.

As a horticulturist, Patty realized that the part of her job she liked the most was answering clients' questions. When she wrote her resume for a job as a travel agent, she emphasized her customer service skills and downplayed her scientific expertise.

Instead of writing: Provided scientific information on thousands of plant species as the lead horticulturist of the country's most prestigious botanical garden.

Patty wrote: Assisted customers in selecting from more than 2,000 options by patiently answering questions and educating them about costs and benefits.

To have effective achievement statements, refer to the aspects of your experiences that paint the picture of your job objective, and therefore, have meaning to your prospective employer.

First Things First

Prioritize your statements so the achievement most relevant to your job goal is first. For example, as a former office manager, 75 percent of Andrea's time was spent processing administrative paperwork, and less than 25 percent of her time was spent on training and supervision. However, she wanted to get a job as a corporate trainer. So she prioritized her achievement statements to stress the training experience, even though it was not her primary responsibility.

The following order reflects the amount of time Andrea spent on each achievement:

♦ Supervised administration of firm's largest litigation department with more than 300 cases per week.

♦ Led office to achieve "#1 Team" award by motivating staff to take a customer service approach to all internal and external interactions.

♦ Trained 13 employees on new automated accounting system, providing classroom sessions, individual coaching, and written instructions.

This order reflects which achievements are most important to Andrea's job goal:

♦ Trained 13 employees on new automated accounting system, providing classroom sessions, individual coaching, and written instructions.

♦ Led office to achieve "#1 Team" award by motivating staff to take a customer service approach to all internal and external interactions.

♦ Supervised administration of firm's largest litigation department with more than 300 cases per week.

The order in which you list your achievements should indicate what tasks you like best and which ones you wish most to perform on your next job.

Career Casualty

Most chronological resume writers make a big mistake: because they're creating a history-based resume, they write job descriptions instead of dynamic achievements. Don't fall for that logic! By writing achievement statements, you'll turn a stereotypically boring document into a winning sales piece.

Lights, Camera, Action Verbs!

A film crew may have lights and cameras, but there's no movie until there's action. Likewise, your resume needs dynamic language to make it move. To deliver the most punch in your achievement statements, use an action verb at or near the beginning of each line. Action verbs make your resume more powerful by emphasizing how you accomplished your goals.

The following list of verbs is categorized under two headings: *Management* and *Communication*. Which verbs most powerfully describe your achievements?

Management

accelerated	consolidated	facilitated	marketed
accomplished	contracted	financed	maximized
achieved	controlled	focused	merged
activated	converted	forced	met
added	coordinated	forged	minimized
administered	corrected	fostered	mobilized
advanced	cultivated	founded	modernized
allocated	cut	fulfilled	modified
analyzed	decided	gained	monitored
anticipated	defined	generated	motivated
appointed	delegated	governed	multiplied
appropriated	delivered	guided	netted
approved	designated	handled	obtained
arranged	determined	headed	opened
assigned	developed	heightened	orchestrated
attained	devised	hired	organized
augmented	directed	implemented	oversaw
authorized	dominated	improved	performed
bid	doubled	incorporated	piloted
boosted	downsized	increased	pioneered
budgeted	drove	induced	planned
built	earned	initiated	positioned
capitalized on	empowered	installed	precipitated
carried out	endorsed	instituted	presided
caused	engineered	integrated	prioritized
centralized	enhanced	intensified	processed
certified	enlarged	introduced	produced
chaired	enlisted	invested	promoted
championed	established	launched	proposed
collaborated	evaluated	led	purchased
completed	exceeded	lowered	ran
conceived	executed	magnified	ranked
concentrated	expanded	maintained	rated
conducted	expedited	managed	reengineered

continues

Management (continued)

reached	restructured	solved	trained
realized	revamped	started	tripled
recommended	reviewed	steered	triumphed
recruited	revitalized	stimulated	turned around
reduced	revived	streamlined	underwrote
regulated	revolutionized	strengthened	unified
rejuvenated	scheduled	structured	united
remedied	secured	succeeded	upgraded
renewed	served as	supervised	upheld
represented	set	synchronized	verified
resolved	shepherded	systematized	won
restored	sold	targeted	

Communication

addressed	compromised	guided	proclaimed
adjudicated	conversed	illustrated	promoted
advertised	converted	impressed	prompted
advised	convinced	influenced	proofread
advocated	corresponded	informed	proposed
annotated	counseled	inspired	publicized
announced	created	instigated	reassured
answered	defined	instructed	recommended
appeased	delivered	interpreted	reconciled
arbitrated	demonstrated	intervened	remarked
argued	demystified	interviewed	represented
articulated	depicted	intonated	settled (disputes)
asserted	described	lectured	specified
assuaged	detailed	litigated	spelled out
assured	developed	lobbied	spoke
authored	dictated	mediated	stated
bargained	discussed	moderated	stimulated
briefed	drafted	motivated	stipulated
campaigned	edited	negotiated	stressed
canvassed	educated	ordered	swayed
clarified	elucidated	outlined	taught
coached	encouraged	persuaded	trained
coined	explained	phrased	translated
collaborated	expounded	pitched	urged
communicated	expressed	preached	verbalized
compelled	facilitated	prepared	voiced
compiled	formulated	presented	won over
composed	guaranteed	pressured	wrote

How'd the Other Guys Say It?

A quick look at what others have written might give you the jump start you need for writing about your own accomplishments. The following achievement statements were taken from several different resumes:

- ◆ Restructured entire Service Department, resulting in more efficient outreach programs.

- ◆ Initiated procedures to increase employee productivity while reducing stress levels.

- ◆ Successfully explained and demonstrated technical products in lay terminology to prospective buyers.

- ◆ Negotiated the sale of $100,000 worth of unprofitable inventory.

- ◆ Created sales and marketing programs that increased shopping center profits by 33 percent.

- ◆ Won more than 80 percent of cases, delivering persuasive arguments as legal representative for corporate clients in administrative law hearings.

- ◆ Increased MediSave's stock value fivefold in nine months by repositioning the product and company.

- ◆ Convinced more than 400 commuters to carpool, reducing the number of vehicles on the road by 225 per year.

- ◆ Managed a national and international sales force of 32 manufacturers' representative companies for Teekel Press, a publisher.

- ◆ Exceeded delivery performance by 10 percent, taking it from 85 percent to a record 95 percent in an industry where the norm is 75 percent.

- ◆ Managed the sales and Profit & Loss for 20 stores in Northern California region.

- ◆ Handled daily news coverage of the San Francisco 49ers and Oakland A's, which involved extensive travel.

- ◆ Authored two published pieces on international touring, which demystified the hardships and emphasized the rewards of independent travel.

- ◆ Reconciled differences among personnel, creating a more cohesive team spirit.

Job Hunt Hint

Name-dropping is the name of the game. Look for opportunities to enhance your image by slipping in names of impressive people, companies, or organizations.

Brainstorming

The following questions will help you think of relevant achievements for your resume. Not all of the questions will apply to your situation, so answer only the ones that do.

1. What projects are you proud of that relate to your job objective?

   Example: Increased productivity 20 percent as lead engineer on Hewlett-Packard's HMS technical team.

2. What are some quantifiable results that point out your ability?

   Example: Drove profits from $20 million to $34 million by directing a national celebrity marketing campaign.

3. When have you demonstrated PAR (Problem, Action, Result)? What was the problem, what was your action to remedy it, and what was the result?

   Example: Reduced theft 47 percent by instituting Shoppers' Spy, a tight yet discreet security program.

4. When did you positively affect the organization, the bottom line, your boss, your co-workers, or your clients?

   Example: Enhanced staff morale through a six-month incentive program that also prompted a major increase in sales.

5. What awards, commendations, or publications have you achieved that relate to your job objective?

   Example: Awarded "Top Salesperson" for three consecutive years.

6. How is success measured in your field? How do you measure up?

   Example: Selected by the NIH to represent the United States at the International AIDS Conference in Brazil.

7. Are you good at using the skills required for this job? When have you demonstrated that to be true?

   Example: Used advanced CAD tools to create a totally new look in video game modeling.

8. What activities, paid and unpaid, have you performed that used skills you'll be using at your new job?

   Example: Offered academic counseling to 40 students at "Make It Happen," a volunteer program at Sanford High School.

9. When did someone sit up and take notice of how skilled you are?

   Example: Commended for achieving 97 percent of production goal in an industry where 85 percent is considered high.

In addition to answering these questions, you might want to browse through the resumes throughout the book, in the Portfolio of Sample Resumes at the back of this book, and at my website, SusanIreland.com, to see which phrases trigger ideas for your resume.

Warning! Functional Resume Ahead

Many times functional resume writers make the mistake of writing achievement statements without indicating where the accomplishments took place. This practice makes potential employers uneasy because they have no way of confirming the experience. The solution? Give each accomplishment credibility by saying where it happened. Here are two ways to indicate where your success took place:

1. Incorporate the name of the organization or your position into the sentence:

   Managed Harrington Department Store's $1.5 million budget.

   Collaborated with executives to create a new marketing strategy as member of the St. Francis Board of Directors.

2. Reference the organization or your position at the end of the statement:

   Managed budget of $1.5 million. (Harrington Department Store)

   Collaborated with executives to create a new marketing strategy. (St. Francis Board of Directors)

You'll notice both of these techniques as you peruse the sample functional resumes in the Portfolio of Sample Resumes at the back of this book.

> **Bonus Check**
>
> A well-crafted functional resume that makes it clear where the job seeker's achievements took place can win over employers, even those who claim not to like functional resumes.

The Least You Need to Know

♦ In a chronological resume, place your achievement statements under the appropriate job title in the body of your resume.

♦ In a functional resume, your skill headings become subheadings under the Relevant Experience section in the body of your resume.

♦ Write powerful achievement statements instead of boring job descriptions.

♦ Use action verbs at or near the beginning of your achievement statements.

♦ Prioritize bulleted points within each section so the statement with the most impact comes first.

♦ Include the information on where an achievement took place in functional resumes.

Michael Wong

123 Adams Street, #1 • Somerville, MA 12345 • (123) 555-1234 • mwong@bamboo.com

JOB OBJECTIVE: A position in Public Relations with an emphasis on Event Planning.

SUMMARY OF QUALIFICATIONS

- Experienced at public relations for a provider of promotional merchandise for national and international concert tours.
- Success in producing events for up to 8,000 people.
- Reputation for achieving goals using a professional yet personable approach.

EDUCATION

MBA, International Marketing, Boston University, Boston, MA, 2000
BA, Marketing, Northeastern University, Boston, MA, 1998

RELEVANT ACCOMPLISHMENTS

Public Relations

- Represented promotional merchandise providers to concert hall managements, bands, and the public. Tours included: Melissa Etheridge   Matchbox 20
  Jimmy Buffett   Faith Hill
- Saved as much as 6% of revenues when negotiating venue contracts for promotional merchandise sales of up to $25,000 per night.
- Developed positive rapport between band and merchandise company by creating a team atmosphere rather than a strictly business relationship.
- Commended for establishing strong working relationships with bands and management companies. Consistently requested by bands for repeat and new tours.
- Acted as tour public relations person, handling questions and comments from fans.

Event Planning

- As event planner on the Arts Board, produced sell-out musical and theatrical programs for up to 8,000 attendees.
- As hospitality director for Musical Event Board, negotiated contracts, supervised catering, and managed backstage accommodations for concerts including:
  U2   Destiny's Child   Eminem
  James Taylor   Brian McKnight   No Doubt

WORK HISTORY

2005-present	**Tour Manager for Merchandise**	DAVIS ENTERTAINMENT, nationwide, 2006-present CARMICHAEL GROUP, nationwide, 2006 tour
2006	**Executive Assistant** (contractual)	AXTELL GROUP (advertising/promotions), Boston
2003-2005	**Department Manager**	SHOE SHOPS INC., Cambridge

Chapter 9

Step Six: Give Yourself Credit for Education and More

In This Chapter

- How to create a proper Education section
- Where to put professional affiliations, community service, and other information on your resume
- How to deal with an employer's request for your salary history
- What not to put on your resume

Your resume is looking pretty good, isn't it? You've resolved your work history problems, written dynamite achievement statements, made claims that blow your competition out of the water—you're on a roll! You need to consider only a few more things, and then you'll be ready to drop your resume in the mail. In this chapter, I share some helpful hints on how to make the most of your academic, professional, and vocational training, as well as other activities that support your job objective. I also explain why some information, such as references, salary history, and personal data, may not belong on your resume at all.

Finish Lines

At this point, you may be left with laundry lists of technical, personal, and professional details that don't fit into the primary sections of your resume discussed so far. Lingering lists might include the following information:

- Education
- Professional training
- Community service
- Professional affiliations
- Publications
- Awards
- Computer skills
- Personal pursuits

Even if you feel like just throwing them in a big pile at the bottom of the page, don't! Instead, create one or more logical sections that will spark the employer's interest. Sneak a peek at the template on the next page to see where you might place your extra goodies.

Education 101

Your education is almost always a point of interest to a prospective employer. The Education section is usually positioned at or near the end of the resume, as noted on the template.

In some cases, however, it's better to place the Education section under the Summary of Qualifications section near the beginning of the resume. You might want to put it here if one or more of the following conditions applies:

- Your education is highly relevant to your new position.

- You're a new graduate and you want to show off your degree.

- You have no employment experience in the field you are going into, but you have a degree or training in that field.

Job Hunt Hint

Instead of listing all the classes and workshops you ever attended, list only the ones that support your job objective.

What If?

Education comes in many forms (formal, independent, professional training, and experiential), and there are as many ways to measure its results (degrees, credentials, certifications, equivalencies, years of experience, lists of acquired skills).

You probably fall into one of the following categories:

- You have one or more college degrees.

- You are about to achieve your college degree.

- You have a college degree equivalent.

- You went to college but didn't complete your degree program.

- You just graduated from high school.

- You graduated from high school some time ago and never went to college.

Let's look at how to present each one of these situations and how real job seekers handled the Education sections on their resumes (found at the end of this chapter).

(Extra Resume Sections)

Name
Street
City, State Zip
Phone, E-mail

JOB OBJECTIVE: The job you want next

SUMMARY OF QUALIFICATIONS
- How much experience you have in the field of your job objective, in a related field, or using the skills required for your new position.
- An overall career accomplishment that shows you'd be good at this job.
- What someone would say about you as a recommendation.

PROFESSIONAL EXPERIENCE
20xx-pres.   Job Title   **Company Name, City, State**
- An accomplishment you are proud of that shows you're good at this profession.
- A problem you solved and the results.
- A time when you positively affected the organization, the bottom line, your boss, your co-workers, your clients.
- Awards, commendations, publications, etc., you achieved that relate to your job objective.

20xx-xx   Job Title   **Company Name, City, State**
- A project you are proud of that supports your job objective.
- Another accomplishment that shows you're good at this line of work.
- Quantifiable results that point out your skill.

20xx-xx   Job Title   **Company Name, City, State**
- An accomplishment you are proud of that shows you will be valued by your next employer.
- An occasion when someone "sat up and took notice" of your skill.

EDUCATION
Degree, Major (if relevant), 20xx (optional), University, City, State

PROFESSIONAL AFFILIATIONS

Association	Position (optional)	Dates (optional)
Association	Position (optional)	Dates (optional)

COMMUNITY SERVICE

Volunteer position	Organization	Dates (optional)
Volunteer position	Organization	Dates (optional)

Hot College Degrees

Perhaps the most common listing for the Education section on a resume is a college degree. So let's begin by talking about degrees and related information. If you have one or more college degrees, keep the following points in mind:

◆ State where each degree (graduate and undergraduate) was received. You don't have to list all the different schools you attended leading up to achieving your degree, just list the one where you obtained your degree.

◆ Dates are optional. They sometimes indicate how old you are and how current your knowledge is, so be conscious of those issues when you decide whether or not to include dates.

◆ Majors, minors, theses, dissertations, internships, projects, papers, and coursework should be listed only if they are relevant to your job objective.

◆ You can spell out a degree (for example, Bachelor of Arts) or use the representative letters (BA or B.A.).

Phillip Riekels listed his Education section near the top of his resume because his degrees are so important to his job objective.

Career Casualty

Don't appear overqualified for the job. For some positions, your Master's or Doctoral degree might scare the pants off an employer because you look too expensive or intimidating. When in doubt, leave the degree off. And if you're tempted to lie about a degree or certification, resist! Getting caught in a lie could put your job in the can.

Getting Credit for Your Pending Degree

If you are currently in a relevant educational or training program but have not yet finished, list the program and name of the institution you are attending, followed by the date you intend to finish or one of the following phrases:

◆ Currently enrolled

◆ Anticipated completion: Spring 2012

◆ In progress

◆ Six months completed

Robyn Jones's resume demonstrates this point.

Interpreting Degree Equivalents

If you achieved a degree equivalency through a less traditional or non-American system, state your experience in terms of its equivalency, for example, "B.A.

equivalent, St. Paul University, Rome, Italy." Grace Deminier's resume presents her degree equivalent.

Don't Have a Degree?

If you went to college, but you do not intend to get your degree in the immediate future, write your area of study and the name of the college, for instance: Liberal Arts, Oberlin College. If you attended several schools without completing your degree requirements, list only one or two schools. Listing more than that might make the reader think you tend to move around a lot without finishing things. Leonora Braun's resume shows how you can present a partial college education.

Hooray! Just Got My High School Diploma

If you're a new high school graduate, write the name of your high school; and year of graduation. Frank Jordan's resume lists his high school diploma.

If you've enrolled in a college, you don't have to list your high school; you can simply say that you're enrolled in college. For example, say "Enrolled in Nazareth College, Rochester, NY."

The Not-So-New High School Diploma

If you received your high school diploma more than two years ago and have no additional schooling, you do not need to have an Education section on your resume unless the job you are applying for specifically asks for a high school diploma. If it does, put "Graduate" or "Diploma," followed by the name of your high school. State your graduation date only if it doesn't blow your cover with regard to your age (as explained in Chapter 7). If you have a high school diploma but no formal higher education, one option is to create a section titled Professional Development or Training. In this section, you can list any training, workshops, seminars, or classes you have attended. Another option is to simply omit the Education section on your resume. Rose Manson didn't put an Education section on her resume because she didn't have a college degree, her high school graduation was many years ago, and her professional experience is all that she needs to qualify for her job objective.

> **Job Hunt Hint**
>
> If you're questioning whether to add another section to your resume, weigh the pros and cons. Does it warrant the extra space it will take, especially if it means the resume will spill onto a second page?

The Last Word

Your destination is within sight; you don't even need binoculars to see the resume shore anymore! Only a few more sections might appear on your resume, such as Professional Affiliations, Community Service, Computer Skills, and Personal Interests. Let's talk about them.

Volunteerism That Pays Off

What you do in your unpaid time may say as much about you as what you do for employment. If you feel that your volunteerism makes a statement about your dedication, character, or social awareness, or in any way enhances your qualifications for your next job, a section called Community Service, Civic Leadership, or Volunteerism is the place to list it.

Dates are optional under the Volunteerism section. If you list them, you should present your volunteer work in reverse chronology (your most recent work first). If you don't use dates, list your community service according to impact (the most relevant first).

Professional Schmoozer

Professional associations to which you currently belong or have once belonged can be listed either alphabetically or in order of relevance to your profession under a section called Professional Affiliations. If you currently hold or have held an office, that should also be noted. Listing dates in this section is optional.

Getting Published

Articles, books, chapters in books, and research papers that you have authored or co-authored belong in a section called Publications. Usually, dates accompany this information, requiring presentation in reverse chronology (the most current date first).

Standing Up for Your Award

In the Awards section, list honors, awards, and grants you have received that support your job objective. You can arrange this list according to date received (if you give the date) or by relevance to your next job (if you don't provide the date).

Key Point: Your Computer Skills

If you have computer or technical skills that are important to your next job, you can highlight them under a special section called Computer Skills or Technical Skills. Your list might include hardware, software, languages, systems, and networks with which you have experience.

Making a Hobby of It

Some job seekers like to have a section called Personal Pursuits, Personal Interests, or Personal Activities in which they can list travel, sports, religious, political, and other personal activities. The Personal Pursuits section is optional and should be included only if you feel your personal activities …

Bonus Check

After you create your laundry list sections, prioritize them on your resume so that the most important and relevant list comes immediately after your Work History section (on a functional resume) or Professional Experience section (on a chronological resume).

- Add to your qualifications as a candidate for your job objective.

- Say something about your character that might be valued on the job.

Although many employers have said they wouldn't hold it against a job seeker for including non-work-related information, consider whether any of your personal activities might create undesired conflict with your employer's views and preferences. A potential conflict of interest could arise over issues such as race, religion, unions, and other controversial topics.

Here are a few assumptions an employer might make from the following listings on resumes:

- An applicant who lists, "Board of Trustees, St. Anne's Episcopal Church," is indicating that she is actively involved in her church. Although some employers may welcome this involvement, others may feel uncomfortable with it.

- The owner of a nonunion company might feel threatened by an applicant who lists, "Organizer, Teamsters, Local Chapter 47092," because he may be worried the applicant will want to unionize his company.

Anything Missing?

Other headings that might appear on your resume include Exhibitions, Research, Lectures, Licenses, and Certifications. If you have just one or two entries for a section, you might combine two similar sections with a double heading, as in the following examples:

Education and Training

Training and Credentials

Awards and Presentations

Cruise through the many resumes throughout the book, in the Portfolio of Sample Resumes at the back of this book, and at my website, SusanIreland. com, to see how various professionals have presented their laundry lists of achievements.

What's Better Left Unsaid

Knowing what to leave off your resume can be just as important as knowing what to include. Do not include the following:

- Salary history or requests

- Reference information

- Personal data

Let's talk about why these items are best left off your resume.

Money Talk

Although some job advertisements ask for a resume and salary history, the two do not go together. Discussion about salary belongs in the interview, not on the resume. It is to your advantage not to make a monetary request before an interview. Indicating salary requirements before the interview may increase your chances of being screened out and decrease your bargaining power during salary negotiations.

If you feel obligated to address salary in order to fulfill the employer's initial application requirements, do so in your cover letter, not on your resume. Turn to Chapter 10 to get ideas for talking about money in your job search correspondence.

Referring to References

Addresses and phone numbers of references should not be a part of your resume. They belong on a separate sheet of paper that you bring to the job interview.

Also, a big thumbs-down on writing "References available upon request" at the bottom of your resume. It's unnecessary, because employers will assume that you have references, and they know to ask for them when the time comes.

Forget the Personal Stuff

Including information about your age, sex, marital status, and health is not appropriate for resumes being used in the United States.

Although personal information doesn't usually appear on a resume, you may want to make an exception if something in your personal life supports your job objective. For instance, if you're applying for a position designing content for a website on diabetes, you might mention in your resume (perhaps in your Summary of Qualifications) that you "have a personal understanding of diabetes" if you think it will increase your chances for an interview.

Likewise, if you have a hobby that's relevant to your job objective, find a way to include it on your resume. For example, if you're looking for work in the solar energy industry, you might write a statement like this under your Personal Activities heading: "Build solar- and wind-powered skateboards for annual county science exhibitions."

Bonus Check

When creating your reference sheet to take to the interview, put it on letterhead that matches your resume and cover letter. In addition to looking spiffy, the letterhead will identify whose reference sheet it is if it gets separated from your cover letter and resume.

The Least You Need to Know

◆ List only the degrees, courses, training sessions, and workshops that are relevant to your job objective.

◆ If you have a degree or credential that makes you look overqualified for the job, don't put it on your resume.

◆ If dates within the Education section tell the reader more than you want to reveal, leave them out.

◆ Take inventory of the relevant information that you still want to include and list that data in appropriate sections such as Community Service, Professional Affiliations, and Awards.

◆ Do not include salary history or references on your resume; include personal data only if it relates to the position you're applying for.

Phillip Riekels, RN, MS, CNA

123 Palmer Avenue • Muskegon, California 12345 • (123) 555-1234 • PhRiekels@bamboo.com

Health Care Administrator with 20 years combined experience:

Project Management

Standards Development/Quality Assessment and Improvement

Staff Training and Development

Client Services

EDUCATION

MS, Nursing Major with dual focus: Administration and Education, 2000
Thesis: Identification of Family Problems During the Treatment Stage of Cancer
University of Oklahoma, Oklahoma City, Oklahoma

BS, Nursing, 1988, University of Arizona, Tucson, Arizona
BA, History of Art, 1982, University of Michigan, Ann Arbor, Michigan

Continuing Education
Numerous courses to maintain **Certified Nurse Administrator** status, 2004-present
Western Network for Nurse Executives, 2003, University of California at Berkeley

PROFESSIONAL EXPERIENCE

2001-present **St. Agnes Medical Center,** Fresno, California
DIRECTOR PATIENT CARE SERVICES, 2006-present
DIRECTOR MEDICAL/SURGICAL, 2001-2006

Managed operating budgets up to $14M, 382 FTEs, and 272 patient beds for this 326-bed accredited, not-for-profit, regional, acute-care facility.

- Revitalized Quality Assurance Program by developing high standards, establishing interdepartmental problem solving, and transitioning to Quality Assessment and Improvement.

- Played primary role in achieving JCAHO accreditation and placement within top 10% of facilities nationwide.

- Improved staff productivity, patient satisfaction, and quality of care.

  - Empowered staff by decentralizing management and decision making within patient-care services. Reorganized, trained, and supported staff.

  - Restructured systems for delivery of care, including staff roles and interdepartmental reporting.

  - Introduced communication and computer technology involving 20 departments.

  - Aligned FTEs with volume and cost variations by introducing staffing by Hours Per Patient Day (HPPD) to replace staffing ratios and static patterns.

  - Improved communication and conflict resolution by providing 20-hour training program, Increasing Personal Effectiveness, for over 500 personnel.

(Continued)

Phillip Riekels, Page 2

St. Agnes Medical Center (Continued)

- Recruited thirteen British nurses (five of whom have stayed for more than five years) as a result of three trips to London. Worked with advertising agency, State Board of Nursing, and immigration attorney.

- Represented the hospital through newspaper and TV interviews about innovative solutions to health care problems.

- Oversaw remodeling of three major units. Merged intensive and cardiac care into one critical care unit.

1998-2001   **HCA Northwest Hospital,** Tucson, Arizona
MANAGER SURGICAL/ORTHOPEDICS

Played major role in the start-up of this new 150-bed, for-profit, acute-care community hospital.

- Developed and managed a 28-bed surgical unit.

- Managed a 24-bed ortho/neuro unit and hospital-wide messenger service.

- Started the nursing Quality Assurance Program and chaired its committee.

- Implemented the HCA Patient Classification System.

- Established HPPD staffing guidelines for all nursing units.

1997-1998   **University of Oklahoma, College of Nursing,** Tulsa, Oklahoma
TEACHING ASSISTANT

1996-1997   **CSI Productions,** Tulsa, Oklahoma
RESEARCHER AND WRITER

Wrote narratives for this producer of health care training materials on Cardiac Monitoring, Medicating the Patient, and Antiembolism Stockings.

1993-1996   **Gila Pueblo College,** Globe, Arizona
NURSING INSTRUCTOR

- Saved the nursing program by achieving 100% graduate passing rate on State Board Exams, a drastic improvement from previous years' unacceptably low rates.

- Redeveloped entire content of first year associate degree nursing program to update information and improve presentation.

1989-1993   **Hospitals in Arizona and Oklahoma**
CLINICAL PATIENT CARE positions: Charge Nurse, IV Therapist, Staff Nurse

AFFILIATIONS

World Affairs Council

Nursing Administrators Council (NAC) of Central San Joaquin Valley
- As President, established NAC as a voice of influence on nursing and health care in the valley.

Organization of Nurse Executives, California (ONE-C)

Sigma Theta Tau, National Nursing Honorary Society

ROBYN JONES

123 Primavera Ct., Portland, ME 12345   (123) 555-1234   robynjones1@bamboo.com

JOB OBJECTIVE

A position in organizational systems management

PROFILE

- Expertise in developing and managing organizational systems that:

Facilitate efficiency	Encourage creativity
Promote responsible behavior	Respond to change
Optimize the group's diversity	Build team spirit

- Committed to improving the environment through research and education.

- Particular skill in empowering others to acknowledge and articulate their value and role in an organization/society.

EXPERIENCE

2002-present **Facilitator, Navy Program for Personal Responsibility**
The Prevent Office, University of Maine, NAS Biddeford, ME

- Facilitate weekly classes for 20 Navy personnel from diverse cultural backgrounds, promoting personal responsibility through communication and appropriate lifestyle behaviors. Topics include:

Decision Making and Problem Solving Strategies	Interpersonal Skills
Personal and Organizational Values and Conflicts	Resistance to Addictions

1998-2002 **Manager, Project Management and Contracts**
Accounting Manager
Loonery & Crosby, Inc., Saco, ME

An international consulting firm specializing in projects that address energy efficiency.

- Facilitated forums for organizational dialogue, encouraging excellent communication among all levels of personnel (president through support staff).

- Improved client relations by establishing procedures and training staff to develop strong consultant-client rapport.

- Worked with staff to provide tools and resources needed to manage projects.

1993-1998 **Independent Bookkeeping Contractor**

1990-1993 **Paralegal**
Raddison, Maloney & Powers, Portland, ME

EDUCATION

Candidate, Master's Program, Social and Cultural Anthropology
Maine Institute of Multicultural Studies, Portland, ME

B.A., Anthropology and Social Studies
Macalester College, St. Paul, MN

Grace Deminier

123 California Street, Fort Wayne, Indiana 12345   (123) 555-1234   graced@bamboo.com

JOB OBJECTIVE: Director of Customer Service

SUMMARY OF QUALIFICATIONS

- 10 years as department manager with experience in internal and external customer service.
- Excellent supervisory skills that enhance employee skills to produce quality work.
- Computer literate in Windows and Macintosh.

PROFESSIONAL ACCOMPLISHMENTS

MANAGEMENT

Paramount Credit Services Corp.

- Monitored $500,000 per month in expenses and compiled data for upper management.
- Decreased expenditures 35% by standardizing purchasing procedures.
- Created and directed all administrative procedures for this 58-person financial firm affiliated with Xerox Corporation.
- Wrote six manuals (70-100 pages each) to clarify responsibilities of accounts payable, telecommunications, records, check processing, and administrative support.

Public Information Group

- As manager of 28 employees, increased productivity, morale, and individual and team initiative by fostering employee career development within the company.
- Improved staff performance evaluations by upgrading job descriptions.
- Created and administered an $850,000 annual budget.

CUSTOMER SERVICE

Public Information Group

- Created system for identifying and notifying past-due accounts, recovering $236,000 of uncollected premiums from previous years.
- Used diplomatic yet firm approach to resolve disputes with customers, agents, and sales staff.
- Encouraged interdepartmental cooperation through excellent internal customer service.

Paramount Credit Services Corp.

- Resolved client issues promptly as liaison to branch offices and attorneys.
- Anticipated and handled hardware and software problems, achieving minimum of downtime for six departments that work with offices in other time zones.

WORK HISTORY

2009	Administrative Assistant	Environmental Review Group, Fort Wayne, IN
2004-08	Supervisor, Administration	Paramount Credit Services, Fort Wayne, IN
1998-04	Manager, Policy Administration	Public Information Group, Toledo, OH
1996-98	Family Management	Les Sables d'Olonne, France

EDUCATION

B.A. equivalent, French, Sorbonne, Paris, France, 1995

Leonora Braun

123 Sea Cliff Drive • San Diego, CA 12345 • (123) 555-1234 • lbraun@bamboo.com

JOB OBJECTIVE

Bookkeeper/Accountant

HIGHLIGHTS OF QUALIFICATIONS

- Experienced Bookkeeper/Accountant for small and medium-sized businesses.
- Ability to work independently.
- Strong list of references.

PROFESSIONAL EXPERIENCE

1991-present BOOKKEEPER/ACCOUNTANT
Selected Clients/Projects
　　　　　Michael Smith, CPA, San Diego, CA
　　　　　Blue Nile Cafe, San Diego, CA
　　　　　Star Mountain Texaco, La Jolla, CA
　　　　　The Walters Marketing Group, San Diego, CA
　　　　　Paintings '86, La Jolla, CA
　　　　　Fleur D'Alsace Restaurant, San Diego, CA
　　　　　Mark-Thomas Corporation, San Diego, CA

Michael Smith, CPA
- Prepared federal and state tax returns for corporations, partnerships, individuals, and estates.
- Maintained general ledgers and prepared financial statements for assigned clients.
- Prepared payrolls, quarterly federal and state payroll tax returns, and state sales tax returns.

Blue Nile Cafe and Star Mountain Texaco
- Set up company books, maintained general ledgers, and prepared Schedule C and partnership returns.

The Walters Marketing Group
- Maintained general ledger, accounts receivable, and accounts payable. Prepared financial statements.
- Prepared payroll, federal and state payroll tax returns, and sales tax returns.
- Assisted in the conversion to computer-generated accounting.

EDUCATION

Accounting:　　University of California, Berkeley Extension, San Francisco, CA
　　　　　　　 Healds Business College, San Francisco, CA
　　　　　　　 San Diego State University Extension, San Diego, CA

Computer:　　 Computer Options, San Diego, CA

Frank Jordan
P.O. Box 123
Bayview Meadow, ND 12345
(123) 555-1234

OBJECTIVE: Bus Driver

SUMMARY OF QUALIFICATIONS

- Dependable, hard worker who can be counted on to "get the job done."
- Excellent driving record; always give first priority to safety.
- Friendly and well liked; good at customer relations.
- Available to relocate.

EXPERIENCE

Driver/Tour Guide   **Trolley Tours, Bay Meadows, ND, 2007-2009**

- Drove small tour bus through scenic parts of this resort, pointing out sites, providing friendly service, and assisting senior citizens.
- Did light repair work as needed.
- Recognized as #1 employee within this company of 15.

Sales Representative   **Recycled Tractor Parts, Townsend, ND, Summer '07**

- Sold used tractor and equipment parts by phone and over the counter.
- Handled inventory, shipping, and nationwide teletype service.

Driver   **Paris Oil Recycling, Paris, ND, Summer '06**

- Picked up and delivered waste oil (until business was sold).

EDUCATION
Diploma, Wells High School, Wells, ND, 2008

ROSE MANSON
123 Fourteenth St., #123
Birmingham, AL 12345
(123) 555-1234
roseman@bamboo.com

OBJECTIVE: To retain insurance company relations as new owner of Highland Insurance Agency

- Reliable reputation among Birmingham attorneys.
- Proven ability to work profitably with home office.
- Currently developing underwriting practice at Highland Insurance Agency.

PROFESSIONAL ACCOMPLISHMENTS

CLIENT RELATIONS

As Branch Manager, Bonding Service, American Insurance:

- Developed and serviced a loyal client base, almost doubling branch premium dollars from $190,000 to $365,000 per year.
  - Gained a reputation among attorneys for providing timely service/markets.
  - Recaptured accounts lost during departure of previous branch manager.
  - Offered additional services to gain accounts.
  - Generated new business through regular court appearances.

As Vice President, Highland Insurance Agency:

- Secured clientele, based upon my established reputation among local attorneys.

UNDERWRITING

As Branch Manager, Bonding Service, American Insurance:

- Authorized to execute under power of attorney in all counties in Alabama, with underwriting authority up to $50,000. Branch bond amounts ranged from $6,000 to $3,000,000.
- Simplified application form to more effectively gather underwriting data.
- Established and implemented more efficient procedures for home office approval, reducing turnaround time from three days to eight hours.
- Dealt directly with surety home office in Springfield, IL.
- Gained extensive knowledge of litigation process as it relates to judicial bonds.
- Negotiated with brokerage firms to perfect surety positions.

MANAGEMENT

As Branch Manager, Bonding Service, American Insurance:

- Developed a user-friendly billing system that increased efficiency of premium collections.
- Managed office relocation, keeping down time to a minimum.

WORK HISTORY

2008-pres.	**Vice President**	Highland Insurance Agency, Birmingham, AL
2003-2008	**Branch Manager**	Bonding Service, American Insurance, Birmingham, AL
1995-2003	**Operations Manager**	Windows Plus, Inc., Birmingham, AL

Part  The Correspondence Connection

With the exception of spam and junk mail, a letter or e-mail is welcomed by almost everyone—and your prospective employer is no exception. In fact, your cover, follow-up, and thank you e-mails and letters might be the elements of your application that send the message that you're the one for the job. Whether it's the way you sell yourself in writing or the personality that comes through in your words, your messages hold the power to make a personal connection between you and the manager.

"Easy for you to say," you mumble. "You're a writer. I freeze at the thought of putting my pen to paper." Relax! Part 3 gives some easy-to-follow advice that will make your fingers fly across your keyboard to create e-mails and letters that work.

Chapter 10

Job Search Correspondence

In This Chapter

- ◆ How to write an e-mail or hardcopy cover letter to accompany your resume
- ◆ E-mail etiquette that can produce great results
- ◆ Making a website cover letter work for you
- ◆ What to say in an e-mail response to a recruiter or hiring manager
- ◆ Let's talk salary

You have a great-looking resume, and you're eager to send it off to Mr. or Ms. Employer. But wait! You need one more thing: a cover letter. And not just any old cover letter—you want a well-crafted letter that makes a great first impression.

This chapter discusses how to write an effective cover letter or e-mail to accompany your resume. It also explains how to write a good follow-up note to a recruiter's request for more information. Because e-mail correspondence has become more prevalent than hardcopy, this chapter focuses on that type of correspondence. However, most of the points also apply when sending hardcopy.

E-Mail or Hardcopy Letters?

In today's job market, e-mail cover letters are sent more frequently than hardcopy letters. Time is of the essence when it comes to applying for a job. The competition is fierce and timing is critical. Within minutes of a company posting a new job opening, a flood of resumes is likely to land on a recruiter's computer. Very often these resumes arrive via e-mail, and the ensuing communication between the recruiter and potential job candidates happens through e-mail.

Job Hunt Hint

How will you know whether to send your letter via e-mail or snail-mail? If the company has a website and conducts recruiting online, send your resume via e-mail. If the company does not have a website, use the good old U.S. Postal Service.

However, there may be times when hardcopy will be the best form for sending your resume and cover letter. If you're applying for a position in a small firm that isn't overly computer-oriented (for example, an old law firm composed of only a few attorneys), a snail-mail resume and letter might make the best impression. For some professionals, there's nothing like holding paper in hand to read a candidate's qualifications.

Here's my secret for writing an outstanding hardcopy cover letter: think of your letter as the basis of the ideal script for the job interview you'll have with the person to whom you're writing. Let your letter indicate the following things to the reader:

◆ What topic could break the ice at the beginning of the interview

◆ What kind of personality you have

◆ What types of things you have to talk about in your meeting

◆ What you hope to get from the interview

If your cover letter can say these four things, it will make an employer start imagining that you and she are having a conversation. When she does that, she'll be more apt to read your resume and then reach for the phone to call you for an interview!

To see how these principles apply, take a peek at Bill Steinberger's cover letter at the end of this chapter.

10 Tips for E-Mail Etiquette

Since Emily Post wrote *Etiquette in Business and Politics*, we've all been conscious of the dos and don'ts of courteous and appropriate communication. As in all business correspondence, polite, well-written job search letters and e-mails can yield powerful results. On the flip side, a poorly written or inappropriate e-mail can get you quickly booted out of the competition for a job. To get it right, pay attention to the following e-mail etiquette tips (slightly updated since Emily Post's time).

1. Write a subject line that's meaningful to the recipient. Many people make the mistake of writing an e-mail subject line that's generic from the recipient's point of view. For example, "Resume, ABC Company," or simply "Resume." A generic subject line like that could result in the e-mail going unnoticed among all the other e-mails in a recruiter's inbox. If you write your subject line with unique wording and include your name, it's more likely to stand out among all others.

   Let's say ABC Company has a job opening for a Landscape Architect that you want to apply for via e-mail. Two hundred people send e-mails to the recruiter, each with a resume attached. Most of those 200 applicants write a subject line that says, "Resume, Landscape Architect," or "ABC Resume." Sure, these subject lines are helpful for the applicants, who are probably applying to several companies, but from the recruiter's perspective, most of the e-mails in his inbox look pretty much alike … until you send your e-mail with its unique subject line. Your subject line says something like, "Amy Hyatt Resume: Landscape Architect." With a subject line like that, you've set yourself apart (and above) the others, simply because you made it easy for the recruiter to distinguish your e-mail among its 200 competitors. That's the power of a well-written subject line.

2. Begin your e-mail with a greeting that includes the recipient's name, if possible. No "Dear sir or madam"! No "To whom it may concern"! If you don't know the person's name, incorporate a logical title into your greeting, such as "Dear Manager," "Dear Recruiter," or "Dear Director." Another option is to write "Hello."

3. Your first sentence should be a grabber—one that captures the reader's attention, while informing him who you are and why you're writing him. Recruiters and managers usually have a gazillion e-mails in their inboxes, and they want to get through them quickly. So get right to the point, using your most relevant strength first. For instance …

   ◆ Drop the name of someone you both know.

   ◆ Speak of something that's uniquely true for that person (reference something in the recipient's background, or an organization he belongs to, or a time when you met).

   ◆ Mention an article or blog post he wrote or is somehow related to him or the company where you want to work.

4. Make sure your e-mail doesn't sound like a form letter. There's no greater turnoff than a form letter, so take the time to personalize every e-mail you send, no matter how many that may be.

5. Make your e-mail visually inviting to read. Here's how:

   ◆ Keep your e-mail short.

   ◆ Break your e-mail into short paragraphs.

   ◆ Insert a space between each paragraph to make it quick and easy to read.

   ◆ Create bullet (or dash) point statements, if appropriate.

6. Use a friendly yet professional writing style. Don't use stilted language that makes you sound like an encyclopedia. Write the way you would speak in a professional conversation so the idea of a telephone conversation or interview is no stretch of the imagination for the recruiter.

7. Your last sentence should suggest what you'd like the next step to be—for example, a job interview. See the samples in this chapter for good ideas for proposing an interview.

8. End your e-mail with a polite closer such as "Regards," or "Thank you," followed by your first and last name on the next line.

9. Make note of how you're sending your resume. If you attach your resume to the e-mail, type "Attachment: resume" immediately under your name. If you paste your resume into the body of your e-mail, introduce it with "Resume follows" immediately after your name. If you attach your resume *and* paste it into the e-mail body, write "Resume attached and below."

10. Proofread your letter very carefully before sending it. Use spellchecker if your e-mail software has it. If not, copy and paste your e-mail into a Word document where you can use its spellchecker. Read the e-mail out loud, or ask another person to proof it for you. You can't be too cautious on this front. One typo can cost you the chance at a great job.

Now let's look at how these tips apply to specific types of job search e-mails.

A Cover E-Mail with Your Resume

Career Casualty

Don't forget to attach your resume to the e-mail before clicking Send. If a recruiter doesn't find your resume, he'll probably delete your e-mail and forget all about you.

Any number of occasions may cause you to send your resume to someone. You could be sending it to …

◆ A recruiter who's interested in your qualifications for a job opening he wants to fill.

◆ A hiring manager with a job opening.

◆ Someone you know who wants to recommend you for a job opening.

◆ A member of your network so he or she can pass it along to a colleague.

Other circumstances that might require you to e-mail your resume include the following:

◆ You're up for a promotion and your supervisor needs an updated version of your resume to support his recommendation.

◆ Your employer is downsizing and all employees must send their resumes to reapply for the jobs they currently hold.

◆ The person you've asked to serve as a reference wants a copy of your resume to use as a cheat sheet.

◆ You need to supply your resume as part of a school application.

Whatever the reason for e-mailing your resume, always write a message in the body of the e-mail to introduce the resume you're sending along with it.

Your cover e-mail should follow the 10 Tips for Written Etiquette, and do the following three things:

1. Break the ice with a concise opening line that says how you know the person to whom you're writing, or how you learned about the job.

2. Announce what job you're applying for, and one or two good reasons you deserve a shot at the job.

3. Introduce your resume, referring to whether you've attached it to the e-mail, pasted it into the body of the e-mail message, or done both.

Take a look at the following cover e-mails to see how all this comes together in a short, effective message.

Job Hunt Hint

The trick to having an excellent cover e-mail is to write each e-mail individually so it never sounds like a form letter.

Your New Buddy, the Recruiter

Liz did her research to learn the name of the recruiter who hires nurses at Alexander Hospital. She did an online search for the recruiter's name and discovered he went to the same school she did, although they didn't graduate the same year. Here's how Liz used that information to her advantage in her introductory e-mail.

Subject line: Wheaton alum seeks R.N. job at Alexander Hospital

Dear Mr. Forman,

You currently have an R.N. job opening at Alexander Hospital, which I would like to apply for. I recently received my R.N. from the state of Maine.

You'll notice in my attached resume (also in this e-mail) that I am a Wheaton graduate (class of 2003). I see from your LinkedIn profile that you also graduated from Wheaton. I'm not sure when you were there, but perhaps we shared some professors.

I am available for employment within the month. Please call me at your convenience (123-555-1234).

Thank you,

Liz Blanton

Resume attached and below

Your Friend Knows a Hiring Manager

Christopher used his network to uncover a job opening at Hemmingway Hardware. The best part of his discovery was that the general manager is a friend of his network associate. Here's how Christopher incorporated that connection into his e-mail cover letter.

Subject line: Henry Hobbs sent me

Dear Mr. Hemmingway,

Henry Hobbs and I have been friends for some time. Based on his knowledge of my professional qualifications and character, he strongly recommended I apply for your sales associate opening.

Is there a time this week or next when we could meet? In the meantime, please find my resume attached (and immediately after this e-mail message).

Thank you!

Christopher Listing

You Don't Know Me

An online job post for a web designer requested applicants send their resume via e-mail. No contact information was given other than the e-mail address where the resume should be sent. Without knowing the name of the hiring person, Rosita wrote the following e-mail to accompany her resume.

Subject line: Rosita Holloway Resume for Web Designer

Dear Recruiter,

Your post on Craigslist grabbed my eye for the following reasons:

- I have three years' experience using WordPress to create nonblog sites.
- My B.F.A. from Hamlyn's School of Design included computer graphics.

Please take a look at my portfolio at rositaholloway.com, as well as my attached resume.

Your request for someone with a background in online subscription services is where I fall short; however, I have no question that I can research this and come up to speed well within your timeframe.

I'd appreciate a phone conversation to discuss the project specs. I can be reached at 123-555-1234.

Thank you!

Rosita Holloway

Mighty Cover Note on a Resume Website

Almost all resume websites (public job boards like Monster.com, and individual company websites that have career sections) have an opportunity for applicants to insert a cover note. Some sites limit the number of characters you can enter; others will allow you to send a message as long as *War and Peace*. Here's what I recommend for your website cover note:

1. Address it: Dear Recruiter.

2. Make a very concise statement as to why you are submitting your resume.

3. Incorporate at least two keywords that define the job you want. Also use the note as an opportunity to include any keywords you didn't get into your resume. (See Chapter 2 for more about keywords.)

4. Give your contact information.

5. Sign off with "Regards," "Thank you," or something similar, followed by your first and last names on the next line.

To get a clearer picture, look at how these job seekers wrote their cover notes for websites.

Setting Your Sights on a Company Website

Aaron did his homework to find the perfect company with a job opening that matched his qualifications as an Electrical Engineer. He went to the Careers page on the company's site and entered his information, including his resume (more on how to do that in Chapter 12). When it came to filling in the field for a cover note, here's what he wrote.

Dear Recruiter,

After much research about GoElectric, I feel certain my resume will be of interest to you. I am particularly interested in working in the Solar Power unit of your organization, where I believe my recent experience in solar panel development will be useful.

My current job is very flexible, so I can meet with you by phone or in person at your convenience. Please contact me at 123-555-1234.

Thank you!

Aaron Smith

Addressing the Big Job Boards

As well as applying to individual companies, Cecily put her resume on one of the big resume websites where recruiters from many companies could find it among the thousands in the resume board's database. Knowing that keywords are essential (see Chapter 2), Cecily packed synonyms for "legal" into her online cover note so the database search engine would find her resume for a job in a law firm.

Here's the note Cecily posted along with her resume on the job board.

Dear Recruiter,

Thank you for discovering me on Monster.com. If you're looking for an energetic new grad to fill a research position in a law firm, here I am! I can do everything from filing to using LexisNexis. And if there's something I don't know, I'll learn it quickly.

My references include lawyers who supervised my internship at Handler and Grissons Attorneys, and my instructors at Lessonson's Paralegal School.

I am eager to start my career in the legal field, and I welcome your response to this post.

Thank you,

Cecily Ambrosio

Follow-Up E-Mail to Recruiter

You might get an e-mail from a recruiter who's interested in talking to you about a job you applied for online. Here's what you should know about writing a good response:

1. Use the Reply function so that a copy of his initial e-mail to you is in the body of your e-mail.

2. Adjust the subject line if necessary to include your name. For example, if the recruiter's subject line was, "Your resume on ABC site," your reply e-mail could say something like, "Re: Betsy Rosen's resume on ABC site," or "From Betsy Rosen re: Your resume on ABC site."

3. Write your response at the top of the e-mail window, not after the recruiter's message.

4. Begin your message with Dear So-and-so. Follow his lead as to how you should address him. For instance, if he signed his e-mail "Ted," then type "Dear Ted," in your response. If he signed his e-mail "Ted Jamison," you should type "Dear Mr. Jamison."

5. Begin your message by thanking the recruiter for his e-mail. Then immediately respond to his request for a telephone interview, more information, your resume, or whatever it is he asked for in his e-mail.

6. In a new paragraph (which starts on a new line with a space after the last paragraph), write a short closing statement, such as an expression of appreciation for the recruiter's time and consideration. Don't be pushy. The recruiter will ask for the next step when the time is right.

7. Sign off with something like "Regards," "Sincerely," "Thank you!" or even "Again, thank you!"

8. Immediately below your closing, type your first and last names. On the following lines put your e-mail address and phone number.

Want to see examples of responses to recruiters and hiring managers? Here you go.

> **Job Hunt Hint**
>
> After writing your follow-up e-mail, send it to a friend for his quick read. He'll be able to tell you if your message is appropriately friendly and succinct. Once you get his thumbs up, send off your e-mail ASAP.

Reply to the Company Recruiter

Louis posted his resume on Bridgestone Realty's career webpage. In just three hours, he got an e-mail from the Bridgestone recruiter asking for a telephone interview. Louis jumped on the opportunity with the following e-mail.

Subject line: Louis Washington re: Job at Bridgestone

Dear Michael,

Thank you for your e-mail. Yes, I would like to speak with you about the opening at Bridgestone Realty. I'm free anytime this morning, and this afternoon from 3:00 on. If you prefer to talk tomorrow, let me know what time and I'll be available.

Thank you for such a quick response to my post.

Regards,

Louis Washington

123-555-1234

Louis@louiswashington.com

Jump on the Job Board

Dominic received an e-mail from a recruiter who found his resume on one of the large job boards. Without revealing the name of the employer he represents, the recruiter said he wanted to speak with Dominic about a job opening in financial management. Here's how Dominic replied to the mysterious recruiter.

Subject line: Re: Financial Management Job response, Dominic Rivera

Dear Mr. Slimm,

Thank you for your interest in my resume, which I posted on CareerBuilder.com. I would be happy to speak with you about the opening in financial management you referred to. I can be reached at 123-555-1234.

Would you be kind enough to send me the web address of the company you represent? That will help me prepare for our conversation.

Thank you!

Dominic Rivera

Getting Back to a Hiring Manager

When a hiring manager e-mails you with a request, send a response ASAP. The manager is most likely very busy, and wants to keep things moving as quickly as possible. If he sent the same request to several job seekers at the same time, which of those job seekers do you think will make the best impressions? You got it—the first few to reply to his e-mail.

Here are a few scenarios in which a quick e-mail response was needed.

Dear Boss

Francine e-mailed her resume to the hiring manager at a cosmetics firm where she hoped to get a position in operations management. Two days later, the manager e-mailed that he liked her resume and wanted to schedule an in-person interview. Here's the e-mail reply Francine sent.

Subject line: Re: Francine Wilhelm for Interview at Face Value

Dear Mr. Bloomingdale,

I was so pleased to get your e-mail expressing interest in me as a candidate for the Operations Manager position. Thank you very much!

If I may have 24 hours notice, I can meet with you at your convenience. I will bring my portfolio to our meeting, as there are a few projects from my past that I think are relevant to your line of products.

Again, thank you for inviting me for an interview. I look forward to meeting you.

Francine Wilhelm

123-555-1234

Yes, I'm Interested!

When Marc got an e-mail from his prospective employer, he didn't hesitate to respond. He knew the competition for jobs at the local utility company was fierce and he didn't want to miss his chance. Here's the e-mail he sent.

Subject line: Marc Armstrong Interview Monday, Installation Job

Dear Ms. Groner,

Thank you for your e-mail this morning. I am very interested in the installation position you mentioned, and I welcome an interview.

You suggested Monday morning at 10:45. I will be at your office then. Please let me know if there is anything other than my resume that you would like me to bring.

Many thanks,

Marc Armstrong

Marc@armstrong.com

123-555-1234

Salary Small Talk

You may run into a job posting that asks for your salary expectations. Most job seekers don't feel comfortable talking about these details before the interview. If you feel compelled to do so in your cover letter (maybe you worry that you'll be disqualified if you don't comply with the ad's request), do so gingerly.

I suggest you first find out what the position typically pays. You can do this by looking at salary surveys online, asking a job counselor or employment agency, or by reading posts for similar jobs online. Then do one of the following:

◆ Mention your salary expectations in your cover e-mail, using language that gives you room for negotiations, such as, "I am looking for a position in the $X to $Y salary range."

◆ Indicate that you would prefer to discuss salary during the interview.

In either case, you've addressed the issue, and you'll likely stand a chance at winning an interview where you can discuss the full compensation package, not just the take-home pay (which is what a salary range implies).

The Least You Need to Know

- ◆ Use good etiquette to make the most of your job search e-mail correspondence.

- ◆ Impress a recruiter or hiring manager with a good cover e-mail that accompanies your resume.

- ◆ Write a concise note that includes keywords when posting a resume on a company website or online job board.

- ◆ Respond to a recruiter's e-mail by answering his questions and showing interest in the job opening.

- ◆ If you're asked about your salary requirements, first find out what the position typically pays before carefully broaching the issue.

Bill Steinberger

123 Terrace Street
El Sobrante, CA 12345
123-555-1234
bsteinberger@bamboo.com

January 5, 2009

Mr. Ron Gratchet, Owner
Tools, Etc.
123 Greystone Road
Portland, OR 12345

Dear Mr. Gratchet,

Linda Zeffer has often spoken highly of you, usually in reference to the likelihood of our meeting someday.

In fact, that's what this letter and resume are about. I'd like to speak with you about the opening for General Manager at Tools, Etc.

I grew up in the hardware business — my parents owned and ran an Ace Hardware store in a small town for 25 years before they sold it to me. As much as I love managing the store, it's time to move on to bigger things ... such as Tools, Etc.

Could we talk soon? I'd like to be the first candidate you consider. I'll call your office to see when you are free to meet with me. Thank you!

Sincerely,

Bill Steinberger

Enclosure: resume

Chapter 11

Thank You Notes

In This Chapter

- Saying "thank you" by hardcopy or e-mail
- The Past-Present-Future formula for writing thank you notes
- How to express gratitude after an interview
- Why you should say thanks for a rejection
- How to respond to a job offer
- A clever way to thank your job search support group

An expression of gratitude goes a long way. Saying "thank you" not only feels good to the person receiving the thanks, it feels good to the person saying it. It's a positive exchange that can only render a positive result, even if that means simply a smile.

This chapter is all about how to say "thank you" in writing. We'll look at how to compose a hardcopy thank you note—yes, those are still in vogue—and how to write an excellent thank you e-mail that keeps your job search moving.

Hardcopy or E-Mail?

E-mail is so commonplace that it's now become very acceptable to write a thank you e-mail. On the other hand, because e-mail is the most common form of written communication, a hardcopy thank you note can make a big impression, just because it will stand out. And a handwritten thank you note, especially if the handwriting is good, will make an even bigger impression.

Here's how to decide whether to send your thank you message via e-mail or snail-mail:

- If time is of the essence (for example, you know the person is going on a trip the following day and a snail-mail letter won't get to him before he leaves), send an e-mail thank you.

Job Hunt Hint

Don't worry that sending a thank you note will pester the employer. Keep it short and to the point. It will take the employer just a minute to read and will send the right message: you sincerely want the job!

♦ If the industry to which you are applying is based online, and most communication is done via e-mail, your thank you should be sent as an e-mail message.

♦ If the employer whom you want to thank is old-school (for example, up to this point most of your correspondence has been hardcopy or by phone), send a hardcopy thank you note.

♦ If there's time for the thank-you to get there by snail-mail (within five days), you have good handwriting, and your gut feeling is that it's appropriate, send a handwritten thank you note.

Now that you know how to send your thank you note, let's look at when you should send one.

Four Times to Say "Thank You"

Here's a safe rule of thumb: every time someone does something for you, say "thank you!" That includes someone in your network who answers a question or shares a contact that brings you just a tad closer to getting your next job.

Thanks don't always have to be formal; they can be quick e-mails that in essence say, "Thank you for *whatever*. I really appreciate it." Or they can be more involved, even offering to do something to help the person in exchange for the favor they've just done for you.

Send thank you notes at every turn in your job search, even if it's in response to a downturn such as a rejection. During your job search, there are four times when official thank you notes should be sent:

♦ After a job interview that goes well

♦ After a job interview that doesn't go so well

♦ When you get a job offer

♦ When you get a job rejection

Before looking at each of these situations, I'm going to give you my quick and dirty formula for writing a good thank you note.

The Thank You Formula

With the ideal thank you note, you'll lead the recruiter or hiring manager to the next step in your job application. In other words, it moves the job search from the past into the future. I call this my Past-Present-Future formula for thank you letters and e-mails:

♦ **Past:** Show gratitude for something the note's reader has done for you (for example, he granted you a job interview).

- **Present:** Continue the conversation about the topic at hand (for example, mention something you're doing or thinking about that's relevant to the job you're going for).

- **Future:** Encourage the next step (for example, refer to a second interview or the job offer).

In the following notes to recruiters and managers, notice how the writers use this formula to establish a connection between the past (previous communications and meetings) and the next step in the job application.

> **Career Casualty**
>
> Unless you're writing to your best friend or sibling, never send text message abbreviations like "Thx." Always write out the full words—"Thank you."

Thank You for Contacting Me

Always acknowledge communication from someone, even if it's with a brief e-mail of thanks. Doing so tells the person …

- You got his e-mail, letter, or phone message.

- You appreciate his having taken the time to do something for you.

Following are a few scenarios of thank you notes that essentially said, "thanks for the communication."

To get a handle on how easy or difficult it might be for her to change careers from a kindergarten teacher to a children's occupational therapist, Leslie posted a message online for all members of her Early Childhood Development group to read. Each time she got a response from a member of the group, she sent him or her a personalized e-mail, which acknowledged her receipt of their message and in some cases nurtured a new relationship that might lead to a job opening in her new career. Here's a sample e-mail she wrote one respondent.

Dear Frank,

That was very kind of you to share your story with me. I'm in a similar position and would love to ask you a few questions. Is there a time when I could call you? Or would you prefer I ask you via e-mail?

Again, thanks for your support!

Leslie Long

Diego received an unsolicited query from a recruiter he didn't know, for a job he wasn't interested in. Because the e-mail didn't sound like spam, he decided to take the time to respond with the following thank-you and query of his own.

Dear Miriam,

Thank you for your e-mail about the position in pharmaceutical sales. You are correct in assuming that I am a sales professional, however I specialize in representing electronic components manufacturers.

Do you handle sales reps in the electronics field? If so, kindly send me your website address. If not, do you know someone who specializes in my field?

Thank you!

Diego Montana

Sylvia didn't waste any time responding to an e-mail she got from her former classmate about an upcoming class reunion that would have a career networking component. Here's what she wrote.

Dear Gail,

What fun to hear from you after all these years! Yes, I'd love to come to the reunion/career networking event. I know we'll have a chance to catch up at the meeting, but let me briefly fill you in on what I've been up to since graduation.

I made it through law school and I'm currently looking for a position in a personal claims law firm. I'd like to stay in the St. Louis area, but I'm open to the idea of relocating if a good opportunity presents itself.

What have you been doing, and what sort of career move are you looking at? Who knows, maybe I know someone who can help.

Thanks for contacting me about the reunion.

Best,

Sylvia Ortega

Can you see the use of the Past-Present-Future formula in these e-mails? Each of them refers to something in the past, speaks about something going on now, and invites future results.

How to Say "Thank You" After an Interview

As soon as you leave a job interview, start thinking about how you will thank the interviewer. Ask yourself the following.

- What went well in the interview?

- Is there something you wish you'd said better in response to a question?

- Did you forget to ask a question?

- Do you know what the next step is in the application process?

Here are some e-mail and hardcopy thank you notes that address these interview results.

James felt very good when he left his interview at Angie's Pet Supplies. He gave confident answers to some pretty tough questions and felt sure he was in the running for the store manager job he'd applied for. As soon as he got home, he turned on his computer and wrote the following hardcopy note to the hiring manager.

James Hartfeld
123 Lazy Duck Lane
Hillsboro, MA 12345
jameshartfeld@hartfeld.com
123-555-1234

January 4, 2010

Christopher Reeney
Angie's Pet Supplies, Inc.
123 Framingham Rd.
Winchester, MA 12345

Dear Mr. Reeney,

It was a pleasure meeting with you today. Thank you for your time and careful explanation of the goals you and your team are reaching for at Angie's Pet Supplies.

I am still thinking about all the ways we can approach the merchandising plan for your new store in Lafayette. In fact, would it be helpful if I put together a presentation of my ideas for our next meeting?

Again, thank you for your time. I would certainly enjoy the chance to work in your forward-thinking organization.

Regards,

James Hartfeld

Billie-Jo left her interview at Angie's Pet Supplies feeling she hadn't performed as well as she might have. Instead of presenting herself as a leader who could manage the stress of a busy retail outlet, she worried her hesitation on a particular question about customer service might have hindered her chance for the job. She decided to address the issue head-on in an e-mail to the recruiter.

Dear Mr. Reeney,

Thank you for your time this afternoon. It was kind of you to give me a tour of the store and I enjoyed meeting the staff.

I feel especially good about the training Angie's Pet Supplies is giving its employees with regards to customer care. In previous jobs, even before I held management positions, I was always seen as the go-to person for resolving customer complaints. My first goal as manager, of course, is to create customer satisfaction and reduce complaints. But when a complaint arises, I've always been able to settle it in a way that meets the customer's needs while maintaining the integrity of the company.

I have several references from former employers and customers who are happy to speak to my management abilities. Would you like me to forward you their names and contact information?

Thank you again for considering me for the store manager position.

Kind regards,

Billie-Jo Harris

Shortly after Graham left his job interview with Angie's Pet Supplies, he realized he'd forgotten to ask an important question about the training program he would be leading as store manager, if he were hired. Here's how he used his thank you e-mail as an opportunity to ask his question.

Dear Mr. Reeney,

I want to thank you for a very informative and friendly interview. I feel as though I belong at Angie's Pet Supplies already. I'm so glad we had a chance to discuss the history of the store and I had the opportunity to meet your excellent staff.

You touched briefly on the training program I would be in charge of. Is that program already developed or is it something you would like me to create? If I would be creating the program, may I meet with you again to give a brief presentation that would simulate an orientation class for the training?

Thank you for your time yesterday. I am available for another meeting at your convenience.

Best regards,

Graham Remington

Nadine had a really good feeling about her interview at Angie's Pet Supplies. In fact, she was so excited during the meeting she forgot to ask when and how she might learn about whether she got the job. To settle the matter, she asked her question in her thank you e-mail.

Dear Mr. Reeney,

Thank you for such a productive job interview this morning. I have been thinking about our conversation, and would like to underscore my passion for working with animals and their owners. I can easily picture myself managing the sales floor and the grooming department.

Understanding that you are eager to bring in your new store manager soon, I wonder what your hiring timeline is. Will you be doing a second round of interviews, and may I call your assistant to learn the status of my application?

Thank you again for meeting with me. I certainly appreciate you taking time from your busy schedule.

Regards,

Nadine Jones

If you were Mr. Reeney, which applicant would you hire, based on those four thank you notes? If I were in Mr. Reeney's shoes, I'd have to call each of them in for another interview to narrow down the choices.

Thanks for the Rejection

No one likes to get rejected, but it happens to all of us at some point in our lives. In these tough times it can be hard not to feel disappointed, if not downright mad, about not getting a job. This is especially true if it's a job you really wanted and felt qualified for.

Don't confuse "job rejection" with "personal rejection." When you don't get offered a job, it simply means someone else got the job and you need to keep looking for one. You're a fine job candidate who's bound to get a job acceptance notice before long.

When you get a rejection letter or e-mail, answer the following questions:

◆ Do you think the race was really close and you lost by just a hair?

◆ Would you want to work at the company even if it weren't in the same capacity as the job you just got rejected for?

◆ If the job opened up again (let's say the new employee couldn't take the job after all), would you accept the job if it were offered to you?

Career Casualty

If you get a job rejection, don't make the mistake most job seekers make—they toss the rejection notice and miss the opportunity of keeping the employment door open by sending a thank you note.

◆ Can you put aside your disappointment and do the right thing—thanking the recruiter or hiring manager for giving you a shot at the job, with no ulterior motive?

If you answered "yes" to even one of these questions, you need to write a thank you note (hardcopy or e-mail) right away. Doing so might take the sting out of the rejection and could even give you an unexpected chance at a job.

Claire went to three rounds of job interviews at a company; each interview seemed more promising than the last. To her great disappointment, she got an e-mail from the interviewer saying she had not been chosen for the job. She knew she must have been one of the top contenders, she thought the interviewer liked her, and she wanted to keep her name on his list of potential hires for the future. She wrote him this hardcopy letter.

Claire Simons
123 Crescent Circle
Buttersworth, NC 12345
claires@clairesimons.com
123-555-1234

February 13, 2010

Mr. William Foster
Health Science International
123 Teedlemeyer Rd.
West Endlake, NC 12345

Dear Mr. Foster,

I want to thank you for your careful consideration of my application for your research and development position. I realize how thoroughly you examined all the job candidates, and I respect your decision, even though I was not chosen for the job.

After three rounds of interviews and much research into your firm, I can say with confidence that I am sincerely interested in an R&D position at Health Science International. Would you be kind enough to keep my resume and contact information on file for another job opening in the future? I would appreciate that very much.

Again, thank you for all the time you put into my application.

Kind regards,

Claire Simons

Raul applied for a research and development job at Health Science International and got his rejection notice after two interviews. He was sad not to get the position, but he wanted to keep his hat in the ring for any other related job at the company. He sent the following thank you e-mail.

Dear Mr. Foster,

Thank you for notifying me of your decision about my application for the research and development position at Health Science International. In the process of applying for the job, I realized how much I would like to work at HSI, in any research-related capacity.

Because you have already reviewed my qualifications, can you suggest another position that would fit my skill sets? I greatly appreciate your thoughts on this matter.

Again, thank you!

Raul Hilago

Rachel also applied for the R&D position and was turned down after her third interview. Knowing she must have ranked high in the competition, she wanted to be the fall-back person should the new employee not work out. She said as much in her thank you e-mail to the hiring manager.

Dear Mr. Foster,

Thank you for your kind consideration in notifying me that the research and development job has been filled. I am sorry not to be the one chosen, but would like to ask that you keep my resume active, should the opportunity re-open for any reason.

Not only is bioscience my career path, it is my passion. I would like nothing better than to work in an environment as socially conscious as Health Science International.

Thank you for all your time and consideration. I hope we will meet again to discuss the exciting projects HSI is involved with.

Warm regards,

Rachel Chin

David also applied for the R&D job at Health Science International. He got a thanks-but-no-thanks form e-mail just days after submitting his application. He was tempted to delete the e-mail and forget about the company, until he thought better of it. After all, the company had been considerate enough to send him a notice rather than string him along with the hope that he was being considered for the job. What could be the harm in his sending a polite thank you e-mail? Here's what he wrote.

Dear Mr. Foster,

Thank you for notifying me so promptly that I am not in the running for the research and development job. Most companies are not as considerate, especially when they are flooded with resumes.

As a young bioscience graduate, I would be grateful if you kept my resume on file for future reference. I will also keep an eye on your website for job openings.

Best wishes for the good work you are doing at Health Science International.

Regards,

David Ralley

I Appreciate the Job Offer

As soon as you get a job offer, acknowledge it with a thank you note. Before doing so, you need to know which of the following three reactions you have to the job offer:

◆ You will gladly accept it because you really want that particular job.

◆ You don't want to accept the job offer.

◆ You want to delay your decision because you're hoping for an offer from a different employer.

Whether you accept the job offer or not, you have to admit it feels pretty darn good to be chosen for a job, especially in this tough job market. A thank you note is in order for both the following reasons:

◆ It's the professional and polite thing to do.

◆ It provides a record of your having received and responded to the offer.

Let's look at some thank you note examples that address accepting, rejecting, and delaying the decision of a job offer.

Glen applied to several organizations dedicated to improving water quality but the job he most wanted was at Green Water Management. When the hiring manager called him to say that he wanted to make Glen a formal job offer, Glen immediately said "yes" on the phone. After hanging up, his first thought was to plan an evening of celebration with his buddies. But before doing that, he went to his computer and wrote the following hardcopy thank you letter to his soon-to-be boss.

Glen Lord
123 Hoover Dam Road
Scottsdale, AZ 12345
glen@lord.com
123-555-1234

March 3, 2010

Dear Ms. Kim,

I was very pleased to receive your call this afternoon in which you offered me the position of Chief Financial Officer of Green Water Management. Thank you! As I said on the phone, I accept the offer and look forward to beginning work on April 8th.

As we have already settled on salary and benefits, I look forward to receiving the employment contract and finishing up those details.

I'd like to express once more that among all my job applications, Green Water Management was my first choice. I'm very pleased to be joining such a fine organization and doing my very best to help it meet its financial goals.

Regards,

Glen Lord

Louise applied for marketing positions at several companies. When she received an e-mail job offer from one of the companies, she'd already accepted the marketing job of her dreams at Green Water Management. She sent the following thank you e-mail to tell her new employment suitor she wouldn't be taking the job. Notice how her e-mail keeps the door open just in case things don't work out at Green Water Management.

Subject line: Louise Angel re: Job offer

Dear Ms. Wright,

Thank you very much for offering me the Online Marketing job. Unfortunately, just yesterday I received an offer from another company, which I accepted.

I regret that I won't be able to join your team. If there is any change in my employment status, I will contact you immediately, as I would be honored to work for your company.

Thank you for your kind offer. I wish you and Anderson Mutual the best.

Warm regards,

Louise Angel

Jerry got an offer from a company that wasn't his number-one choice. He really wanted to work at Green Water Management, but he hadn't yet heard from them and he was still holding out hope that they would offer him a job. He wrote the following e-mail response to the employer, to express his thanks and stall for time.

Dear Mr. Helmet,

Thank you for your e-mail offering me the position in your accounting department. It is a wonderful opportunity and I am honored to have won the job offer.

All things look good for my accepting the position; however, I would like to ask for a little time before making a final decision. I will get back to you with a definite answer next Monday, May 12th.

Again, thank you for your vote of confidence.

Regards,

Jerry McNally

Job Hunt Hint

Feel free to borrow any of the lines or concepts from these examples. And don't be afraid to use your own style and creative ideas for expressing gratitude and asking for what you want.

Don't delay in sending your thank you letter or e-mail. The sooner you send it, the more impressed the employer or recruiter will be. Saying "thank you" makes the right impression and is part of advancing your career, as well as being considerate of the many people who helped you along your job search journey. It takes only a few minutes to compose and send a short thank you, and it might lead to a long and fruitful relationship.

The Good News Letter

Once you get your new job, be sure to send a thank you note to everyone in your personal and professional networks who …

- ◆ Gave you hot tips and practical advice.

- ◆ Introduced you to contacts, even if those contacts didn't lead to your new job.

- ◆ Served as job or character references by writing letters of recommendation or speaking with your prospective employers.

- ◆ Helped with your resume, interviewing skills, or salary negotiations.

- ◆ Provided a shoulder to lean on when things got emotional.

- ◆ Lent you a hand when it came to personal matters (such as childcare or financial help) so you could pursue your job search.

Here's an easy way to thank your support group: write a good news letter. This is a form note that announces the good news that you've landed a job, and thanks everyone for helping you achieve that goal. At the end of the message, you write a short personal note that acknowledges the specific way the recipient helped in your job hunt.

To understand this kind of thank you note, here's a sample, which can be sent as hardcopy or e-mail. If sent via e-mail, each e-mail should be sent individually, not as a bulk e-mail, so you can include a personalized note at the end of the form message.

Dear Friends,

The journey is over! I landed a new job—one I'm really going to enjoy. I'll be the new Project Manager of Technical Support at Hardware Inc. in Cupertino.

Every one of you played a special role in my seemingly endless pursuit of this job. I want to personally thank each of you. I look forward to returning the favor when you need help with something.

Thank you all!

Ricardo

Preston, my special thanks for introducing me to Willard Scott. He turned out to be key to getting my foot in the door at Hardware. I couldn't have done it without you! Give me a call sometime and we'll go out and celebrate! —Ricardo

---

The Least You Need to Know

◆ It's perfectly acceptable to send an e-mail thank you note; however, a hardcopy version will make an excellent impression as long as it arrives in a timely manner.

◆ Each time someone contacts you by phone, letter, or e-mail, acknowledge that communication with a thank you note.

◆ No matter how well or poorly a job interview goes, send a thank you note immediately afterward.

◆ Send a thank you note to the hiring manager or recruiter even if you get a job rejection. Doing so may keep your resume alive in his mind and database.

◆ Whether you accept or reject a job offer, do it in writing as a thank you note.

◆ Send a group letter along with a personal note of thanks to everyone who helped you get your new job.

Part 4

Your Job Search on the Web

Because most recruiting now takes place online, your resume needs to be ready for its adventure in cyberspace. It will travel at lightning speed, be looked at by search engines from every angle, and finally land in the inbox of the right hiring manager. How will it find its way to the right inbox? You're going to use all the technology at your fingertips to spread the word about your professional qualifications.

You've already filled your resume with the keywords and accomplishments recruiters will zoom in on. Now it's time to get your resume e-mailed to employers, posted to Internet job boards, transformed into a social network profile, and maybe even posted to your blog.

Sound good? Then let's get clicking!

Chapter 12

E-Mail Express

In This Chapter

♦ The five steps for sending your resume via e-mail

♦ Pasting your resume into the body of your e-mail message

♦ Making your resume look good in the body of your e-mail

♦ Sending your resume as an e-mail attachment

♦ Launching your cover e-mail and resume into cyberspace

"Please e-mail me your resume." When an employer or recruiter says that, you need to be ready to send it off lickety-split. It's important for you to know how to put your resume in an e-mail-friendly format so it arrives on the manager's screen looking its best.

In this chapter, I'll explain the details of how to attach a resume that's in the right version of Microsoft Word and has a memorable file name. I'll also cover how to format your resume so it can be pasted into the body of your e-mail message as well and why this extra measure serves as insurance for your resume transfer.

The instructions in this chapter are for Word 2007 for Windows. If you have an earlier version of Word or you're on a non-Windows platform, consult your Help menu for instructions.

Easy E-Mail Resumes

E-mailing your resume isn't complicated at all. With an understanding of the process, you'll be zipping your resume through cyberspace in minutes. In a nutshell, here's what to do:

1. Go online, open a new e-mail message, and address it to your prospective employer.

def•i•ni•tion

Plain Text is the most basic form of computer document. Its formatting is so rudimentary, it can be transferred, read, and used by all computers. On Windows computers Plain Text is also called Notepad and has the .txt extension.

2. Write a brief cover note, following the suggestions in Chapter 10, including a good subject line.

3. Copy and paste a *Plain Text* version of your resume into the e-mail message.

4. Attach a Word 97–2003 (.doc) version of your resume to the e-mail.

5. Click Send.

To do these five steps, you need two versions of your resume (Plain Text and Word 97–2003) specially prepared for e-mail transmission. Let's look at how to create these e-mailable versions so you can send them on their way quickly.

Pasting Your Resume into the Body of the E-Mail

Why paste your resume into the body of your e-mail if you're going to attach it? It's all about valuing the recruiter's time. If you can give him a quick look at your resume without him having to download and open it, you've done him a favor. If he sees what he's looking for in the first few seconds of opening your e-mail, you could be put in the Yes pile (or folder) immediately.

Another benefit is the assurance that if the recruiter forwards your e-mail to someone else, the second recipient will also see your resume. With many e-mail programs, an attachment (such as your resume) doesn't remain attached to an e-mail that's forwarded. If your resume is in the text of the e-mail message, it will definitely get forwarded.

Granted, the Plain Text resume in the body of your e-mail isn't going to look fancy, but that's okay because the employer won't expect it to. Besides, I'm going to show you how to make it look pretty darn good, considering the layout limitations of e-mail.

Here's an overview for how to prepare your resume for pasting into the body of your e-mail:

1. Make a copy of the Word document that contains your resume. Open the copy so that you can make the following adjustments to it.

2. Use all CAPS for words that need special emphasis.

3. Make sure to use straight quotes in place of smart quotes. (I'll show you the difference a little later in this chapter.)

4. Save the document as Plain Text.

5. Adjust the spacing and text in your Plain Text resume.

Now let's look at each of these steps in detail to see how to accomplish them.

Make a Backup Copy to Work In

You'll need to make some changes to your Word document resume before you convert it to Plain Text. To be sure you don't mess up your original resume, make a copy of it, open that copy, and continue with the following steps.

Add Emphasis with CAPS

If you used features such as bold, italics, and underlines in your resume to highlight particular words, retype them in all CAPS. Why? Because the conversion to Plain Text will strip your document of special effects but will maintain the capped letters. All caps will give those words a little extra emphasis within the limits of Plain Text formatting.

Career Casualty

Don't go overboard by making too many words all-capped in your Plain Text resume. An overwhelming number of caps will make it look like you're shouting. Used judiciously, your caps will give just the right highlight.

Use Straight Quotes

There are two types of quotation marks: straight and curly.

- Curly quotes look like "this" and are known as smart quotes.
- Straight quotes look like "this" and are called stupid quotes.

You don't want curly quotes in your Plain Text resume because they sometimes translate as unreadable symbols (shaded rectangles) when sent via e-mail or posted online. If you have quotes in your resume, now's the time to make sure they're straight quotes. Here's how to do that:

1. With your Word resume open, click the Office button (the circle in the upper left corner of the screen with the colorful logo in it), and click Word Options in the lower right corner of the pull-down window.

2. When a new window opens, click Proofing in the left column.

3. In the next window, click AutoCorrectOptions.

4. The AutoCorrect window will open, which has several tabs at the top. Click the AutoFormat tab.

5. In the new window, deselect "Smart quotes" with "straight quotes."

6. At the top of the window, click the AutoFormat as you Type tab.

7. In the new window, deselect "Smart quotes" with "straight quotes."

8. Click OK and the job is done.

At this point you need to find each quotation mark in your resume, delete the quotation mark, and retype it. It should automatically type as a straight quote, which is what you want for your Plain Text conversion.

Save the Document as Plain Text

The following eight-step process will transform your handsome resume into a very blandly formatted, Plain Text document. Here we go:

1. Open the Word document that contains your resume.

2. In the upper left corner of your screen, click the Office button.

3. Hold your cursor over the Save As option, and a side panel will open. From that panel, click Other Formats.

4. When you have the Save As window open, rename your document using a name that will identify it accurately (such as "resume_plain_text").

5. Still within the Save As window, go to the Save As Type pull-down menu and click Plain Text.

6. Click Save.

7. Close the document.

8. Reopen the document you just closed, which you've named resume_plain_text. There's your document, completely stripped of fancy formatting!

You've now converted your document into Plain Text, and you're ready to make just a few more adjustments before pasting it into your e-mail.

> **Career Casualty**
>
> Keeping organized as you make multiple versions of your resume can be a challenge. Develop a plan to name your files logically and place them in folders that keep things straight.

Make a Few More Minor Adjustments

Take a look at your Plain Text resume on your computer screen. Depending on how your original resume was formatted, you may need to use your space bar and Enter key to rearrange things. For example:

- If you had items listed in two or more columns side by side, you need to combine those items into one list or put them in a paragraph with commas between each item.

- Where there were indents or spaces created by tabs, delete those spaces and use the Enter key to create one or two spaces where the tab space once was.

- If your bullet point statements seem squished together, give them a little breathing room (and increased attention) by inserting a space between each statement.

Bite the Bullet

Can you have bullet points in your Plain Text resume? The answer is yes! The latest version of Word hangs on to bullet points when a document is saved as Plain Text. The bullet points are smaller but they're bullet points, nonetheless. However, once your resume is in Plain Text, there's no easy way to create new bullet points. You can, however, copy and paste bullet points from within the Plain Text document. So, yes, you can have bullet points in your resume, which gives it a little more pizzazz than Plain Text resumes of yesteryear.

Alternatively, you can delete each bullet point and replace it with one of the following keyboard characters:

- ◆ Dash (-)

- ◆ Plus sign (+)

- ◆ Asterisk (*)

- ◆ Greater-than sign (>)

- ◆ Dash and greater-than sign (->)

- ◆ Equal sign and greater-than sign (=>)

Don't use the tab key to create indents. Instead, press the spacebar to place a single space after each symbol or bullet point (before the first word of the statement).

> **Job Hunt Hint**
>
> If your Plain Text resume is more than one page, eliminate "Continued" at the bottom of page one and your name and "page two" at the top of page two. You won't need these when your resume is in an e-mail message.

Using Your Notepad

Some e-mail software inserts a space after every line of a Plain Text document when entered into an e-mail message. To avoid wasting space with those extra lines, you need to open the document as a Notepad document. To do that, close your Plain Text document, find it on your hard drive, and open it again by clicking its Notepad icon.

If you print out your Notepad resume, you may see that a header and footer have been added (which weren't visible onscreen). Don't be concerned—the header and footer won't show when you copy and paste the document into an e-mail message.

Staying Above the Fold

In Chapter 10, we talked about how to write a cover e-mail that introduces a resume. By keeping your e-mail message brief, the resume that you paste into the body of the e-mail will appear above the fold—that is, the reader can see it without having to scroll down his e-mail window. Having the resume within easy sight immediately tells her what your e-mail's about.

Give yourself the three-word test when it comes to writing a good subject line for your e-mail. Because most e-mail systems show only a few words of a subject line, make the first three words of your subject line strong enough to make the employer open your e-mail.

Sending Your Resume as an Attachment

Most employers and recruiters like to receive resumes as e-mail attachments. Their computers have powerful virus protection, so they don't worry about opening e-mails with attachments or downloading documents to their hard drives. The most commonly preferred form for an attachment is Microsoft Word, for the following reasons:

- It's a word processing program almost everyone has.

- A Word document can easily be dumped into a database and searched for keywords.

- It holds its formatting through the e-mail transfer process, as long as it's in the correct version of Word (more about that later).

Although the recruiter's mail system has an icon that indicates an e-mail has an attachment, it's a good idea to briefly mention your attachment in the text of your message. That way, if for some reason the resume doesn't follow the e-mail (let's say you forget to attach it, or the e-mail gets forwarded to a hiring manager and the attachment isn't successfully transferred), the manager will know from reading the e-mail that something's missing. If he likes what he sees in the resume pasted in the e-mail message, he'll send you a reply asking you to resend the attachment.

Job Hunt Hint

To grab the reader's attention, keep your cover note short so the beginning of your resume shows in the body of the e-mail message without the reader needing to scroll down his e-mail screen.

Document Success with Old Versions of Word

Although most people use Word 2007, there are still some who haven't upgraded from the previous version. Unfortunately, pre-Word 2007 folks can't open and read Word 2007 documents (which have .docx extensions). If you're not sure which version the recruiter or employer is using, it's best to save your document as Word 97–2003 (which has the .doc extension).

It's easy to do. Here's how:

1. Open your resume document (resume.docx).

2. Click the Office button in the upper right corner of your screen.

3. Select Save As.

4. Select Word 97–2003 Document.

5. When the Save As window opens, go to the Save as Type window and select Word 97–2003 Document from the scroll down menu.

6. Click Save.

Your resume is now saved in the earlier version of Word, which works for both you and the employer. You can make edits in this version, and the employer will be able to open and see it exactly as you intended.

3-2-1, Take-Off!

You've done a great job of preparing your resume as both a Plain Text document and an attachable Word version. Now you're ready to drop it into an e-mail message, attach your Word version, and launch it into cyberspace. The following steps will get the job done:

1. Write an e-mail message to the recruiter or employer, following the suggestions in Chapter 10.

2. Without closing your e-mail message, open the Plain Text document (.txt) that contains your resume.

3. Copy the entire text of your Plain Text resume, and paste it into the e-mail window, immediately after your brief message.

4. Now that your resume is in the e-mail message window, check that it looks the way you want the employer to see it.

5. Attach the Word 97–2003 version (not the Plain Text or Word 2007 version) of your resume to the e-mail.

6. Double-check that you really *did* attach your resume to the e-mail, so you don't look careless by forgetting it.

7. Give everything one last check and click Send.

Congratulations—you're now an e-mail resume pro!

The Least You Need to Know

- To preserve your perfect Word resume, make a copy and work in that copy to prepare a Plain Text version.

- Use all caps instead of bold, underline, or italics to give emphasis to important words.

- After saving the Word resume as Plain Text, make adjustments so spacing looks right and text is aligned properly.

- Copy and paste your Plain Text (.txt) resume immediately after your message in the body of your e-mail.

- Attach a Word 97–2003 version of your resume, and send.

Posting Your Resume Online

In This Chapter

- ◆ Resume websites that work for your job search
- ◆ Going straight to a company's website
- ◆ What the big online career sites offer
- ◆ Weighing the pros and cons of posting online
- ◆ Steps for uploading your resume online
- ◆ Making changes to your online resume

Online job boards (also known as job banks) have changed the face of job hunting. Almost all job searching is conducted online, and for good reason: it's highly effective! There's no precedent for the kind of access applicants now have to job openings. And it's a two-way street: employers have never had such a huge talent pool to select from. Because online recruiting is so successful, most companies now use it as their primary means of finding job candidates.

In this chapter, I'll talk about how to find the right resume site for your job search. Then we'll take it step by step until you've posted your resume on that site.

Picking a Bank

When online resume banks first came on the scene, they were used primarily by high-tech companies to find high-tech applicants. Gradually, the range of industries that use online resume banks for recruiting has grown. Today almost all industries use online recruiting to fill most levels and types of employment. It's very likely that your profession is represented somewhere online—your job is to track down where.

Job Hunt Hint

If your resume is in an employer's database you could be considered for a fantastic job you didn't even know you were qualified for. The search engine might select your resume based on keywords an employer entered to find the perfect candidate for a job you hadn't even thought of.

Resume banks can fall under one or more of the following categories. They might …

◆ Specialize strictly in one industry (such as IT or health care).

◆ Focus on a particular profession (such as human resources or sales).

◆ Provide recruiting services to special interest groups (such as women, the disabled, or other minorities).

◆ Cater to a geographic region (such as a state or metropolitan area).

◆ Cover a wide range of industries and professions so applicants are considered for lots of job titles.

Let's look at how to find resume banks in these categories.

Specialized Industries or Professions

Many websites specialize according to industry, profession, or both. Here are ways to learn of those that apply to your job search:

◆ Use your Internet search engine (such as Google), inserting keywords that indicate your area of expertise or industry (such as *jobs*, *e-commerce*, and *marketing* for a marketing position in online business).

◆ Read professional magazines in your field or visit their websites to see what online recruiting sites they suggest.

◆ Ask your colleagues what resume sites they recommend (assuming you can speak freely with them about your job search).

There's no harm in posting your resume on multiple sites. Think of it as spreading your net wide on the World Wide Web.

Specializing in Special Interests

Many resume websites focus on special interests, such as a social cause or an ethnic population. These sites have a couple of advantages over the large generic sites in that they may …

◆ Offer current employment information that's specific to that interest group.

◆ Provide job search support through articles, blogs, and member profiles to enable individual networking.

Good ways to find your special interest websites include asking friends in your special interest group, using your search engine, and looking for website addresses in literature from your interest group.

It's a Regional Thing

A website that represents regional recruiting efforts is highly valuable, whether you live in that geographic area or are planning to relocate to it. Such sites are often sponsored by the following organizations:

◆ Career centers

◆ Libraries

◆ Local media (TV, radio, or newspapers)

◆ Special interest groups for the area

◆ Recruiting agencies

◆ Specific companies

In addition to supplying their resume databases to local employers, the sites frequently announce (and sometimes sponsor) career fairs, lectures, workshops, and other networking events that you might attend online or in person.

The Big Guys

You've probably heard of online career sites such as Monster.com and CareerBuilder.com. This type of megasite is well managed and usually features a resume bank that offers the following:

◆ A large client base of employers

◆ A wide range of industry job categories

◆ National and international job openings

◆ A job agent (a service that e-mails you job listings that fit your criteria)

◆ Online job search advice (for instance, how to write a resume)

◆ E-newsletters sent to you via e-mail

◆ The option to keep your resume anonymous

◆ The ability to update your resume after it's been posted

These large resume sites have a high volume of recruiters who search their databases regularly. This means that you could get a response within hours of submitting your resume.

Company Websites Pay Off

If you have a company in mind you'd love to work for, go straight to its website and find the Careers or Employment webpage. Most companies have a resume submission process right on their site, with instructions for submitting your resume and applying for specific positions.

Applying directly through the company website can be beneficial because …

♦ It can save time. Rather than going through a third-party site such as Monster.com or CareerBuilder.com, you go straight to the source.

♦ You can browse the company's database of job offerings, possibly finding other jobs that fit your skill set.

♦ Some company sites (such as Kaiser.com) give you more responsibility for your job search, insisting that you check in to see new job openings and submit specific requests for jobs. Although this requires more work on your part, it's a good way to draw the attention of company recruiters by keeping your application active.

Using company websites gives you the advantage of knowing where your resume has been submitted, because you—not a third party—are the one submitting it.

The Downside of Uploading

Not surprisingly, there are some possible downsides to posting your resume online:

♦ Your current employer could find out about your job search.

♦ You could get pigeonholed into a career path.

♦ Your personal and professional information becomes public knowledge.

These points are worth examining, because they'll help you weigh the pros and cons of posting online.

Hello, Ms. Employer!

Your employer may be using an online database to search for future employees, and she could run across your resume in the process. Yikes! The cat would be out of the bag about your job search.

To spare you from such an embarrassing and potentially job-threatening situation, some banks offer to block out information on your resume (such as your name, contact information, and current employer). If you choose this option, the job bank's system acts as your agent, notifying you of each employer's request for information about you. Then you can decide which opportunities to pursue.

Pigeonholed

Announcing your career intentions by posting your resume online can be very helpful in the short run as it might very well bring your next job to you quickly. However, what goes online often stays online. Often resumes get archived in databases, both on- and offline. This means that at any point in the future, a recruiter may find your old resume when he conducts a search using keywords in your resume. That's no problem if you're still in the same line of work. But what if you have changed the focus of your career and your old resume doesn't reflect your new direction? That old resume could send the wrong message to a potential employer and you might not get considered for a job you really want.

For example, a scientist who posts her resume today for a position in a specific subspecialty of nanoscience might later decide to shift her career to a different subspecialty. With her old resume online (which can happen even if she made efforts to delete it from the job boards), she could get trapped in her first sub-specialty because her original resume keeps surfacing when recruiters search for the keyword "nanoscience."

Your Personal Info Becomes Public

Sad to say, but there *are* dishonest people in the world—identity thieves who pose as recruiters and collect personal information from resumes posted online. Some job boards allow you to keep your address and contact info private. But today's search engines make it easy for thieves to use a name and limited information (such as your previous employer or college) to dig deeper and eventually get more information about you than even your mother knows.

To reduce your risk, read the privacy policies posted on job boards and follow them carefully.

Go to the Bank and Fill Out the Forms

Online resume banks are constantly changing the layouts of their websites and fine-tuning their procedures as they become more sophisticated. At most resume banks, you'll be presented with a two-step process:

1. Fill in the blanks of an online form (also called an e-form).

2. Submit your resume into a large window.

Both steps are straightforward, but let's look at a few tricks that will ensure your success.

Fill In the Blanks

Here are the items you will probably be asked to type in:

◆ Your name, address, phone, and e-mail address

◆ The location where you'd like to work

◆ Your job objective or professional title

Career Casualty

It's so easy to make a typo when entering familiar information such as your address or job title. To prevent that from happening, when you fill in the blanks for your e-form, first type the info in a Word document, proofread it carefully and run your spellchecker, and then copy and paste the info into your online resume form.

Filling in your name and contact information should be no problem. (If you have questions, review Chapter 5 for advice on what to put in the Heading section of your resume. The same concepts apply to the e-form.) Selecting the geographic area where you'd like to find employment is usually done through a pull-down menu where you choose from what's listed.

The Big Submission

Job banks usually offer three ways to submit your resume:

◆ Build a resume on the site

◆ Upload your resume as a Word document

◆ Copy and paste a Plain Text version of your resume

Let's take a look at each of these options to see which will work best for you.

Online Resume Builder

Using the site's resume builder means you type your work history and details into an online form. This may seem the quickest and easiest, but keep in mind …

◆ Typos lurk! Typing directly into a form increases the likelihood of typos and spelling errors because most systems don't have a spelling and grammar checker.

◆ One size doesn't fit all. Online forms typically force you to use a chronological format. This doesn't work if you want to present your qualifications in a combination or functional format (see Chapter 4).

For these reasons, I don't recommend the resume builder option.

Plan A: Upload Your Resume

This is the way to go—when it works. Many sites can successfully take your lovingly crafted resume and present it perfectly as-is—with all the wonderful bold, indents, and other special effects you've used to accent your features. However, some sites haven't mastered the technology to accept and present a resume without jumbling the formatting, which won't serve you well in your job search.

How will you know if this option works with your resume? Try it and see what the results look like.

1. Click on the Upload button.

2. Use the Browse option to locate and select your resume on your hard drive.

When your resume appears on the site (you may have to click the Review button to see it), examine it carefully to see the quality of the upload.

If your resume doesn't look the way you want it to, click the Edit button and "massage" the formatting to get it into shape. Not all sites offer online editing, and on some sites the edit function doesn't fully function, leaving you with a less-than-desirable resume on the screen. If that happens, click the Delete button to remove your uploaded resume, and move on to Plan B: copy and paste.

Plan B: Copy and Paste

Copying and pasting your resume into the site's resume field won't render the prettiest online resume, but it's a safe way to go. It also provides you with a resume you can use for other sites that offer the copy-and-paste option.

To create a Plain Text version of your resume, follow the instructions in Chapter 12. Once you've adjusted the spacing, capitalization, and quotation marks, and you're satisfied that it looks as good as possible (given the limitations of Plain Text formatting), it's time to post it online. Here's what to do:

1. Place your cursor in the body of your Plain Text resume.

2. Select all (press the Ctrl and A keys simultaneously).

3. Copy the text of the document (press the Ctrl and C keys simultaneously).

4. Go to the resume webpage and place your cursor in the Copy-and-Paste Your Resume window.

5. Paste your resume into the Resume window (press the Ctrl and V keys simultaneously). Your Plain Text resume should appear in the window.

Before you click the website's Submit button, click the site's Preview button. Doing so will bring up a window that shows you how your resume will look to the employer. If there's anything you want to change in your document, click the Back button and make your edit.

Keeping Up-to-Date

Most online resume banks offer you the capability to edit your resume even after it's submitted. This is an important feature for several reasons:

◆ You can keep the info on your document up-to-date.

◆ You can improve your resume if it's not drawing the response you want.

◆ You can correct typos should you detect them after submitting your resume.

◆ You can extend the life of your resume in the bank if you need to. Some banks will list your resume for a limited number of days (typically 60 to 90). By editing your resume, you essentially reset the clock.

◆ In some systems, new resumes are listed at the top of the entire list of resumes or may be categorized under a section such as "New Listings," which employers are apt to look at first. By editing your document, you can re-enter the New Listings category.

Update your online resume by following the instructions on the resume website. If your edits are extensive (let's say you want to rewrite your Summary of Qualifications section), compose your points in a Word document, run your spellchecker, and proofread carefully. Then copy and paste it into your online resume. Alternatively, you could make edits to your resume on your hard drive, and upload your new version to replace your old one.

As soon as you land a job, be sure to delete your resume from the resume banks where you've posted it (check with the sites for instructions). You don't want your resume in circulation after you're happily employed (unless you do contract work, in which case you may want to have your resume on the market permanently). After all, you don't want your new boss to find your resume floating around in the job market and think that you're already looking elsewhere.

The Least You Need to Know

◆ Online resume banks can be a very efficient way for you to find a job and for employers to recruit job candidates.

◆ Some resume sites specialize according to profession, industry, special interest, or location. Others offer a wide range of criteria that can be narrowed to fit your search.

◆ You can find online resume databases by using your Internet search engine, asking friends for recommendations, and reading professional journals.

◆ To post your resume online, fill out an e-form, which includes uploading or pasting your resume into the form.

◆ Before submitting your resume on a website, click the Preview button to see how your resume will appear on the employer's computer screen.

◆ Be sure to keep your resume up-to-date after you post it online, and delete it after you've found employment.

Chapter 14

Your Social Network Profile as Your Resume

In This Chapter

◆ Why use social networks to find a job?

◆ Creating your LinkedIn profile like a resume

◆ Getting your profile in the online spotlight

◆ Augmenting your online presence with Twitter and Facebook

Networking has been around since hydrogen was introduced to oxygen to form H_2O. When it all comes down to it, people knowing people is what makes the business world turn. Your job hunt is much the same.

In this chapter we'll explore the world of online social networking to see how a keyword-rich profile can connect you with your next boss.

The Good Ol' Network

No one can argue the benefit of a job seeker having connections—friends and associates who can do one or more of the following:

◆ Introduce you to people in their networks who might help your career development.

◆ Turn you on to job openings they know of.

◆ Give you insider industry advice regarding job applications, answers to interview questions, and salary negotiations.

◆ Serve as job and character references.

Consciously or unconsciously, you've been developing your network for years. Now that you're in job search mode, you'll want to build and capitalize on your network because doing so might very well lead you to your next paycheck. That's where online social networks come in.

The Buzz About Social Networking

Online networking is a must for job seekers in almost all fields. Why?

- ◆ Recruiters often look within their social network for job candidates. If you're not a member, you might not get discovered.

- ◆ Employers search social networks as part of their background research on potential employees. With just a little effort on your part, you can have an online presence that wins an employer's approval!

Most networks cost nothing to join, and they're fun to be a part of. Social networking has become so popular and business-oriented, it is quickly becoming the hub of job searching and recruiting.

Get LinkedIn

Bonus Check

Social networks aren't just about improving your social life. Online communities are often used by professionals who want to network for business reasons, such as hiring new employees.

There are hundreds of social networks on the Internet and many more in the making as you sit holding this book. LinkedIn (linkedin.com) is one I highly recommend for career development. Its online instructions are easy to follow and the community is friendly, yet professional. Most important, it's used widely by job seekers and recruiters looking for perfect matches.

Because LinkedIn is one of the largest professional sites and offers specific job search and recruiting tools to its members, I'll use it in this discussion as a prime example of how social networking can further your job hunt.

Sign Me Up!

What does it take to join LinkedIn? Simply go to the site's homepage (linkedin.com) and register. LinkedIn offers paid and unpaid levels of membership. Before you pony up money for a premium membership, register for a free account to start. Not to worry, LinkedIn will let you upgrade later if you decide to.

Once you're registered, take the plunge:

- ◆ Create your profile (sort of your online resume).

- ◆ Invite members to connect with you, and accept invitations to connect with other people.

- ◆ Start participating in the network's activities like special groups, job search functions, and Q&A forums.

Your Profile: Your Online Resume

Your LinkedIn profile holds tremendous marketing potential for your job search. Create it as you would a resume, following the principles outlined in Part 2. Much like your resume, your profile will have sections such as:

- Name
- Headline
- Summary
- Work history
- Achievements
- Education
- Memberships
- Links to your website and blog

Here are some tips for making the most of each of these sections.

Your Number-One Keyword: Your Name

When you open your account, you're asked to enter your first and last names. That becomes your account name, which appears in bold at the top of your profile. But what if there are a few, or a few hundred, other people with the same name as yours? Well, that's where the second section of your profile, the headline, comes in.

Headline That Follows You Everywhere

The headline is a short descriptive that distinguishes you from others. It's the most important part of your profile because it follows you wherever you go on the LinkedIn site.

For example, if you ask a question, or make a comment through one of the LinkedIn forums, your name and headline will automatically be placed along with your question or comment. This snippet from your profile contains a link that allows someone (like a recruiter who's interested in your headline) to click through to your profile.

On your profile, the headline appears at the top, immediately under your name (as a job objective statement or professional title appears below the heading on your resume). It's the first thing a recruiter or employer sees (after your name), so this isn't the place for that story about your fishing trip. Keep it simple: tell the recruiter something about yourself as concisely as possible, using the most important keywords in your statement. For example:

- Sports Industry Marketer
- Energetic Sales Trainee
- Ph.D. Medical Librarian

Job Hunt Hint

If you have a website or blog that's relevant to your job search, include the web address in the headline of your profile.

To grab the attention of a recruiter, add either the word "seeks" or "seeking" to your headline. These two keywords are often typed into the search engine by recruiters to find available candidates. Adding these keywords, the previous headline examples might read:

◆ Sports Industry Marketer seeks job in North Carolina

◆ Energetic Sales Trainee seeking a job in financial services

◆ Ph.D. Medical Librarian seeks a position at college or university

What keywords can you string together to concisely say who you are and what job you're looking for? If you have trouble coming up with a great headline, put yourself in a recruiter's shoes, and enter keywords in the social network's search engine to see what profiles pop up. With enough browsing, you'll get the hang of it, and be able to compose a headline that's rich with your keywords.

Sum It Up

The Summary section appears near the top of your profile and should be loaded with keywords.

This section is automatically set in paragraph format. Instead of having a big chunk of text, break your information into short paragraphs—one or two sentences each. The shorter the paragraph, the more likely it is to be read in a quick scan by a recruiter. It's the bullet point statement concept without the bullet points.

A terrific and perfectly acceptable way to ensure that all your important keywords are in your profile is to simply list them in your Summary section. That's right, one long list of every keyword you can think of that defines you and your job search. You can put the keywords in a column, or in paragraph form. Either way the search engine will find them.

Another trick is to list misspelled keywords (including your name, and shortened versions of your name), which you think might be typed into the search engine incorrectly by a recruiter. If he makes that mistake, he'll still find your profile because you've anticipated his possible error. For example, at the end of my profile I might have a statement like this: "Commonly misspelled keywords: resumee, auther, Sue, irland."

Longer the Better Work History

The online profile has no limit as to how long it can be. So feel free to:

◆ List all the jobs (even small ones if they're relevant to your job objective) you want to, without worrying about how many pages your history stretches to.

◆ Be sure not to have gaps in employment (see Chapter 7 for details on how to fill such gaps).

◆ Use real job titles and consider putting more meaningful titles in parentheses if it makes the relevance of the position more evident. For example, Administrative Assistant (supervisor of three clerks).

Search other network members' profiles to get good ideas for presenting your own history.

Think Achievements, Write Achievements

Achievement statements tell your reader that you have the experience, you're good at using your skills, and you enjoy putting your talents to use. Just as on your resume:

◆ State your experience in terms of achievements.

◆ Use quantifiable results whenever possible and appropriate.

◆ Prioritize your statements so the most impressive is first.

◆ Keep your statements to three or four lines long.

As you progress in your current position, update your profile with your latest achievements. Each time you make an update, your network connections will be notified via e-mail, which might increase your chances of someone spotting you for a job opening.

Education with Extra Credit

Listing your education on your profile is easy and has some amazing benefits built into the system. LinkedIn will alert you to alumni who are also registered on that social network, allowing you to invite them to connect with you. So, you'll not only get credit for the education you gained at an institution, you'll also have the chance to benefit from others who went there.

Case in point: Janice wanted to break into a new industry and found someone in that industry via her LinkedIn alumni group. Janice sent her fellow alum, Charlie, a LinkedIn message saying she wanted to chat about his company. Charlie checked out Janice's profile, which presented some good experience and listed a degree from the same school he had attended. Charlie figured he'd help Janice out, so they set up a time to talk on the phone. Charlie passed Janice's info along to a colleague at work, who then set up a job interview with Janice.

It was the college-in-common in both their profiles that won a level of trust between Janice and Charlie, which led to Janice's job interview.

Memberships

Like the Education section, once you identify professional organizations and online groups you belong to, you'll have access to members of that group who are registered on LinkedIn. This can be extremely powerful because group members tend to trust and refer to other group members. That's what networking is all about—meeting people who know people who know people.

> ### Bonus Check
>
> LinkedIn has the ability to create special effects like stars and bullet points to highlight items in your profile. Use these effects sparingly, as too many can be distracting for your reader. To learn how to incorporate these elements, read the site's Help menu.

Pointing to Your Online Presence

Your profile also has a special section for listing your website and blog so people can see who you are outside the social network environment. You don't have to have a website or blog to have a terrific network profile, but if you have those extras, the profile is a great place to list them. Your profile visitors are apt to click on those links, which increases traffic to your site or blog. (See Chapter 15 for more about setting up a blog.)

Likewise, you can direct people to your network profile by listing your profile address on your resume (for example, in the heading of my resume I wrote linkedin.com/in/susanireland). If you have a website or blog, you can add a link to your profile. You might also include the link in the auto signature of your e-mails.

Seeing Is Believing

Take time to make your profile a great one, then keep it up-to-date as you move through your career. Just like your resume, keep tweaking your profile until it brings the results you want.

Here's a story of a new Pharm.D. grad who used his LinkedIn profile to get discovered by a recruiter.

Bryan Zembrowski was a member of LinkedIn for about a year, but didn't seriously format his profile until he began his job search. About three months after rewriting his profile, Bryan received the following message (with real names deleted) through the LinkedIn mail system.

Hello Bryan,

My name is (recruiter's name). I am the Director of Research & Recruitment at (name of recruiting firm), specializing in the placement of professionals within the pharmaceutical industry. I am presently working on a search for a client located in (name of location) who is seeking to hire a (name of job opening) to join their team. Your profile appears to be an excellent match to the experience my client desires.

I would welcome the opportunity to speak with you further about this position. Please accept my invitation to connect on LinkedIn and provide your contact information where I may reach you.

Not only were Bryan and the recruiter both members of LinkedIn, they were members of LinkedIn's Professionals in Pharmaceutical Industry and Biotech Industry group, which is where the recruiter first found Bryan.

Initially the recruiter contacted Bryan regarding a clinical position (a drug information position), probably because of the Pharm.D. and medical affairs terms in his profile, along with his industry experience. After the first contact, the recruiter sent him another job description for a product manager role after seeing that he had marketing experience from his post-doc at Novartis.

As you can see from Bryan's profile at the end of this chapter, he now has his first real job—as Product Manager at American Regent.

Job Hunt Hint

In addition to LinkedIn, check out niche networks that are especially geared to your profession and industry.

Tweeting on Twitter

Another popular social network is Twitter (twitter.com). This network is very dynamic, almost like a huge online chat room composed of overlapping circles of conversation. How can it help your job search?

◆ You can keep up with what's new by "following" recruiters, professionals in your field, and career development folks (like me, twitter.com/ susanireland).

◆ You can post comments that add value to the online conversation about your profession or industry, thereby drawing positive attention to yourself.

◆ You can see who trusted colleagues are following, and start following those folks as well.

Even network gurus find Twitter hard to explain. The best way to grasp its value is to sign up and start "tweeting."

Staying Connected on Facebook

Facebook (facebook.com) is one of the largest social networks and is used primarily as a casual online social medium. The chatter is often personal in nature and it offers a place where people let their hair down and talk about personal stuff.

Although Facebook doesn't have a job search component or a profile that lends itself to being an online resume, you might consider joining this network anyway. It's fun and even in casual exchanges you might well run into a valuable contact for your job hunt.

Career Casualty

Behave yourself online. For example, it's okay for an employer to see that you love sailing. It's *not* okay for him to discover that you swear like a sailor.

Buyer beware: when a recruiter or employer conducts an online search using your name as the keyword (for example, through Google or Yahoo!), the search engine will pull up all your social network profiles. If you have more people linking to your Facebook page than to your LinkedIn page, your Facebook page will appear above your LinkedIn profile in the search engine results. No problem, as long as your Facebook profile doesn't contain anything that might dampen a recruiter's enthusiasm to contact you.

Because a recruiter or employer can search for you using any number of keywords, all your online activity should be considered part of your job application.

With that in mind, always be conscious to:

- Say things that look good for you career-wise.

- Avoid writing things or uploading photos that could hold you back professionally.

No matter what type of online social network (personal or professional) you join, follow this rule: never write anything online you wouldn't want an employer to see. No matter how hard you try, there's always a chance he could come across it. And be cautious about uploading photos that can come back to haunt you. That shot during spring break that you or a friend posted for fun might be seen by a recruiter. That's probably not the impression you want to make with someone so crucial to your job search.

Now that you know the ins and outs of social networking, hop online and network your way to a new job!

The Least You Need to Know

- Recruiters use social networks to find qualified job candidates.

- LinkedIn is the most professional and job hunt–friendly network.

- Your LinkedIn profile serves as your online resume.

- Keywords in your profile are important for grabbing a recruiter's attention.

- Twitter and Facebook can also support your online job search.

- Whether you're on a professional or casual social media site, don't type or post anything you wouldn't want an employer to see.

Bryan Zembrowski's public LinkedIn profile.

Bryan Zembrowski

Product Manager at American Regent

bryan.zembrowski@gmail.com

Summary

Industry focused PharmD. with over 2 years of pharmaceutical industry experience spanning marketing, medical affairs and discovery research

Specialties

Respiratory Marketing, Managed Care Marketing

Experience

Product Manager at American Regent
May 2009 - Present (2 months)

Rutgers Pharmaceutical Industry Fellow at Novartis
July 2007 - May 2009 (1 year 11 months)

Managed Markets - KAM Marketing (Year 1)

- Compliance/Persistency Relationship Marketing
- KOL Program Management
- Managed Care Pull-through Tactics

Respiratory Marketing - Brand Marketing (Year 2)

- Professional Promotions
- Convention Planning
- Strategic Launch Planning
- Alliance Management

1 recommendation available upon request

Education

The University of Connecticut
PharmD., Pharmacy, 2003 - 2007

Boston College
B.S., Biochemistry, 1999 - 2002

Chapter 15

Blogging Your Way to a New Job

In This Chapter

- ◆ What the heck is a blog?
- ◆ Getting your job search blog up and going
- ◆ Posting your resume on your blog
- ◆ Your online video resume
- ◆ Driving recruiters your way

Would you like to have your own online billboard—a blog that touts your career qualifications for all to see? Imagine the convenience of offering your blog site address to an employer and then letting her browse through it to grasp why you should be hired for that dream job.

Creating a blog isn't all that hard or expensive. In this chapter I'll discuss how you can put your resume under a website address that bears your name, and gives a recruiter's search engine lots of keywords to find you.

It's a Website, It's a Blog, It's Your Online Billboard!

Blogging has become commonplace. We easily go to websites for TV networks, companies, and organizations, click the link for their *blogs*, and read *blog posts* to see what pundits have to say about this and that. Most blogs are interactive, which means readers can write a comment after the blog post. In fact, it's that interactivity that makes blogging so popular.

def•i•ni•tion

A **blog** (a contraction of *weblog*) is a website of articles by the blog's author, with the most current article appearing at the top of the page. A **blog post** is an article on a blog. An interactive blog post allows readers to write comments after a post.

As a job seeker, you might create a blog and use it to …

◆ Get your name and lots of keywords out in the blogosphere where recruiters will find you when they search for job candidates in your line of work.

◆ Put your resume online as a blog post, which you can link to in e-mails to potential employers.

◆ Add value to your professional community, which helps build your reputation and your online network.

◆ Create a conversation among colleagues in an online environment that has your look and feel.

If this sounds worthwhile for your job search, read on to find out how to create and promote your job search blog.

Blog Nuts and Bolts

Blogs can be configured online in one of the following ways:

◆ Hosted by a blogging community such as blogger.com

◆ Created as an independent blog site, such as the Career Coach Cafe at workcoachcafe.com

◆ Part of a website, such as Job-Hunt.org's blog at job-hunt.org/job-search-news

Let's figure out how you want to set up the blog for your job search.

Joining a Community

Joining a blog community is the easiest way to set up a blog. In fact, your blog can be up and running in a matter of minutes. Here are three popular blog platforms that are very user-friendly and offer blog hosting services:

◆ WordPress (wordpress.com)

◆ Blogger (blogger.com)

◆ Typepad (typepad.com)

These three provide more than just blogging software and hosting; they're online communities where fellow bloggers discuss the latest upgrades and enjoy lending a hand to answer even the most basic questions. How do you think they do their Q&A sessions? You got it—through blogs.

Each blog platform is slightly different, but basically the sign-up process is like this:

1. Register (through the site's homepage).

2. Create a blog title (your name would be a good one).

3. Select a theme (a ready-made page design).

4. Write a profile.

5. Create a header (your blog title and a tag line).

6. Enter your first post.

Going It Alone

Instead of going with one of the large blog communities, you may decide to create a blog with your own website address. In that case you'll need to:

◆ Purchase a domain name.

◆ Sign up with a website hosting company.

◆ Install blogging software.

If you're unfamiliar with how to do all that, consider taking a website development class or hiring a professional to help you with it.

Adding a Blog to Your Website

If you already have a website, you can add a blog to that site. Then you can direct traffic to your blog by incorporating links in your site's navigation bar and in page content. Depending on how old your website is, you may need to upgrade your site's coding to accommodate blogging software.

Once you have a blog up on your site, be sure to gather a loyal audience by joining Twitter, LinkedIn, and other social networks (see Chapter 14). These are excellent places to announce blog posts as you publish them to your site.

Look at Me, I'm Blogging!

Once you have your blog set up, it's time to start blogging. Do some practice posts to get the hang of your new typing environment. (You can delete those posts later if you decide to.) Here are things you'll learn as you poke around on your blog:

◆ You create posts in the editing section of the blog, which is accessible only to you (the administrator) and anyone else you designate (such as your technical support person).

◆ In the editing section, you can compose posts using familiar techniques such as bold, indents, bullet points, and so on.

◆ You can create hyperlinks that take your readers to other webpages on your blog or on other websites.

◆ You can organize your posts by category, and create an easy-to-use navigation system for your blog.

◆ You can assign keywords (called tags) to each blog post. These tags are used by search engines to identify the content in your posts.

Career Casualty

Don't let frustration keep you from having a job search blog. If you're not familiar with the ins and outs of blog programs, ask a blog-savvy friend or hire a professional to help you.

Feature Your Resume

Now that you have a blog, you're ready to create and post your blog resume. Where should you do this on the blog? I suggest one of the following:

◆ Put your resume on your homepage, making it "sticky" to keep it permanently there even when other posts are added to your blog. To learn how to do this, you may need to consult the Help menu of your blogging platform, or ask an experienced fellow blogger for guidance.

◆ Create your resume as a blog post. This is the easiest option that even a newbie can do.

For the second option, create a concise title for the post (for example, Resume or Susan Ireland Resume) that unmistakably identifies it as your resume. Because the title of the post becomes part of the web address, your title should be succinct and meaningful. For example, here's what would happen if I created my resume post with various titles:

◆ If the title of my resume post was Resume, the web address for my resume might be susanireland.com/resume or susanireland.wordpress.com/resume.

◆ If the title of my resume post was Susan Ireland Resume, the web address might be susanireland.com/susanirelandresume or susanireland.blogspot.com/susanirelandresume.

See how your blog post title determines the web address? Create a title for your resume post that makes a concise, logical web address.

Load 'er Up

You've already written your resume (see Part 2); now it's time to put it up on your blog. Here's how to do it:

1. Create a Plain Text version of your resume (see Chapter 12).

2. Copy and paste your Plain Text resume into your blog post window.

3. Incorporate features such as bold, italics, indents, and bullet points to make your resume more attractive.

4. Create hyperlinks for selected terms and phrases.

Your blog software will have a toolbar in the window for your post. This toolbar is similar to the one in Word. With a little practice, you'll get the hang of how to use it to create the special effects mentioned in steps 3 and 4 above.

Adding Links

Now that your resume's on your blog, it's time to take advantage of website technology—primarily the ability to link to other webpages. First, identify what links you'd like to create:

◆ Your e-mail address can be created as a link to enable someone to contact you with the click of a mouse.

◆ Place a link to your social network profile near the top of your blog resume.

◆ Statements could be enhanced with links to more detailed information on other pages of your blog. For example, if you mention working on a certain project, you might link to a post elsewhere on your blog that speaks in detail about that project and your role in its success.

◆ Direct your visitors to a publication, article, or website that features you or your work. By linking to that site, your reader can go there and read it on the spot.

◆ Link to your employers to make it easy for a recruiter to see what type of company you worked for.

◆ When speaking of volunteer work or even personal interests, you can link to relevant websites or blog posts.

◆ "References available" has new meaning when you link to a page with written letters of recommendations for your professionalism.

Links in your resume create a new dimension. Imagine how much depth you can give to your presentation, and how much a recruiter can learn from just a few minutes on your blog.

Once you've identified what links you want to have in your blog resume, use the toolbar to create those links. If you need help figuring out how to do that, check the program's Help menu.

Job Hunt Hint

Create a blog profile that includes a friendly photo of yourself and brief tag line that states your professional goals.

Learning the Ropes

If you're a first-time blogger, you don't have to start with a grand production. Begin by posting your resume in its simplest form with no links, if you like.

Gradually, tweak your resume to include links, which may require you to create additional blog posts for those links to point to.

If you think of your blog resume as a work in progress, you'll always be adding to and editing it. This has a double advantage:

◆ You keep your resume up-to-date.

◆ Search engines will reprioritize your resume page in their rankings because they "see" the latest date it was published (or republished) to your blog. Searches in the blogosphere often pull up pages by most recent dates, as well as keywords.

Making the Best of a Good Thing

Have fun with the blog technology. There's a lot you can do to create a professional presentation that has your own personal touch. Take time to pick your blog theme, as the look and feel of your blog will influence how a recruiter perceives you.

Here are recommendations for setting up your blog site:

◆ Choose a theme that gives good contrast between the print and the background. If a recruiter wants to print your resume from your blog, you want it to come out of his printer as legible as possible.

◆ Organize your posts by category, not by date. By looking at your posts by category, a recruiter will better understand what you're offering.

◆ Use your navigation bar to list links to relevant sites (such as your social network profile), even if those links are duplicated in your resume.

◆ If you want your blog to be interactive, you can allow your readers to leave comments after each post. Otherwise, you can disallow comments after posts. A third option is to allow comments that require your approval before they can be published to your blog.

Special Effects

Now that you've got a great written blog resume, how about stepping it up a notch with a video? They're not for everyone, but for those who enjoy playing with online technology and are in a profession where visual media are appreciated, here's your chance to wow your audience.

It's easy to create a video resume using a digital video camera, microphone, and simple video software. Here are ideas for your video resume:

◆ Be a talking head, speaking into the camera about your qualifications.

◆ Take your camera to various sites, showing yourself in different environments. Then add a voiceover or speak directly into the microphone while the video camera is rolling.

Bonus Check

If your blog contains your resume and informative articles about your profession and industry, it can serve as your personal career agent, working for you 24/7.

- Do a scrolling text video along with an audio recording of you reading it and perhaps adding comments here and there.

- Ask a friend to interview you on camera, asking questions that draw out your best qualifications.

- Put together a digital slideshow about your professional accomplishments.

I'll bet you can think of even more, so go for it!

Topic Thunder

Some blogs are static, others dynamic. If your job search blog is static, it might be no more than one or two pages that remain the same all the time; or it could have multiple layers that allow interested visitors to delve deep into your professional achievements and history. In either case, it's perfectly fine for it to have no activity other than serving as an online brochure about your professional life.

If you have a dynamic blog, you might write a new post regularly (once a week, every few days, or even daily) about topics that are relevant to your profession and industry. This type of blog can draw lots of traffic, not only from recruiters and employers, but from colleagues in your field and the general public. No harm in that. The more traffic to your blog, the greater your chances of being discovered.

Think how impressed a recruiter will be when he reads posts on your blog that show you really know your stuff. By adding value to your online community through blog posts, you add value to your job search. Not a bad deal … especially if you enjoy blogging.

Job Hunt Hint

When writing posts on your blog, include keywords in your sentences so a recruiter will find you when using a search engine to find a professional in your field.

Driving Traffic to Your Blog

Once you get your resume (and maybe a few relevant posts) on your blog, how are you going to get people to visit it? Here are some ways:

- Add your blog address to the heading of your resume.

- When you send e-mails to recruiters and members of your network, include the web address of your blog resume.

- Write comments after posts on other blogs in your field. When you do this, include your name and blog address so interested readers can seek you out.

- Link to your blog from your social network profiles.

- If you write articles or are interviewed for the print media, include your blog's web address.

- When doing any online activity that's even remotely related to your occupation, include your blog address.

◆ Tell your friends and followers on Facebook and Twitter about your new posts. On LinkedIn you can have the first few lines of your blog posts appear on your profile page. (See Chapter 14 for more about these social networks.)

Your blog can be a great online brochure. Once created, drive as much traffic as possible to it, knowing that even if someone isn't in a position to hire you, they may know someone who knows someone who knows someone who's hiring. Or they may put a link to your blog on their blog, which then gets picked up by a recruiter.

Sample Blog Resume

Blogs have a lot of room for creativity, and blog technology is advancing all the time. I hardly ever see two blogs that are alike. Without much trouble, you can make yours one that represents your professionalism as well as your personal character. And you can do it for next to nothing!

Paul Boyette built his blog resume in a few hours, then tweaked it over time to create the one you'll find at the end of this chapter. (See Paul's complete resume in the Technology section of the Portfolio of Sample Resumes.) Use your imagination to see the red and gray design with a white background for each post. He chose this theme to give a sense of organization and clarity, which appeals to his technical audience.

The Least You Need to Know

◆ Establish your job search blog on one of the large blog communities, as an independent blog, or as an add-on to your existing website.

◆ Make your resume "sticky" on the homepage of your blog, or create it as a blog post.

◆ Copy and paste your Plain Text resume onto your blog, which you can then adjust with bold, indents, and bullet points.

◆ Use links in your blog resume to allow readers to easily contact you and learn more about your professional qualifications.

◆ Keep your resume up-to-date and generate traffic to your blog by writing blog posts from time to time.

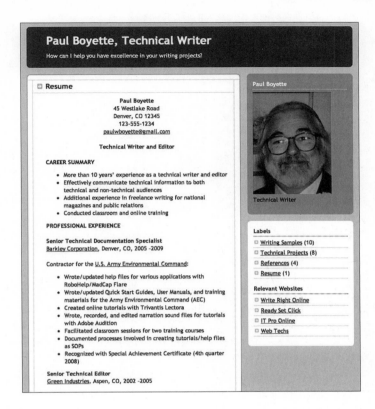

Paul Boyette, Technical Writer

How can I help you have excellence in your writing projects?

□ **Resume**

Paul Boyette
45 Westlake Road
Denver, CO 12345
123-555-1234
paulwboyette@gmail.com

Technical Writer and Editor

CAREER SUMMARY

- More than 10 years' experience as a technical writer and editor
- Effectively communicate technical information to both technical and non-technical audiences
- Additional experience in freelance writing for national magazines and public relations
- Conducted classroom and online training

PROFESSIONAL EXPERIENCE

Senior Technical Documentation Specialist
Barkley Corporation, Denver, CO, 2005 -2009

Contractor for the U.S. Army Environmental Command:

- Wrote/updated help files for various applications with RoboHelp/MadCap Flare
- Wrote/updated Quick Start Guides, User Manuals, and training materials for the Army Environmental Command (AEC)
- Created online tutorials with Trivantis Lectora
- Wrote, recorded, and edited narration sound files for tutorials with Adobe Audition
- Facilitated classroom sessions for two training courses
- Documented processes involved in creating tutorials/help files as SOPs
- Recognized with Special Achievement Certificate (4th quarter 2008)

Senior Technical Editor
Green Industries, Aspen, CO, 2002 -2005

Paul Boyette

Technical Writer

Labels

□ Writing Samples (10)
□ Technical Projects (8)
□ References (4)
□ Resume (1)

Relevant Websites

□ Write Right Online
□ Ready Set Click
□ IT Pro Online
□ Web Techs

Portfolio of Sample Resumes

Following is a collection of resumes written or critiqued by professional writers on Susan Ireland's Resume Team. As with the other sample resumes in this book, they have been made anonymous, with the exception of the resumes for Roberta Rosen, Catherine Sutton, Maureen Nelson, Jan Johnston-Tyler, Katie Baird, Marc Korchin, and, for the most part, Peter Dubro.

The resumes are categorized according to industry, aligned with the Job Objective statement or professional title on each. The exception is the first category, Executive Management, which spans various industries. The categories are labeled by shaded tabs on the side margins of the resumes.

If you're looking for a particular profession (such as Sales or Marketing), look within the category that comes closest to your industry. Also browse other industries to find resumes with occupational titles/job objectives that are similar to yours.

Turn the page for an itemized list of the resumes within each category.

Executive Management

Kevin King—Chief Operations Officer

Rebecca Walton—Senior position in Operations and Supply Chain Management

Alana Chang—Executive Director of Major Business Projects and Initiatives

Isabel Harper—Executive Director, American Charitable Giving Association

Career Development

Loretta King—Career Center Director

Maureen Nelson—Career Counselor

Jan Johnston-Tyler—Neurodiversity and Career Counselor

Roberta Rosen—Career Consultant

Catherine Sutton—Resume Writer

Education

William Miller—Middle School Science Teacher

Matthew Crosby—Elementary School Music Educator

Karen Chung—Preschool Head Teacher

Regina Andrews—College Enrollment Counselor

Timothy Arnell—Business Process Consultant specializing in University Systems

Environmental

Peter Dubro—Solar Energy Engineer

Thomas Perkins—Senior Research Associate in the Environmental Energy Technology Division

Andrea Cooper—PR position with an organization devoted to renewable energy

Brooke Maddox—Environmental Impact Assessment (EIA) Research Analyst

Marc Korchin—Sales Representative for Manufacturer of Electric Vehicles

Darrell Kramer—Environmental Attorney

Financial Services

Mark Butler—Senior Level Risk Manager

John Blitzer—Position in Accounting in the Insurance Industry

Veronica Lipton—Personal Lines Underwriter for HomeSmart Solutions

Healthcare

Anthony Ruiz—Healthcare Management Specialist

Brenda Lincoln—Senior Business Analyst with focus on the healthcare and pharmaceutical industries

Amy Moore—Project/Program Management position within a healthcare setting

Kayla Wong—An Executive/Administrative Assistant position within a healthcare setting

Nora Quinn—Nurse Practitioner

Kathleen Canfield—Nurse Technician

Andrew Carpenter—Emergency Medical Technician (EMT)

Loretta Nash—Medical Transcriptionist

Kate Warren—Research position with a biotechnology or pharmaceutical company

Technology

Martin Hersch—Chief Technology Officer/Vice President of Product Development for Advanced Tech

Beth Crawford—Marketing Professional in the High-Tech Industry

Graham Phelps—Senior IT project management position

Paula White—User Experience/User Interface Architect

Taylor Thompson—Database Developer, Statistical Analyst, Visual Basic Programmer

Kerry Wainwright—Software Programmer

Maureen Teeton—Web Designer

Katie Baird—Certified Virtual Assistant offering Website Development & Maintenance and Project Management

Ryan Seymour—Multimedia Developer and Web Designer

Paul Boyette—Technical Writer and Editor

Tawny Hall—Technical Writer

KEVIN KING, MBA

7701 Maple Drive • Johnson City, TN 12345 • (123) 555-1234 • kevinking@unknown.com

Chief Operations Officer

SUMMARY OF QUALIFICATIONS

Profile: A focused and energetic management professional with 10+ years of operations and financial management experience in diverse industries.

Leadership: A respected leader, able to set clear goals, recruit top candidates, and foster cohesiveness in achieving results.

PROFESSIONAL EXPERIENCE

2007-2009   CEO, **IMAGINEX, INC.,** Johnson City, TN
- Identified target markets and set goals for innovative online brokerage offering life insurance products.
- Secured and allocated appropriate resources for product development and management. Recruited and led experienced team of senior executives.
- Consulted with industry leaders to determine product focus and features and to generate funding for development.
- Negotiated strategic partnerships with major insurance companies and real estate brokerages.
- Supervised operations team in setting goals and reaching budget objectives.

2005-2007   Vice President, Corporate Development , **FORD GROUP,** Nashville, TN & Denver, CO
- Opened and operated Denver office during initial phase of industrial manufacturing project.
- Negotiated with financing sources and participated in development decisions for a $100M high-end office complex.
- Hired and supervised management company in the development of a championship golf course, including planning, construction, and alignment of goals to meet bottom-line objectives.
- Developed business plan, financial goals, and corporate support structure; negotiated franchise agreement with national restaurant chain.
- Conducted financial analyses for each project and developed appropriate metrics to set goals, evaluate results, and ensure budgetary accuracy.

2002-2004   Investment Banking Analyst , **JAMAICA TRUST,** Kingston, Jamaica
- Collaborated with cross-functional team to develop a creative financing mechanism to restructure $400M in non-performing assets.
- Handled highly confidential materials and projects, prepared board reports, coordinated audits, and managed treasury operations.
- Advised Jamaican manufacturing company in its sale to a U.S. firm.

1998-2001   Financial Analyst / Internal Auditor, **FIRST BOSTON BANK,** Boston, MA

EDUCATION

Nashville School of Business, Nashville, TN, 2005
M.B.A., Global Financial Management

REBECCA WALTON

45 Flint Street • Fargo, ND 12345 • (123) 555-1234 • rebeccawalton@unknown.com

OBJECTIVE

Senior position in Operations and Supply Chain Management

SUMMARY OF QUALIFICATIONS

- More than 10 years in business operations within the technology industry, with proven experience and success in operational effectiveness, strategic planning, manufacturing and production, process improvement, and supply chain logistics.

- Skilled in leading cross-functional teams in business turnarounds, with a track record of significant increases in revenue generation and cost savings.

- Enthusiastic, dedicated and organized, with strong attention to detail.

- Effective communicator, able to build relationships with individuals from diverse backgrounds and organizational levels. Fluent in Italian.

PROFESSIONAL EXPERIENCE

2006-pres. **CYBERION CORPORATION,** Fargo, ND
A leading IT product distributor of multiple brands, with $7B in annual revenue; a Fortune 500 and Forbes 400 company.

Director of Process Development & Supply Chain
- Oversaw supply chain and third-party logistics for two top customers, with $60M-$70M in monthly revenue. Improved supply chain metrics and customer satisfaction from 85% to 95%, resulting in CDW Supplier of the Year Award 2007 and Dell Top In Class.

- Developed and implemented processes for new business requirements, working closely with IT to write specifications, create checkpoints and proofpoints to ensure on-time completion and user-friendly application. Processes include:
  - Established Customer Consignment program for major retail accounts such as One-Stop Supply, Good Buy, and Office Warehouse. Program generated $2.4M in additional revenue within six months.
  - Built Buy&Hold program to target online stores, including amazon.com and buy.com, increasing revenue by $500K in six months.
  - Worked with IT team to determine specifications and create formulas to accurately calculate inventory as key component of the Purchasing Decision Suggestion System, resulting in standardized purchasing decisions and optimal levels of the $400M daily inventory.

- Collaborated with senior product management, operations and financial teams to identify needs and select value-added vendors.

- Educated senior-level, cross-functional team in clarifying bottom-line goals for the contract review process. Successfully shortened contract negotiation turnaround time from five months to two months and phased in 50 new vendors.

- Negotiated and reviewed vendor contracts, and contributed $70M from new vendors in first six months.

-continued-

2003-06   **Tech America,** Fargo, ND
An OEM with its own channel and brand.

Vice President of Sales & Marketing

- Invited to return to company to direct the North and South American territory. Reopened sales channel and turned a $20M operations loss into a $40M profit in the North American region within 18 months.

- Worked closely with Marketing and R&D teams to complete the product line, adjust selling price and cost, capturing additional market share and significantly increasing profit margin.

- Analyzed market and customer trends, sales channels, and product levels to maximize resource utilization and improve sales forecasting from 60% to 85%.

- Developed manufacturing production plans to meet market requirements and maintain appropriate inventory levels.

- Key player in helping company enter into super retailer stores, increasing annual revenue by $10M. Stores include: P&L, Kavanaugh's, and Computerland.

- Leveraged brand recognition as an award-winning technology leader to drive marketing efforts, and built excellent relationships with print and online media editors to keep current with trends and maintain a consistent media presence.

- Actively participated in company merger and acquisition by Worldwide Industrial Widgets (WIW) in 2006.

2000-03   **Cyberion Corporation,** Fargo, ND
Senior Manager of Material Control

- Oversaw all purchasing decisions for manufacturing assembly and material control, including strategic planning to ensure smooth and efficient production.

- Supported manufacturing assembly division to settle surplus material; reduced loss to zero.

1992-00   **Tech America,** Fargo, ND & Rome, Italy
Director of Sales   *1995-00*
Senior Sales Manager   *1992-94*

- Worked closely with manufacturing team to develop successful production plan, producing the right product at the right time to continually improve profit margin, revenue generation, and customer satisfaction.

- Managed Asia Pacific and European regions, increasing client base by 150%.

- Identified and worked directly with customer to obtain exclusive sales agreement with key account, doubling revenue in the European region.

EDUCATION / PROFESSIONAL DEVELOPMENT

B.A., Economics, Rome University, Rome, Italy

Certificate, Federal Tax and Payroll Seminar, John Taylor, CPA, CMA, Fargo, ND

Certificate, ISO 9002 Management Representative, Robert Spaugh, Principal, M.S.I.E., Fargo, ND

Computer skills: MS Word, Excel, Power Point; PageMaker, Dream Weaver, Word Perfect, and Lotus 1-2-3

Alana Chang

50 Burbank Street, Des Moines, IA 12345
123-555-1234, alanachang@unknown.com
Linkedin.com/alanachang

Executive Director of Major Business Projects and Initiatives

PROFILE

Leadership: Twelve years of progressive leadership of major business projects. Exceptional team management in critical collaborative contexts. Robust record of success in achieving complex objectives and timelines.

Character: Dynamic, articulate, analytical, and results-oriented; I love a good challenge.

PROFESSIONAL EXPERIENCE

2002-pres.   HOMESTYLE, INC., Des Moines, IA

Director, Project Management Department, 2006-pres.
Led multimillion-dollar business initiatives and created a highly effective new department including an intranet and training program; dramatically reduced time to market with a new project management process.

- Planned and launched distribution in 4,000 retail stores in 60 days.
  - Selected and led cross-functional team from 16 departments, and served as point person, ensuring high levels of synergy between companies.
  - Established and attained detailed action plan, milestones, and timelines, and created efficient documentation system available to all involved via intranet.
  - Ensured installation of 4,000 in-store kiosks and live demo units on tight time schedule.
  - Won internal support through presentation of objectives and benefits.
  - Resolved countless questions daily, weighing costs and benefits, creating solutions, and consulting with others; provided weekly executive updates.

- Wrote and persuasively presented proposal to executive team, and directed initiative for a major e-Business program projected to save $20M per year.
  - Created online functionality in troubleshooting, ordering, account activation, installation scheduling, and bill payment, updating to an entertainment theme with new hosting and content management.

- Oversaw development, beta, and launch of three new products with other companies, including a digital video recording product and the largest interactive television platform in the U.S. with over 3 million customers.

- Managed $1.5B partnership with MSN, implemented acquisition and integration of Broadwide (a broadband service).

- Continued -

Alana Chang, Page Two

Senior Project Manager, Media Company Acquisition, 2005
Directed smooth transition planning for technically complex migration of 3 million customers following $2B acquisition, achieving high retention.

Senior Project Manager, Media Company Acquisition, 2005
- Led steering committee of key department heads from both companies and three critical vendors to develop and implement an elaborate plan for a very risky customer migration of 100,000 customers per day for 31 days.
- Negotiated sensitive vendor agreements, and managed $30M transition budget.
- Held daily conference calls and weekly meetings to track and troubleshoot progress, frequently creating multi-layered contingency plans.
- Comprehensively evaluated business management and personnel strengths to consolidate operations, and elegantly arranged transition assignments.

Senior Project Manager, Customer Service, 2004
Launched joint technical call center handling 300,000 calls per month, consistently meeting specified performance metrics.

Project Manager, HomeStyle, Inc. Milan Launch, 2003
Selected by CFO to collaborate with five Italian partners on enterprise start-up.
- Developed policies, procedures, and processes for all aspects of operations, including dealer approval, sales, customer support, and billing.

Senior Project Specialist, Financial Planning, 2002
Led multi-department finance team to develop support process for sales and marketing promotions, and served on vendor selection team.
- Negotiated and managed vendor contracts, and launched two employee programs.

2001-02   BIG PICTURE INVESTMENTS, Lansing, MI
Corporate Insurance Analyst
Managed $500M portfolio of 12 Fortune 500 clients, consistently achieving high returns.
- Led re-engineering team to dramatically improve operating efficiencies.

EDUCATION
B.S., Business Administration, 1997, University of Topeka, Topeka, KS

ISABEL HARPER

5545 Portman Circle, Rochester, NY 12345
123-555-1234
isabelharper@unknown.com

OBJECTIVE: Position as Executive Director, American Charitable Giving Association

HIGHLIGHTS OF QUALIFICATIONS

- Eight years of highly successful nonprofit management experience for national and regional affiliated organizations such as the Bakersfield Foundation and the Dewey-Grant Association.
- Educational accomplishments: MPA (2006) and BA in Broadcasting, Public Relations, and Advertising.
- Adept in public awareness utilizing community events, public speaking, the media, and networking.
- Developed and wrote long- and short-range strategic plans for a variety of nonprofit organizations, many of which did not have this critical planning tool.
- Proven history of significantly exceeding financial goals while holding costs to a minimum.
- Skilled in expanding memberships, sponsorships, partnerships, and community involvement.

PROFESSIONAL EXPERIENCE

Regional Manager, Northeast, NY   2006 to Present
THE BAKERSFIELD FOUNDATION OF GREATER NEW YORK, NEW JERSEY & PENNSYLVANIA
- Hired by Foundation to open and manage one of first, "satellite offices" as part of Chapter's implementation of Shared Services Model; due to success, Chapter has become a national model.
- Set up and manage a one-man, virtual office for three-county area with culturally diverse and economically challenged population of nearly 600,000.
- Starting from "zero," exceeded goals by raising over $500,000 during the first two years; on target to exceed current year's goal of $300,000, while keeping expenses significantly below corporate budget.
- Integral member of Chapter Task Forces: Corporate Giving, Individual Giving, Internal/External Events; work collaboratively with Chapter staff members via onsite meetings, conference calls, and written communications.
- Developed highly productive regional and local relationships with both large and small corporate sponsors including: Motor Systems; the Pascal Group; Butch's Creamery; Moline's; Craftworks; Automobile Dealers and Realtors Associations; and many other organizations.
- Build strong community relations through involvement in events, Chambers of Commerce, and outreach to children's hospitals, regional hospitals, civic groups, local schools, and universities.
- Plan, coordinate and manage large- and small-scale external and internal events; created Casino Night, a signature event that generated over $106,000 in its second year.
- Customize innovative marketing packages matching corporate giving goals with Foundation objectives.
- Cultivate, increase, and maintain individual giving through one-on-one donor relationships; created and developed successful corporate "levels of giving" initiative.
- Research and write up to seven grants a year for funds from community and corporate foundations, ranging from $12,000 to $42,000; responsible for all grant reporting.
- In past two years, received $90,000 in funding with grant awards growing steadily; undertook a "challenge grant" that was completed in less than two months and raised $42,000.
- Cultivate and productively utilize very strong relations with regional media, including: press conferences, TV appearances, radio segments, press releases and articles, and event coverage; produce video segments.
- Organize and run quarterly Board Meetings for satellite office; actively recruit new Board Members.
- Hire and supervise college interns in nonprofit administration; increased office volunteers from 16 to 45; recruit and coordinate up to 75 volunteers for any one event.
- Received President's Award (2008) for exceptional achievement in chapter growth.

Isabel Harper – page 2

Director of Youth   2003 to 2005
LEADERSHIP MONROE VALLEY, Rochester, NY
- Directed and produced programming for youth organization of regional leadership program for 40 high school students selected annually from diverse population across Monroe and Wayne counties.
- Responsibility for 100 percent of program funding; developed and successfully implemented new program, Alumni Giving Campaign and newsletter that increased revenue by 10 percent.
- Instituted a yearly "class project" where youth selected and raised funds for a local nonprofit.

Director of Public Relations / Marketing   2000 to 2004
DEWEY-GRANT ASSOCIATION, Peekskill, NY
- Hired to fill new position within growing chapter in need of innovative marketing and event development.
- Created new programs still in effect today, including the Pro Ladies Lunch and Hallmark Festival.
- Designed new concepts for annual reports, brochures, and invitations; created newsletter; updated website.
- Wrote PSAs, press releases, and articles, located and built productive relationships with local media.
- Redesigned, updated, and implemented four large fundraising mail campaigns annually.

Previous Work History   1995 to 1999
- Agent Assistant: Albert, Wyckford, Caldwell, Best; Aspen, CO (1998-99)
- Assistant Stage Manager: Maybelle Theater Company, Estes Park, CO (1995-98)

EDUCATION & PROFESSIONAL DEVELOPMENT

Masters in Public Administration, University of Rochester, Rochester, NY
- Thesis: "Think Like a Business with the Heart of a Charity," with focus on skills required for nonprofit leadership in modern day organizations; particularly performance measurement standards, leadership vs. management skills, and important role of marketing in today's competitive donor climate.
- Graduate Assistant: Center for Nonprofit Leadership, American Humanics Program

B.A. in Telecommunications, University of Rochester, Rochester, NY
Major: Broadcasting, Minor: Public Relations and Advertising

Recent Professional Development:
- Strategic Planning: The Raymond Ball Foundation (2007)
- Board Development: The Raymond Ball Foundation (2007)
- Grant Writing: University of Rochester, The Grant Center (2003, 2006)
- Corporate/Individual Giving: AFP, The Plymouth Group (2004, 2007)
- Media Relations/Effective Wealth Advisory Practices: Chase Bank Govt. for Nonprofit Series (2008)
- Leadership Monroe Valley, Class of 2007: Class Coordinator

Technical & Professional Skills:
- Tools: Raiser's Edge, MS Office (Word, Excel, PowerPoint, Publisher), SPSS, Adobe PageMaker and Illustrator
- Skills: Internet Research, Multimedia Production, Technical and Creative Writing

COMMUNITY SERVICE & RECOGNITION

- **Strategic Planning, Writing & Collaboration:** Center for Nonprofit Leadership, Howell House, Junior League of Rochester, Monroe Valley Professionals 20/30 Club
- **Awards & Recognition:** MVP 20/30 40 Under 40 Award, Regional Chamber Athena Nominee
- **Active Volunteer:**
  Rochester/Warren Regional Chamber: Chamber Ambassador, Member of Government Affairs Committee
  Amber Sisters HIV/AIDS Ministry: Fund Development Board, Past Chair
  Mayor's Community Foundation: Board of Trustees
  Junior Cooperative of Rochester: Past Vice President, Chair of Marketing
  Rochester Friends: Vice-Chair of Achieving our Potential Council
  Monroe Valley Professionals 20/30 Club: Past Trustee, Co-authored Brain Gain Report

Loretta King
123 Main Street
Westfield, NH 12345
(123) 555-8888
lking55@unknown.com

OBJECTIVE: Career Center Director

HIGHLIGHTS

- Twelve years' experience as director of a college career center
- Counseled hundreds of students in all aspects of career development
- Sensitive and caring career counselor who believes in the value of change as a means of personal growth

PROFESSIONAL EXPERIENCE

1997-present Director of Career Development and Placement
COLLEGE OF LAMONT, Westfield, NH
Directed all aspects of the college's career development center

Administration
- Created and implemented on-campus recruiting program. Tripled the number of students interviewing with companies.
- Increased use of career center by 50% in the first two years.
- Partnered with Wheels Rent-a-Car to sponsor "Lunch with a CEO" and developed paid internships for students.
- Scheduled and staffed 12 units of career development courses a year.
- Developed and administered budget.

Counseling and Teaching
- Counseled students and alumni at all academic levels and from a wide variety of backgrounds.
- In academic undergraduate and graduate classes, made numerous presentations on all aspects of career development.
- Created and taught a class (for credit): "Career Strategies for the Working Professional."

EDUCATION

M.A., Career Development, University of New Hampshire, Durham, N.H.
Member, Eastern Association of Colleges and Employers

MAUREEN NELSON, M.A.
925.708.7476 • mpn@dorsey.org

CAREER COUNSELOR

ASSESSMENTS • JOB PLACEMENT • WORKSHOPS • RESUMES • INTERVIEWS • EMPLOYER RELATIONS

Experience: Career development professional with four years' experience coaching clients in educational, career and life planning. Qualified to administer assessments of values, interests, skills, personality. Ten years delivering workshops on career topics. Background in publishing, technology, business, education.

Populations: Culturally competent to work with clients of all ages, races, nationalities, incomes, abilities. Significant experience working with displaced workers and ex-offenders.

Settings: One Stop, non-profit, community college, university. Organized career events and led job clubs.

M.A., Career Development, John F. Kennedy University, 2007
~ Co-author of GETTING YOUR IDEAL INTERNSHIP ~

CAREER DEVELOPMENT EXPERIENCE

CURRENT EMPLOYMENT (2008–PRESENT)

Business Relations Specialist, One Stop Career Center, Goodwill Industries, *San Francisco, CA*
Help dislocated workers and low-income adults (WIA) to obtain training and employment. Create individual development plans and assist with resumes. Co-Chair of San Francisco Job Developer Assn.

- **Help clients overcome multiple barriers to employment:** poverty, poor work history, lack of housing/childcare/transportation/education, language barriers, disabilities, criminal backgrounds.

- **Perform outreach to employers** to facilitate placement of clients in jobs. Invite employers to recruiting events, find job leads, visit employers onsite, follow up with employers after interviews.

- **Keep accurate and detailed records** of clients served and placed in jobs. Monitor and document progress; follow up on referrals. Confer with clients' case managers. Write reports.

- **Build relationships with community organizations,** developing connections with One Stops, training programs, businesses and non-profits. Lead SFJDA meetings in Chairman's absence.

CONTRACT WORK DURING GRADUATE SCHOOL (2006–2007)

Resume Writer, Ladybug Design, *Columbus, OH*
Trainer, Eureka Career Exploration System, *Richmond, CA*
Freelance Writer, various career publications, *Pleasant Hill, CA*

CAREER COUNSELING INTERNSHIPS (2004–2007)

John F. Kennedy University Career Center, *Pleasant Hill, CA*
Western Career College Career Services, *Pleasant Hill, CA*
Diablo Valley College Career Center, *Pleasant Hill, CA*
EastBay Works (One-Stop Career Center), *Concord, CA*

CAREER PRESENTER (1998–Present) — VENUES INCLUDE:

UC Extension	CSU East Bay
Contra Costa College	Jewish Vocation Service
Diablo Valley College	Western Career College
John F. Kennedy University	Rainbow Gender Association

"Maureen is a wonderful career counselor! She is very professional as well as inspiring. She not only helped me with resume, cover letters, and interviews, but also helped me to find my own strengths and power through her great listening skills and thoughtful and encouraging comments."

— K.T., client hired as a
Therapist Intern
at counseling center

OTHER PROFESSIONAL EXPERIENCE

Product Manager, Pivotal Resources (training & consulting), *Walnut Creek, CA* (2001–2006)
Writer/Editor/Researcher, self-employed, *Richmond, CA* (1999–2001)
Webmaster, HR Technology, Bank of America, *San Francisco, CA* (1998–1999)

EDUCATION

M.A., Career Development, John F. Kennedy University, Pleasant Hill, CA, 2007. GPA 3.96.

Resume Writing	Counseling Practicum	Career Counseling Interview
Creative Assessments	Introduction to Coaching	Clinical Issues in Counseling
Interviewing Techniques	MBTI Intensive Seminar	Research in Career Development
Assessment Approaches	Workplace Issues & Trends	Counseling Diverse Populations
Organizational Approaches	Human Resource Management	Technology & Career Development
Career Planning Resources	Theories of Career Development	Business Models: Systems Thinking

B.A., Liberal Studies, California State University East Bay, Hayward, CA.

PROFESSIONAL DEVELOPMENT

Re-Entry Workforce Development (6 hrs), Walden House Institute, San Francisco, CA, Nov 2008
— Introduction to Motivational Interviewing
— Impact of Incarceration on Re-entry/Post-Prison Shock Syndrome

METSYS (database software for case management), Goodwill Industries of San Francisco, CA, Oct 2008

Powerpoint Pizzazz, Goodwill Industries of San Francisco, CA, Oct 2008

Workforce Development Programs Serving Ex-Offenders Training (20 hrs), Larry Robbins, Fall 2008
— Assessing for Hidden Assets and Barriers to Employment in Ex-Offenders
— Ex-Offenders and the Employer Connection: Job Development and Job Search Strategies
— Keep Working and Don't Live Your Life Behind Bars: Job Retention as an Anti-Recidivism Strategy

Third Annual Rentry Summit, Nor Cal Service League and Safe Communities Reentry Council, Sept 2008

Workers' Rights (8 hrs), Office Fed Contract Compliance (OFCCP) & Eq Emp Opp Comm (EEOC), Aug 2008

Workforce Re-Entry seminar, National Employment Law Project (NELP), Oakland, CA July 2008

Distance Credentialed Counselor training (16 hrs), University of Santa Clara, July 2008

Domestic Violence seminar, La Casa de Las Madres, San Francisco, CA, June 2008

Fundraising Fundamentals seminar, Transgender Leadership Summit, Berkeley, CA, June 2008

Strong Interest Inventory (update training), Sacramento State University, May 2008

SkillScan Advance Pack (update training), Los Medanos College, Pittsburg, CA, March 2008

Introduction to Nonprofit Management (8 hrs), John F. Kennedy Univ, Pleasant Hill, CA, 2007

Strategic HR: Metrics and Analytics Conference, NCHRA, San Francisco, CA, 2007

Succession Planning for Small Business, NCHRA, Walnut Creek, CA, 2006

Radical Collaboration in Adversarial Environments, NCHRA, Walnut Creek, CA, 2006

Six Sigma Training: Green Belt & Black Belt, Pivotal Resources, Walnut Creek, CA, 2004

National Career Development Association Conference, San Francisco, CA, 2004
— "No One is Unemployable" seminar on how to help difficult-to-place candidates, 2003

International Career Development Conference, worked as volunteer, Oakland, CA, 2003

Marketing • Public Relations • Project Management, UC Extension, Berkeley, CA, 2000-01

AWARDS AND HONORS

"Author with the Most Impact" Award, National Career Development Association, 2008
Outstanding Student of the Year, School of Management, John F. Kennedy University, 2008
Celebration of Scholarship Award, John F. Kennedy University, Pleasant Hill, CA, 2007, 2008
First Place, BrassRing.com's Writing Contest on Careers and Technology, 2000

MEMBERSHIPS & COMMUNITY LEADERSHIP

Co-Chair, San Francisco Job Developers Association (SFJDA), 2008–Present

Member, National Career Development Association (NCDA), 2004–Present

Member, Association of Career Professionals International (ACPI), 2004–Present

Volunteer Host, San Francisco Career and Talent Development Forum, ACPI, 2006

Member, Outreach Committee, St. Paul's Episcopal Church, *distribution of funds,* 2003-2004

Executive Committee Member, Contra Costa Interfaith Housing, *supportive housing,* 2002-2004

Project Lead, Angel Tree/Red Bucket benefitting clients of Wardrobe for Opportunity, Christmas 2003
   Gifts for disadvantaged women entering the workforce

Facilitator, Business Education Volunteer Program, Richmond High School, 2000

Mentor, Welfare-to-Work Partnership, Bank of America (6-month commitment), 1998

Conference Facilitator, "An Income of Her Own," Independent Means, 1997
   Providing incentive for poor teen girls to becoming financially independent

Literacy Tutor for gang member, LEAP (Literacy for Every Adult) Richmond Public Library, 1996

CLIENT COMMENTS: "Helped me quite a bit with confidence" • "Extremely helpful in my job search"
"Solid resume guidance and good interview preparation" • "Gave me leads to people" • "Fast time to value"

SPEAKING & PRESENTATIONS

"Great Resumes for Every Client," BEST Pro Train-the-Trainer Series, Jewish Vocational Service, SF, 2009
Guest, "At Work with Marty," KALW, FM 92.7, Transgender in the Workplace, April 30, 2008
"Job Hunting Advice from Employment Experts" (panel), LGBT Center, San Francisco, CA, 2008
"Counseling Transgender Clients," Graduate Panel of California Career Development Association, 2008
"Resumes & Cover Letters that Get Results," Career class, Diablo Valley College, Pleasant Hill, CA, 2007
"Projecting A Professional Image," brown-bag talk, Diablo Valley College, Pleasant Hill, CA, 2006
"Knock 'em Dead Interviews," EastBay Works (One-Stop Career Center), Concord, CA, 2004
"Informational Interview Etiquette," Cal State East Bay, Hayward, CA, 2002
"High Tech Jobs for Low Tech People, Contra Costa College, San Pablo, 2000
"Creating A Career Portfolio for Any Industry," Cal State East Bay, Hayward, CA, 1999

PUBLICATIONS

"Systems Thinking in Organizational Career Development Programs," *Career Convergence,* NCDA, 2008
"30 Tips for New Career Counselors," *Career Convergence,* NCDA, 2007
Getting Your Ideal Internship, WetFeet, San Francisco, CA, 2006
"Beyond Training: Mentoring for Skills Transfer," *Support World,* November/December 2003
"Informational Interview Etiquette," Webgrrls International website, 1999
"Working for Nonprofits Can 'Profit' Your Career," The Creative Group, 1999
"Do You Need a Career Coach?" The Creative Group, 1999

EVOLIBRI

Neurodiversity &
Career Counseling

Jan Johnston-Tyler, MA
Neurodiversity Counselor
650 961-7073
janjt@evolibri.com
www.evolibri.com

Summary of Qualifications

- Career counselor with expertise in working with high-functioning teens and adults diagnosed with:
Autistic spectrum	Brain trauma injuries
Attention deficit	Learning difficulties
Pervasive mood disorders	
- Background in corporate management, which brings real-life understanding to my counseling.
- Author of two books, *Heaven and Hell: The Guide to Asperger Adolescence*, and *The Mom's Guide to Asperger Syndrome*.
- Seasoned presenter and lecturer at universities and professional conferences.
- Smithsonian Laureate for Innovation.

Education

Master of Arts, Counseling, Career Emphasis

Santa Clara University

Bachelor of Arts, English
University of California at Berkeley

Professional Experience

EvoLibri Consulting, Palo Alto, CA   **2006-Current**

Principal / Career Counselor

Career counseling and referral services for those facing neurodiversity issues.

Direct services include:
- Case management, individual, and family counseling
- Career and post-secondary education assessment and planning
- Job and volunteer coaching and placement services
- Transition-readiness assessment, planning, and training
- Social communities, camps, workshops, and psycho-educational groups
- IDEA and ADA advocacy
- Educational and intervention program development for schools and non-profits

Indirect services include:
- Therapeutic treatment with clinicians specializing in neurodiversity
- Academic and executive functioning tutoring
- Legal representation with attorneys specializing in ADA and IDEA

Harper & Associates, San Jose, CA   **2005-2007**

Associate Counselor (contract)

Worked with clients who were difficult to place due to disability or length of time out of workforce.

(continued)

Informed Publishing, Portland, OR   **2005-2007**
Director, Content Architecture and Systems

Juniper Networks, Inc. Sunnyvale, CA   **2003-2005**
Technical Publications Manager, E/M/T Series Hardware

Cisco Systems, Inc. San Jose, CA   **1994-1999**
Senior Manager, Central Documentation Services   *1997-1999*
Senior Manager, Technical Documentation   *1997*
Manager, Technical Documentation   *1995-1997*

Memberships

American Psychological Association (APA) – American Counseling Association (ACA) – California

Association for Counseling and Development (CACD) – National Career Developers Association

(NCDA) – National Association for Mental Illness (NAMI)

Related Work, Presentations & Publications

- *Team lead:* **Challenge Success Project,** Mountain View High School, in conjunction with the Department of Education at Stanford University (ongoing)

- *Guest lecturer:* **Special Education Masters Program,** Santa Clara University (ongoing)

- *Guest lecturer*: **Career Counseling Masters Program,** Santa Clara University (ongoing)

- "Hidden Disabilities in the Workforce," ICDC, Fall 2007, Sacramento, California

- *Heaven and Hell: The Guide to Asperger Adolescence*, AAPC, in press

- *The Mom's Guide to Asperger Syndrome*, AAPC, April 2007

ROBERTA J. ROSEN

415-885-4804   roberta_careers@yahoo.com

Career Consultant

Executive Coaching   **Career Counseling**   **Personal Coaching**

HIGHLIGHTS OF QUALIFICATIONS

- More than 15 years of experience providing career consulting and mentorship to individuals and groups at all organizational levels.
- Adept at quickly engaging each client, establishing rapport, and assessing needs and goals.
- Expertise in combining creativity, humor, intuition, and an in-depth understanding of the job market to assist clients in developing a strategy for personal growth and professional success.

PROFESSIONAL EXPERIENCE

2000-pres.   **ROBERTA J. ROSEN CONSULTING,** San Francisco, CA
Career Consultant

- Developed thriving career consulting practice through referrals, an extensive network of contacts, and client satisfaction.
- Provided coaching to individuals and groups, utilizing in-depth assessments to identify career objectives, role-playing to prepare for interviews, and tools for successful cold-calling and follow-through.
- Conceived, designed, and implemented pilot program on Group Coaching with Marin Coaches Alliance.
- Facilitated Group Coaching sessions, providing coaching and mentoring to help groups of diverse individuals achieve personal and professional goals.
- Presented outplacement workshops and other individualized outplacement services for small organizations.
- Trained IBM Sales Executives in sales and communication strategies. Provided Executive Coaching Services to Directors at U.C. Berkeley.

1986-2000   **ALUMNAE RESOURCES,** San Francisco, CA
Career Advisor

- Guided 100+ clients through the informational interviewing process, provided assistance with goal-setting and identifying career opportunities, and suggested methods for navigating the ever-changing job market.

1985-2000   **HEWLETT PACKARD COMPANY,** San Francisco, CA
(concurrent) *Account Manager*

Leadership & Coaching

- Selected to mentor new sales reps with presentations and meeting facilitation, utilizing shadowing, debriefing, and role-playing techniques to quickly bring them up to speed as productive team members.
- Coordinated and led teams in developing business solutions for customers to reduce costs and increase revenues.

-continued-

Career Development

ROBERTA J. ROSEN
PAGE TWO

- Member of task forces on increasing effectiveness of sales managers and improving job satisfaction for technical and sales staff. Invited by company executives to present results to 600 field employees.

Sales & Account Management

- Established and cultivated strong relationships with CEOs and CIOs of $500M+ accounts, and developed successful strategic partnerships.
- Negotiated bids for highly competitive contracts.
- Consistently exceeded sales quota for 15 years.
- Wrote and presented proposals to executive committees of target accounts to ensure Hewlett Packard's place as partner of choice for technology decisions.
- Facilitated communication between in-house and customer executives to ensure establishment of ongoing, mutually beneficial relationships.

Previous experience includes:

Teacher Trainer, Upper Valley Regional Center for Education for New Hampshire and Vermont schools, co-sponsored by Dartmouth College and the Office of Education in Washington, DC.

Sales Manager, Control Data Corporation, San Francisco, CA. Directed the 12-member team responsible for the sale and marketing of the Plato Learning System.

Regional Director of Admissions and East Bay Coordinator, Interstudy, San Francisco, CA. Hired and trained 120+ representatives in the coordination of language/homestay programs for international students here in the U.S. and for Americans abroad.

EDUCATION & TRAINING

B.A., cum laude, Education, minor in Psychology, City University of New York, NY
Graduate studies in Psychology, John F. Kennedy University, Orinda, CA

Ongoing Coaches Training, The Coaches Training Institute, San Rafael, CA

Professional Certified Career Coach, Career Coach Institute

Key Executive Seminars with CEOs from major corporations worldwide, led by John Donovan, Cambridge Executive Enterprises, Inc., Cambridge, MA

Coursework in Conflict Resolution, Mediation, and Entrepreneurship, The Amos Tuck School of Business Administration, Dartmouth College, Hanover, NH

PROFESSIONAL AFFILIATIONS

International Coaches Federation
San Francisco Coaches
Career Coach Institute
Hewlett Packard Alumni Association

Catherine Sutton

510-528-2261 | catherinesutton@resoundingresumes.com

Professional Résumé Writer

PROFILE

- A practiced writer with a flair for creating compelling résumés and cover letters that get results, and a portfolio of over 700 résumés in every career field.
- Warm and insightful, a careful listener who specializes in eliciting achievements from even the most reticent of clients, whether in person or on the phone.
- Adept at fashioning individual résumés to reflect unique accomplishments and skills, and at highlighting transferable skills to promote career objectives.
- British-born and educated, with solid knowledge of American grammar and syntax; comfortable with non-native speakers; familiar with French and Russian.

RELEVANT HIGHLIGHTS

Susan Ireland's Resume Service, Berkeley, CA   2002-present
Writer

- Collaborate with clients both locally and worldwide in corporate, academic, white-collar and blue-collar fields to produce powerful, individualized résumés.
- Utilize the latest in computer technology to facilitate communication and to increase speed and efficiency of the long distance process by up to 25%.
- Consistently receive referrals and testimonials from clients who have used their new résumés to find better jobs; satisfied comments include:

    "The résumé...gives me a boost of confidence to see that I really do have the skill sets that can be translated into the work force."

    "I am very pleased with the result and enjoyed working with you. Thanks for making me look so good on paper." (Senior corporate executive)

    "What a privilege to watch your process in transforming my original drab document into a dynamic, engaging piece." (Business manager)

    "I never thought that it was possible to summarize 15 yrs of experience in one page. I got multiple interview requests...and received the job I wanted."

- Conducted onsite interviews with staff anticipating layoff from a variety of positions at a manufacturing facility and, respecting a tight timeline, produced résumés that emphasized their transferable skills.

Vector Marketing, Olean, NY   1993-02
Senior Sales Leader, Western Region

Previous Positions: office administrator, network marketer, editor, interpreter, business owner, personal growth trainer, promoter, head waitress and dance teacher.

EDUCATION & TRAINING

In-depth training in the art and science of résumé writing, Susan Ireland, Berkeley, CA
B.A. (Honours), Russian Language and Literature, Leeds University, Leeds, UK

Career Development

WILLIAM MILLER

35 Ashley Blvd. Trenton, New Jersey 12345
123-555-1234, willmiller@unknown.com
linkedin.com/williammiller

OBJECTIVE

Middle School Science Teacher

PROFILE

- Twelve years as a middle school science teacher, with a talent for sharing my enthusiasm for science with young minds.
- Consistent record of providing a safe learning environment.
- Enjoy working with parents to help students meet educational goals.

EDUCATION

BS, Chemistry, 1995
Bigelow University, Hoboken, NJ

New Jersey Department of Education Science Standard Certificate

Fieldwork: Student Teacher, General Science, Grant Middle School, Gladstone, NJ

EXPERIENCE
2004-pres.

Bradley Howell School, Trenton, NJ
Science Teacher

1997-04

Millstone Middle School, Montclair, NJ
General Science Teacher

CURRICULUM DEVELOPMENT
- Developed general science curriculums for 7th and 8th graders, which included geology, biology, anatomy, and astronomy, as well as emerging topics such as renewable energy.
- Incorporated field trips to local sites of scientific interest.
- Created lesson plans and homework assignments that, as much as possible, met the individual needs, interests, and abilities of the students.
- Within the district's guidelines, adjusted curriculum as school year progressed to accommodate learning styles, and topical news.
- Provided written evidence of lesson plans upon request of principal.

WILLIAM MILLER
(continued)

CLASSROOM MANAGEMENT
- Create a classroom environment that is conducive to learning according to the maturity and interests of the students.
- Strive to instill a sense of excitement in the sciences and an appreciation for the role of science in the world.
- Augment classroom participation by including PowerPoint presentations, video, Internet, elementary lab experiments, and field trips.
- Encourage students to "buy into" acceptable classroom behavior and standards of respectful conduct.
- Emphasize safety in the classroom, especially when handling equipment and science models.
- When required, provide disciplinary measures that are in compliance with district guidelines.

PARENT-TEACHER RELATIONS
- Actively participate in parent-teacher events such as PTA meetings, open house, and individual parent conferences.
- Maintain open communications with parents by providing student progress reports and through contact by phone or in person when necessary.
- Invite parents whose careers are in the sciences to make classroom presentations.

MEMBERSHIPS

New Jersey Science Teachers Association
New Jersey Earth Science Association
American Association of Science

Education

Matthew Crosby

123 Clipper Street, Hazeltown, ND 12345   (123) 555-8888, mcrosby@unknown.com

Elementary School Music Educator

Summary of Qualifications
❖ GRAMMY Award 2005 for excellence in music education
❖ Experience in evaluating teachers and students with a positive critical eye
❖ Superlative evaluation skills and the ability to communicate need for improvement

Professional Accomplishments
HAZELTOWN ELEMENTARY SCHOOL, Hazeltown, ND, 2003-present
Choir Director (grades 3-8), **Music Teacher** (grades K-2)
❖ Develop excellent vocal production, and prepare for school and community concerts.
❖ Offer Kodaly-based curriculum with Orff and Dalcroze incorporated.
❖ Prepare 60 3rd-graders for May Pole celebrations, and 120 1st- and 2nd-graders for spring concert.
❖ Develop Music Education lessons, which incorporate activities for special learners.
❖ Awarded grant for the music department from the Philanthropic Ventures Foundation.

BRUSHMOOR CHILDREN'S CHORUS, Brushmoor, ND, 2003-2004
Music Director and Kodaly Specialist for Training Choir (ages 5-8)
❖ Taught in-tune singing, memorization, posture/breath support, and solfeggio sight singing.
❖ Prepared singers for winter and spring concerts.
❖ Worked with all levels from beginners to advanced chamber choir.
❖ Communicated weekly with parents.

GRAIGMONT SCHOOL, Leechmere, ND, 1999-2003
General Music Teacher, Drama Director (grades PK-8)
❖ Conductor for annual All School Concert.
❖ Prepared middle-school students for MENC vocal competitions.

Education
Master's in Music Education (Kodaly), St. John's College, Berring, ND, 2004
North Dakota Credential Program, St. John's College, Berring, ND (Professional Clear), 2003
Whiley College, Windham, ND, Orff Schulwerk Graduate Level Certification Program, Level I, 2000
Bachelor of Music, Music Education, Honor Student, University of Kansas, Kansas City, 1998

Professional Development
CLAD certification program, University of North Dakota, 2007
TRIBES Learning Community Training, Center Source Systems, Hazeltown, ND, 2005
Attendance to OAKE National Conference, 2003 and 2007
Attendance to ACDA National Conference, 2005

Awards/Honors
NDAKE Scholarship to attend OAKE National Conference, April 2003
St. John's College Kodaly Graduate Fellowship, 2001, 2002, 2003
University of Kansas, Music Department Scholarship, 1996, 1997, 1998
Pamela A. Hastings Scholarship for excellence in the performing arts, 1995
State of North Dakota Single Subject Credential (Music) grades PK-12
State of Kansas Beginning Educator Certificate (Music) grades PK-12

Affiliations
MENC, Music Educators National Conference
OAKE, Organization of American Kodaly Educators
NDAKE, North Dakota Association of Kodaly Educators, Board Member (Membership)

Karen Chung

2876 Grove St. ! Miami, FL ! 123-555-1234 ! karenchung@unknown.com

OBJECTIVE: Preschool Head Teacher

PROFILE

- A knowledgeable and compassionate head teacher with six years' experience encouraging culturally diverse preschool and elementary children to thrive.
- Observant and passionate to learn, with infectious enthusiasm and a positive approach to emergent curriculum for the young child.
- Hands-on knowledge of arts and crafts in a preschool setting and a reputation for developing creative, play-based programs.
- Proficient in Spanish; field experience with Miami Unified School District.

EXPERIENCE

Tiny Tots Nursery School, Miami, FL   2006-present
Head Teacher
- Introduced a more process-based curriculum, in partnership with staff, for a group of 30 culturally diverse three- to four-year-old children in a full-inclusion, play-based parent co-operative, and demonstrated the power of creative arts in motivating children to learn.
- Built a sense of community and consistency into the daily children's circle time with age-appropriate songs and stories, music, yoga, and movement, encouraging individual contribution, participation, and cooperation.
- Developed structured outdoor play area, observed individual behavior, and encouraged children in activities that challenged them and helped them in specific areas of concern.
- Built strong relationships with parents of diverse socio-economic backgrounds by listening to what they have to say, engaging them in their children's education, and providing them with tools and resources to help their child succeed.

Citrus Grove Development Center, Orlando, FL   2003-06
Associate Teacher
- Assisted in a classroom of 26 three- and four-year-old primarily Spanish-speaking children at this bilingual school, communicating with parents, students, and staff.
- Enhanced the morale of the classroom with a beautiful gallery of the children's art, and maintained portfolios of individual work.
- Completed state-required assessments.

Clarkson School, Orlando, FL   2002-05
Art Teacher (concurrent with study)
- Designed and led mixed media art class for a broad spectrum of elementary students. Participated in staff meetings and program enrichment.

VOLUNTEER WORK

Volunteer, Roberta Price Elementary School, Orlando, FL   2003

EDUCATION & PROFESSIONAL DEVELOPMENT

19 units, Early Childhood Education, City Colleges of Naples & Miami, FL	2008
First Aid and CPR Certified	2008
Attendee, Kids and Stuff Workshop with Marianne Phillips, Miami, FL	2007
Site Supervisor Permit, Commission on Teacher Credentialing	2006
Bachelor of Arts in Fine Art, minor in Education, University of Orlando, Orlando, FL	2002

Education

REGINA ANDREWS

123 Sprockett Way • Houston, TX 12345 • (123) 555-8888 • randrews@unknown.com

OBJECTIVE

Enrollment Counselor, Rangeley College of the Law, University of Texas

SUMMARY OF QUALIFICATIONS

- Organized and motivated, with more than 10 years of success in cultivating rapport with people from diverse cultural backgrounds.

- Excellent listener; able to assess needs, synthesize and articulate information, and assist clients in making appropriate choices to fulfill their goals.

- Motivated and focused; able to work independently and as part of a team to complete tasks within strict deadlines.

PROFESSIONAL EXPERIENCE

2007-09   **TEXAS STATE UNIVERSITY**, Houston, TX   *Student*
- Worked closely with professors, advisors, and top-level administrators in Admissions, Financial Aid, and Arts & Sciences to submit transcript and financial aid requirements, and ensure complete and accurate paperwork.

- Advised and informally advocated for fellow students, providing suggestions to make wise academic decisions, fulfill requirements, and excel in their university experiences.

- Collaborated with students of varied ages and ethnicities to develop questions for tests, and co-wrote mid-term and final exams.

- Wrote extensively, with a focus on critical thinking and analysis, clarity of thought, and grammatical accuracy.

2003-07   **ADHERENT COMPONENTS, INC.**, Longchester, TX   *Sales Manager*
- Interviewed clients to assess needs and limitations; identified products for optimal fit.

- Communicated effectively with clients in Europe and Asia, despite differences in language and culture.

- Conducted site visits, built strong relationships, and delivered convincing presentations to improve client loyalty and retention.

2002-03   **TRUE-TIME MERCHANTS, INC.**, Louisville, KY   *Sales Account Manager*
2002   **INTERSTATE HOTELS, INC.**, Huntsville, KY   *Front Office Manager*
1997-02   **EXPRESS INN**, Crainacre, KY   *Guest Services Supervisor*

EDUCATION / AWARDS

B.A., English Literature, Kentucky University, Lexington, KY, 2009

Graduate, Champlain College Preparatory School, Champlain, KY, 1994

Studies included Forensics, Parliamentary Process, and Oratory Skills

Timothy Arnell

987 Random House Lane, Cleveland, OH 12345
123-555-1234, TimothyA@unknown.com

Business Process Consultant

Specializing in University Systems

- ➢ Business process analysis and improvement
- ➢ Project planning, management, and implementation
- ➢ Strategic planning
- ➢ Relationship management
- ➢ Organizational development and coaching
- ➢ Writing, editing, and intergroup communications

BUSINESS EXPERIENCE

Project Leader/ Business Process Consultant, 1992-Present
Ohio State University, Controller's Office (2006-Present) *Independent Consultant*
- Led information-gathering focus groups; currently planning a new online directory system.
- Prepared Project Cost Analysis training materials for PeopleSoft web-based financial system.
- Documented critical financial system processes for OSU's financial system, including: Year End Close, Reorganizations, Combo Edits, and Budget Checking.
- Conducted initial screening and interviews for recruitment efforts.

Ohio State University, Information Technology, 2001-2006, *Independent Consultant*
Administrative Computing Services (ACS)
- Created plan for implementing new stand-alone Oracle Workflow business process technology at OSU and managed business side of this web-based technology start-up.
- Managed business process design, requirements gathering, user testing, implementation, and documentation of web-based workflow financial application. Led initial phases of HR and service-request workflow systems. Worked with DBAs and programmers to design user interface and flow.
- Interfaced with departments throughout OSU to determine whether they would benefit from automating and streamlining their business processes.
- Performed interviews and organizational analysis for integrating new 11-person SIS group into ACS. Prepared detailed findings and recommendations.
- Helped with organizational development, including recruitment and individual coaching.
- Assisted with strategic plan documents, critical reports, and audit responses.

Organizational Redesign
- Provided comprehensive recommendations for organizational redesign of a large student services department within the University.
- Coached key staff to help them prepare for change.

Client Services Center
- Developed start-up and deployment of new plans for IT Help Desk staffing and coverage.
- Provided recruitment assistance and coaching/support for expanded coverage start-up.

(continued on page two)

Timothy Arnell
(page two)

Ohio State University, School of Medicine, 2001, *Independent Consultant*
- Assessed performance and applicability of new Electronic Medical Records (EMR) software.
- Worked with Strategic and Program Planning group on projects, including creation of high-level recruitment process and assessment of large-scale medical research proposals.

Ohio State University, School of Medicine, 2000, *Project Manager*
- Planned and implemented 10-area process redesign for conversion/migration of existing financial system.
- Directed school-wide user communications and training for the migration.
- Worked closely with users and service providers to ensure continuity of services.

Trading Up, Inc., 1998-2000, *Project Manager*
- Planned and supervised point-to-point and end-to-end Y2K testing for Global Market systems.
- Documented procedures for administering security for all of Trading Up's trading systems.

Environmental Defense Fund, 1996-1997, *Project Manager*
- Managed start-up of national demonstration for an environmental software product.
- Coordinated management of project among nonprofits headquartered in different cities.
- Created and implemented marketing plan; published articles; presented concept at conferences.

Women's Prison Association, 1994, *Project Manager*
- Managed start-up of transitional facility for formerly incarcerated homeless women.
- Negotiated contracts, budgets, and client eligibility requirements with City.

Santa Fe Department of Human Services, 1992-1993, *Consultant*
- Member of Mayoral Task Force created to start new agency for homeless services.
- Developed organizational structure as well as MIS and HR budget plans.
- Coordinated strategic planning workgroups and designed start-up policies and procedures.

Santa Fe Personnel Office, 1988-1991, *Director of the Bureau of MIS, Research, and Legislative Analysis (BMIS)*
- Managed unit that provided ongoing analytic support to the adult and family shelter systems, AIDS Services, Homecare and Protective Services.
- Initiated and guided evaluations and studies within the shelter system.
- Led 30-person task force and wrote plan to improve shelter intake/assessment policies and procedures.

EDUCATION
Ohio State University, MBA in Finance; minor in Economics
New Mexico University, BA in Political Science; minor in Psychology
Hastings Law School. Completed first year. Moot Court. Constitutional Law internship

COMPUTER SOFTWARE: MS Office (Word, Access, Excel, PowerPoint), MS Project, Visio

PETER C. DUBRO
peter@unknown.com
Thistown, MA 12345
(123) 555-1234

SOLAR ENERGY ENGINEER

EDUCATION
Masters of Science in Energy Engineering - Solar, 2007
University of Massachusetts, Lowell, MA (GPA 3.6/4.0 – Dean's Medal)

Bachelor of Science, Electrical Engineering; Minor, Computer Science, 1997
Rensselaer Polytechnic Institute, Troy, New York (GPA 3.1/4.0)

EXPERIENCE
Senior Energy Engineer – Solar Design Company, MA 2004 - present
- Engineering and project management of renewable energy systems.
- Solar photovoltaic systems installation and commissioning.
- Grant, proposal, commissioning, and feasibility report writing.
- Data acquisition system development, programming, and consulting.

Energy Engineer - Energy Logic Inc, Dennisport, MA 2004 - present
- Set up office computer network and provided technical support.
- Researched applicability of solar PV application for large business use.

Substitute Teacher - Mansfield HS, Mansfield, MA 2001 - 02
- Various subjects, including five weeks as a permanent substitute in Biology and Chemistry.
- Helped students design and build robot for FIRST robotics competition.

Senior Software Engineer - Bizland Inc., Burlington, MA, 2000 - 01
- Small Business Resource Center Platform involving co-branded business web hosting.
- Developed and refined member tools utilizing mySQL, PERL, with some JavaScript.
- Integrated third-party unified login and registration.
- Performed technical lead and point-of-contact role on several projects.
- Role of Perl coach to guide junior team members and report project status in senior meetings.

Engineer - Raytheon Electronic Systems, Portsmouth, RI, 1997 - 00
- Web development for Smart Product Model using PERL, Java, JavaScript.
- Integrated Engineering tools for Web/WAN based deployment.
- Active Server Page Web/database integration using VBSCRIPT ADO and ACCESS.
- Block1C Open Systems Module FDDI network designer.
- FIM - AN/UYK43 testing interface.

Research Assistant - Rensselaer, Troy, New York, 1997
- Software Engineer - Transportation Environmental Management.
- SQLWindows Database design for the New York Department of Transportation.
- Developed Database and GUI for Environmental tracking.

(Continued)

PETER C. DUBRO
Page Two

Jr. Engineer - Nortel Technologies Inc., RTP, North Carolina, 1994 - 96
- Developed Web Page, employing JAVA, CGI scripts, and PERL, in HTML.
- Hardware/ Firmware Engineer - TOPS Hardware Design.
- Worked on development of hand-held prototype to test digital telephony equipment.
- Debugged and wrote C and DSP code for the user interface and signal processing functions.
- Developed a proprietary database management system in FoxBase+ to track sales, which saved the company $150k in outside consulting.

SKILLS
Programming Languages: Java, Javascript, Visual Basic + ASP, Perl, HTML, C++, C, Assembly, SQL, FoxBase+, PASCAL, FORTRAN, BASIC, CMS2Y
Computer Systems: Windows95/98/2000/XP, UNIX, LINUX, VMS, DOS, OS/2, and Macintosh
Web Servers: Apache, Microsoft, Tomcat
Computer Software: ArchiCAD Pro-Engineer, AutoCAD, XACT, FUNDES, Sprig, PowerView, MAPLE, PSPICE, Matlab, Mathcad, MS Word, Excel, Access, Lotus 123, Power Point, Frame, SAS

PROJECT MANAGEMENT
- 15 custom designed car canopies with 15kW of PV on each for a total of 225kW.
- Dual roof system at PBS studios with 60kW low slope ballasted for inclusion in a green roof and 40kW flat roof PV systems. First PPA in MA.
- 50kW system on supermarket chain.
- 44kW installation on a hospital on Martha's Vineyard.
- 22kW system on a fire station in Western MA.
- 11kW Roof integrated system at a museum with second phase renovation that moved part of the roof into a rack system with additional PV.
- 5kW residential system with 800 Ahr battery backup capacity.

DATA ACQUISITION
- Worked with Solar Design Company to develop improvements for Linux back-end and National Instruments front-end data acquisition system. Code written in Perl and PHP and used in a dozen systems. Systems meet revenue grade monitoring and exceed MA State reporting requirements.
- Created web-based tools and alerts for quick analysis of systems.
- Founded Solar Design Company's website to independently develop inexpensive small scale systems. Back-end code primarily written in Perl using MySQL databases and flat files incorporating PHP.
- Developed second generation commercial system for Solar Design Company to reduce costs and improve reliability as well as offering better on-site user interface while reusing existing code for web-based interface.
- Developed algorithms to more accurately determine PV performance metrics and shade characteristics.
- Specified and developed materials list for acquisition system in Abuja Nigeria for integration with Alabama controls DAQ.
- Specified DAS components for Cape Systems data acquisition project in the Bahamas involving five renewable energy systems of mixed wind and solar using string level monitoring on a battery backup and grid-tied system over three facilities.

Thomas Perkins
123 Walker Street, Reno, NV 12345
(123) 555-8888, tomperkins@unknown.com

Objective	Sr. Research Associate in the Environmental Energy Technology Division
Education	University of Utah, Salt Lake City, B.S., **Mechanical Engineering,** 2009 *Graduated with High Honors (3.85 GPA)* University of Nevada, Reno, B.A., **Philosophy,** 2007 *Graduated with Highest Honors*

Work Experience

2009-present   **Project Engineer,** Hyden Associates, Reno
Provide due-diligence services for publicly funded, demand-side management (DSM) programs directed at commercial and industrial customers, including large office buildings, oil refineries, and various manufacturing facilities

Energy Engineering and Analysis
- Oversee metering, measurement, and verification of energy and demand savings
- Monitor data analysis
- Perform and assess energy audits
- Knowledge of end-use technology, including pumps, fans, compressors, condensers, electric motors, variable-speed drives, and fluorescent lighting

Program Management
- Advise participants on energy savings estimates, and measurement and verification methodology
- Write detailed project reviews for utility clients
- Ensure compliance with energy program rules
- Approve applications and savings reports
- Work directly with service providers and customers on projects

Additional Projects
- Reviewed a proposed revision to the Federal Energy Management Program (FEMP) Measurement and Verification Guidelines, chapter on Renewable Energy Projects
- Assisted in developing and implementing measurement and verification plans for projects participating in the Nevada Energy Commission's summer demand initiative

2008   **Research Assistant,** University of Utah Combustion Laboratories, Salt Lake City
Participated in experimental modeling of combustion kinetics; experiments involved shock tube tests with acetylene

Computer Skills

FORTRAN	Excel	Word
MatLab	Pascal	PowerPoint

Environmental

Andrea Cooper
800 Bingham Street, Apt. 1A, Concord, NH 12345
andreacooper@unknown.com; 123-555-1234

Objective: PR position with an organization devoted to renewable energy

Education

Chelsea College	May 2007	Concord, New Hampshire
St. Andrews University	Semester Abroad	Scotland, United Kingdom
Major: Classical Languages		Major GPA: 3.98; Cumulative: 3.91
Minors: Art History and Environmental Studies		

Awards Received

Summa Cum Laude: Title denoting the highest possible honors upon graduation
Phi Beta Kappa: National academic honor society
Order of Wailatpu: Chelsea honorary award for exceptional service to the college

Leadership

- Compiled literature review on environmentalism and regional tourism within the middle classes of India for Geography professor at St. Andrews University (2007).
- Assisted Environmental Sociology professor at Chelsea College in her research focusing on environmental toxins and the Native American tribes of the Pacific Northwest (2007).
- Organized an extremely successful, entirely student-run fundraiser for the environmental program of Hillside High School (2002).

Work Experience

Personal Organizer: The Arnsley Family, Concord, NH (2007-present)
- Implemented a systematic organization of files, photographs, and slides. Advised family about interior design and environmentally sound landscaping.

Project Aide: Project for Employed Families, Dover, NH (Spring 2008)
- Assisted in the creation of America's only contract language database by compiling and analyzing information from union contracts and a contract language lawyer's evaluations.

Library Intern: The Museum of Contemporary Art, Boston, MA (Summer 2007)
- Provided support in this widely renowned research institution, requiring attention to detail, commitment to assignments, independence, and enthusiasm.

Serials Assistant: Chelsea College Library, Concord, NH (2003-2007)
- Executed extreme care for details in updating databases and daily maintenance of the thousands of journals and newspapers; worked on many independent projects, such as taking inventory of all paper items currently held by online catalogs.

Resident Assistant: Chelsea College Residence Life, Concord, NH (2005)
- Planned 20 academic and social events, in addition to 3 meetings weekly; learned the value of effective communication with one's peers.

Trail Conflict Surveyor: Upstate Regional Park District, Geneva, NY (Summer 2004)
- Utilized diplomatic communication skills when asking controversial questions.

BROOKE MADDOX
School: Harvard University, Box 345 • Cambridge, MA 12345
Home: 123 Northlake Road • Los Angeles, CA 12345
(123) 555-1234 • brookemaddox@unknown.com

Environmental Impact Assessment (EIA) Research Analyst

EDUCATION

Harvard University, Cambridge, MA *Class of 2009*
- Honors Major: Environmental Science and Policy
- Overall GPA 3.4; Major GPA 3.75
- Honors Thesis: How effective are invasive species removal programs? A case study from the Yosemite National Park, CA

RESEARCH

Nature First, *Intern,* Yosemite, CA *Summer 2008*
- Designed and executed my own research experiment on the effectiveness of herbicide treatment in reducing invasive species cover in preserved under-story forest communities
- Worked independently in the field for eight weeks collecting 8500m^2 of data
- Completed literature research and statistical analysis (manuscript in preparation)

Dept of Organismic and Evolutionary Biology, *Research Assistant* *Fall 2007-Present*
- Perform terrestrial biogeochemical laboratory techniques, such as plant sample preparation and strontium isotope analysis
- Participate in weekly lab meetings with graduate students and faculty

---

BUSINESS EXPERIENCE

Phillipstown Financial Group, *Intern* , San Diego, CA *Summer 2007*
- Worked directly under the financial advisor to organize financial data on over 1,500 clients
- Corresponded with 700 clients, with regular follow-up

Rich & Sons Hardware, *Green Researcher,* Santa Barbara, CA *Summer 2007*
- Researched and catalogued a myriad of green product suppliers into the master database

---

LEADERSHIP EXPERIENCE

Sustainability Consulting & Investment Partnership, *Member* *Spring 2009-Present*
- Advise local businesses how to reduce their impact on the environment and overall efficiency

Career Development Center (CDC), *Peer Career Advisor* *2008-Present*

Women in Science and Engineering (WiSE), *Mentor* *Fall 2007-Present*
- Advise freshman women students interested in the sciences on coursework and student life

Capital Outdoor Leadership Training, *Participant,* Culver City, CO *Fall 2006*
- Practiced leadership skills while backpacking and peaking two mountains

UC Davis Science and Sports Camp, *Group Leader,* Davis, CA *Summer 2005&2006*
- Helped teach science and math courses to young students at University's Hall of Science

---

VARSITY ATHLETICS

Women's Varsity Crew, *Oarswoman* *Fall 2005-Present*
- 2006 Season: Personally undefeated. Boat 2nd at Ivy League Championships
- 2007 Season: Personally undefeated. Boat 3rd at Ivy League Championships
- 2008 Season: 5 wins/1 loss. Boat 3rd at Ivy League Championships
- 2009 Season: Personally undefeated. Boat 2nd at Ivy League Championships

---

SKILLS AND INTERESTS

Computer: Stata, SketchUp, Basic MatLab, and Microsoft Office
Interests: Alpine skiing, sculling, backpacking, and hiking in the High Sierras; baking desserts

MARC KORCHIN

1500 San Pablo Ave.
Berkeley, CA 94702
(510) 845-4743
info@gogreenmotors.com

Sales Representative for Manufacturer of Electric Vehicles

Summary

- Established Neighborhood Electric Vehicle (NEV) dealer in San Francisco Bay Area, with strong media and community relationships.
- Aggressive and successful sales professional with over 9 years experience in direct sales and sales management; over 17 years experience in retail sales.
- Proven track record of growing small start-up companies to profitability and/or sale.
- Background includes business management, retail, inside and outside sales, account management, training, and customer service.

Professional Experience

Green Motors (Berkeley, CA)   **2007-present**
Manager

- Founded and grew the nation's #1 NEV dealership, which sells trucks, cars, motorcycles, mopeds, scooters, and bicycles.
- Operate a 3,500 sq. ft. retail store; and became the #1 ZENN dealership within the first year of operation.
- Manage onsite service department, which offers warranty and nonwarranty services for all electric vehicles, as well as plug-in conversions for hybrids.
- Build ongoing relationships with government and university officials, including Assemblyperson, Barbara Lee, Mayor Tom Bates, and Tim Lipman of UC Berkeley.
- Frequently interviewed for print, TV, and radio features about green cars and environmental issues.
- Active participant in community events, including city parades, How Berkeley Can You Be?, and Earth Day.

SoftChalk, (Richmond, VA)   **2004-2006**
Vice President, Sales

- Took company from $18,000 in total sales on April 9, 2004, to $749,898 on June 30, 2006. Achieved sales of $109,000 in 2004, $306,000 in 2005, and $317,000 in the first 2 quarters of 2006, thereby breaking the sales record for 2005 in the first 2 quarters of 2006.
- Hired, trained, and managed new Sales and CRM team while continuing to mine and close new business and increase revenue from existing clients.
- Strategically targeted "high profile" prospects in the e-Education industry in Higher Ed and K-12; successfully closed sales to major universities, including the University of Kansas, Duke University, and the University of Maryland; and several major system-wide sales, including Dallas Community College District, Maricopa Community College District, and the Los Angeles Virtual Academy.

continued

MARC KORCHIN   **Page 2**

Blackboard (Washington, DC)   **2000-2004**
Sales and Account Manager
- During Blackboard's purchase of MadDuck Technologies, personally converted over 85% of MadDuck clients to Blackboard software within 4 months (after being given 18 months to do so), thereby increasing the sale price of MadDuck from $1.4 million to $2.9 million, and generated an additional $200,000 dollars in initial revenue to Blackboard by generating multiple-year deals.
- Direct Sales Manager responsible for increasing revenue from existing clients as well as generating new sales of products, service, and third-party hardware and software.
- Consistently maintained greater than 95% annual retention of existing customer base.

Awards and Recognition at Blackboard include:
- "Sales Rep of the Quarter"
- 2003 Presidents Club

MadDuck Technologies (Richmond, VA)   **1999-2000**
National Sales Manager

- Global responsibility for sale of "Web Course in a Box" Course Management Software (CMS) to K-12, Corporate, and Higher Education markets.
- In one year, doubled the sales that MadDuck had made in the company's history. Products included the CMS, a "Suite" of services and training.
- Increased the perceived value of MadDuck Technologies, which led to subsequent sale of MadDuck to Blackboard for $2.9 million.

Computown (San Francisco, CA)   **1998-1999**
Computer Sales Specialist
- Sold over $1.5 million per year in hardware, software, and support contracts.
- Over 85% of hardware sales included support and maintenance contracts resulting in a 25% increase in revenue for the company.
- Top salesman of the year for two years in a row.

Charles Schwab (San Francisco, CA)   **1996-1998**
Client Relations Manager
- Managed relationships with Schwab One credit card customers.
- Responsible for securities negotiation and estate reconciliation of stock; successfully renegotiated greater than 97% of all stocks in any given quarter.

Whole Earth Access (San Francisco, CA)   **1984-1992**
Computer and Electronics Salesman
- Sold consumer electronics and computers in a retail environment.
- Top salesman of extended warranties on products.

Education

Bachelors Degree, Cognitive Science, University of California, Berkeley
    Awards and Recognition
- Irwin P. Diamond Scholarship for "Most Outstanding Transfer Student"
- Florence Gastonguay Scholarship for "Outstanding Mathematics Achievement"
- Kathleen D. Loly Scholarship for highest grade point average in the Alpha Gamma Sigma Honor Society

Environmental

Darrell J. Kramer, JD, MPA

123 62nd Avenue, San Francisco, CA 12345   123-555-1234   djkramer@unknown.com

CAREER PROFILE

- Environmental attorney specializing in federal, state, and local environmental laws for water, air, solid waste, and hazardous materials.
- Skilled at administrative law and transactions such as reviewing and drafting construction contracts and consulting agreements.
- Experience as legal counselor, mediator, and facilitator for parties including community organizations, corporations, and government agencies.
- Adept at dispute resolution, both internal and external to an organization.

EDUCATION

Columbia University, New York, Masters of Public Administration, 2006
   National Urban Fellow, 2005, 2006
Hastings School of Law, San Francisco, Juris Doctor, 2000
   New California State Regents Professional Scholar, 1998, 1999
   Clinical Internship, USEPA, Office of Regional Counsel, Region II, Fall 1996-Spring 2000
Boston University, Massachusetts, Bachelor of Arts, Political Science, 1995

BAR AFFILIATIONS

California Bar: passed exam, 2000; admitted, 2001
New York State Bar: passed exam, 2000; admitted, 2001

EXPERIENCE

2005-pres.   OAKLAND INTERNATIONAL AIRPORT, Oakland, CA
Environmental Manager, 2008-pres.
Developed and direct the Environmental Program, which ensures environmental compliance of medium-hub airport servicing 12 million passengers annually. Program includes:

- Fueling systems oversight
- Recycling and reuse
- Air quality permitting
- Groundwater remediation
- Hazardous materials management
- Storm Water Pollution Prevention Program
- Underground and aboveground storage tanks
- Tenant and employee training and multi-medium inspections

- Implement the mitigation measures required of the airport's $3 billion master plan.
  - Execute systems and policies for landside and airside operations.
  - Negotiate tenant/permittee commitment to the program.
  - Act as project manager for construction of alternative fuel infrastructure and procurement of vehicles.
- Interpret environmental regulations and respond to internal inquiries regarding airport environmental issues.
- Serve as regulatory contact for the airport to outside agencies and professional organizations.
- Create and administer contracts; write consulting agreements; develop and oversee environmental section workplan, staff, and budget.

Special Assistant to the Director of Aviation, 2005-06
Assisted Director of Aviation in management of international commercial operations and personnel.

- Advised administrators on federal environmental and transportation laws and regulations.
- Resolved disputes and provided dispute resolution training for management and staff.

—Continued—

Darrell J. Kramer, JD, MPA, page 2

2001-05   CA ENVIRONMENTAL JUSTICE ALLIANCE, San Francisco, CA
Counsel and Executive Director
Served as Counsel to San Francisco communities during negotiations with local, state, and federal
Environmental and Transportation Agencies.

- Analyzed and evaluated compliance with federal and state environmental laws including
SEQRA, NEPA, RCRA, CERCLA, CAA, FWPCA, FSWA, and ISTEA.

- Advised clients about environmental enforcement, compliance, siting, risk management,
permitting, and land use; and negotiated with government agencies on clients' behalf.

- Planned and directed projects and policies in the areas of solid waste, water quality, air quality,
Brownfield development, and alternative fuels.

- Testified at national and local hearings and lobbied state, city, and federal governments for
transportation and environmental regulations.

- Served as Principal Investigator (2003-05) to the CA Environmental Worker Training Program
to develop a federally sponsored superfund waste site and emergency response operation job
training program. Training included:
  - Asbestos removal   - Environmental site monitoring
  - Lead abatement   - Confined space entry

- Interacted with environmental remediation and construction businesses to place 100% of trained
students from the Environmental Worker Training Program.

2003-04   SAN JOSE STATE COLLEGE, San Jose, CA
Adjunct Professor, Federal Environmental Law and Policy

RELEVANT COMMITTEES

American Association of Airport Executives, 2006-pres.
California State Bar Association: Environmental Law Section, 1998-05
The Association of the Bar of the City of San Francisco: Transportation Committee, 2002-05
San Francisco City Environmental Benefits Fund: Board Member, 2003-05
Department of Environmental Conservation Comparative Risk Project, 2004-05
Mayor's Task Force on Brownfields, 2004-05

Environmental

MARK BUTLER
Senior Level Financial Risk Manager

100 Parkside Drive, Richmond, VA 12345
123-555-1234   markbutler@unknown.com   linkedin.com/markbutler

Background: Highly successful career in financial marketing, planning, and trading. Strong knowledge of foreign exchange and capital markets; CFA, CCM, and MBA.

Professionalism: Customer focused and proactive; skilled in cultivating new and lucrative business. Goal oriented and highly motivated professional who excels in high-pressure situations. Excellent communication and interpersonal skills; a leader and team player.

CERTIFICATIONS & EDUCATION

CFA (Chartered Financial Analyst), AIMR, 2009
CCM (Certified Cash Manager), AFP, 2007
MBA, Finance & Accounting, Penn State University, 2002
BA, Business Economics, University of Virginia, 1999

PROFESSIONAL EXPERIENCE

Third Bank, Richmond, VA & Charlotte, NC   2005-pres.
VICE PRESIDENT, FOREIGN EXCHANGE MARKETING (2007-pres.)
- Currently rebuilding bank's Foreign Exchange presence in western United States. Tripled client base of middle to large cap customers and increased earnings by over 200%.

- Work closely with clients' executive officers in the management of financial strategies, following through to successful outcomes and ensuring customer satisfaction.

- Identify and quantify clients' accounting and economic cash flow risks, then develop and execute custom solutions, utilizing foreign exchange tools.

- Structure and execute spot, forward, and option contracts in accordance with customers' cash management forecasts.

- Work with clientele in the construction and accounting evaluation (FASB 133) of interest rate and currency derivative products.

- Perform online research to develop economic and political profiles pertaining to foreign currencies.

- Generate technical analyses including economic models, forecasts, and projections.

ASSISTANT VICE PRESIDENT, FOREIGN EXCHANGE TRADING (2005-07)
- Worked as Senior Spot Trader for Asian and London markets.
- Built productive working relationships with 180+ foreign corporate and institutional clients.

- Continued on Page 2 -

MARK BUTLER
- Page 2 -

ASSISTANT VICE PRESIDENT, FOREIGN EXCHANGE TRADING (continued)
- Quoted prices and provided overview for clients of Asian and London market developments.
- Developed supportive team structure on trading floor, fostering cooperative efforts in highly dynamic and oftentimes volatile environment.
- Provided liquidity for trading desk and covered currency prices in absence of primary dealer.
- Continually increased and maintained large relationship base in Asia and Europe.

Assurance Bank, Charlotte, NC   2002-05
FOREIGN EXCHANGE SPOT TRADER (2003-05)
- Provided liquidity for trading desk in spot USD/DEM.
- Quoted prices on interbank basis, developing relationships in Europe, Asia, and North America.
- Solicited new order business.

FOREIGN EXCHANGE TRADER - DERIVATIVES GROUP (2002-03)
- Traded in the forward risk for the global OTC and Exchange Options Books.
- Assisted in pricing of options.

College Intern, Boston, MA & London, England   2001-02
Treasury Department, Boston (2001-02)
- Assisted City Controller in management of pension and cash funds.

Foreign Exchange, Assurance Bank, London (2001)
- Developed strong working knowledge of Foreign Exchange Market by assisting in all aspects of currency trading.

AFFILIATIONS, SKILLS, & CONTINUING EDUCATION
Richmond Society of Financial Analysts, AIMR Local Chapter   2009
AIMR, National Chapter   2007
AFT, National Chapter   2002

Coursework in Preparation for CPA Exam: 2009-pres.
University of Virginia Accounting, Auditing, Tax, Accounting Information Systems

Information Systems Skills:
- Bloomberg   - Reuters   - FENICS   - EBS   - Microsoft Office   - Internet

John Blitzer

123 Ford Street, Plymouth, IN 12345

123-555-8888, jblitzer@unknown.com

OBJECTIVE

Position in Accounting in the Insurance Industry

SUMMARY OF QUALIFICATIONS

- Experienced using QuickBooks, Peachtree, and other accounting software.
- Two years of experience in accounting in the insurance industry.
- Energetic self-starter with strong communication skills; work well independently or on a team.
- Highly productive managing projects; a creative problem solver who rapidly adapts to changing demands.

ACCOUNTING & COMPUTER SKILLS

QuickBooks	Accounts Payable	Vendor Management
Peachtree	Accounts Receivable	Producer Commissions
Quicken	Finance Agreements	Payroll
MS Office	Collections	Benefits Administration

WORK HISTORY

2005-present   **Hugh and Grant Insurance Inc., Plymouth, IN**   **Comptroller/IT Manager**
- Managed: Accounts Receivable
            Accounts Payable
            Automation of Accounts
            QuickBooks

2004-2005   **Family Therapy Associates, Wilkinson, IN**   **Bookkeeper**
- Handled: Insurance Billing
            Customer Billing
            Vendor Management
            Banking

2001-2004   **Littleton Bank of the West, Promise, IN**   **Business Systems Analyst**
- Administered network and data warehouse security IDs for employees.
- Designed and implemented various databases to manage information.
- Coordinated vendor activity.

1999-2001   **Timely DataGathering Inc., Promise, IN**   **Office Manager**
- Managed: Accounts Receivable
            Banking
            Customer Service
            Vendor Management

EDUCATION

Bachelor of Science in Business, Highland College, West Fork, IN

VERONICA LIPTON

P.O. Box 5678
Pittsburgh, PA 12345
555-555-1234
veronicalipton@unknown.com

OBJECTIVE: Personal Lines Underwriter for HomeSmart Solutions

SUMMARY OF QUALIFICATIONS

- Experienced Personal and Commercial Lines Underwriter and top producer during 16 years in the Insurance Industry.
- Proven history of increasing business, and in softer markets, maintaining business; skilled in new product introduction, training, and marketing.
- Outstanding skills in relationship marketing; upbeat and enthusiastic, highly reliable, follow up promptly, solve problems, and establish and maintain positive communication at all times.
- Exceptionally knowledgeable in all aspects of underwriting Personal Lines business.
- Collaborated with IT Department in development of new proprietary online quoting system.
- Utilize high level of proficiency in administrative functions such as writing and implementing procedures, training personnel, and analyzing overall production results.

LICENSURE, EDUCATION, & SKILLS

- **License:** Pennsylvania 2-20 General Lines   1995 to Present

- **Bachelor of Science;** Major: Business Administration   1989
  UNIVERSITY OF PENNSYLVANIA, Pittsburgh, PA

- **Relevant Computer & Internet Skills:** Microsoft Office (Word, Excel, Outlook, Access), RiskMeter, ISO, ChoicePoint, Property Appraisers' websites, GoogleEarth, research using various search engines

- Member, Pittsburgh Association of Insurance Professionals

PROFESSIONAL EXPERIENCE

CANTERBURY INSURANCE, Pittsburgh, PA   2006 to Present
Senior Underwriter
- Top producer for a dynamic MGA managing a $20 million book of high value homeowners' insurance business placed through Gates of London and Biltmore Insurance; company currently handles over $2 billion in Pennsylvania aggregate.
- Proven skill working in current, volatile market utilizing a fluid approach whether concentrating on keeping current agencies or finding new quality business and cultivating relationships.
- Judiciously exercise autonomy in underwriting decisions and contracting with new clients.
- Senior team member of a staff of two Underwriters and one Assistant Underwriter; train staff on underwriting techniques and practices.
- Develop and manage audit team during underwriting audits.
- Collaborated with the IT Department during the design and development of new proprietary online quoting system; introduced and trained clients on new system.
- Work directly with inspection companies; order, follow up, and evaluate inspection reports to complete underwriting files.

VERONICA LIPTON - CONTINUED

HANDY INSURANCE, Erie, PA   2005 to 2006
Production Specialist
- Top producer bringing in new business, cultivating agency relationships, underwriting, and marketing.
- Skillfully managed up to 25 agencies; traveled throughout Pennsylvania to accomplish this goal.
- Active in underwriting high value homeowners' products in all lines of business.

BRYON, STAFFORD & TILFORD, Harrisburg, PA   2003 to 2005
Insurance Defense Legal Assistant to Managing Partner
- Utilized insurance background to assist attorneys in commercial claims liability litigation cases.
- Maintained professional relationships with commercial liability litigation specialists and corporate counsel; coordinated meetings, conferences, and events for the managing partner.
- Acquired valuable knowledge of claims litigation.

PETER SMYTHE, Pittsburgh, PA   2002 to 2003
Commercial Lines Broker
- Acted as liaison between producers and commercial insurance underwriters; adeptly handled placement of commercial policies nationwide.
- Worked effectively with carriers always obtaining the best possible rates for clients.
- Maintained "Top 10%" in monthly production volume; successfully managed integrated network of commercial insurance underwriters from over 15 major insurance companies.
- After the 9/11 crisis and with aggregates down, honed skills in people and relationship building and became extremely effective in maintaining business.
- Trained new hires for future broker positions; one of these brokers is very successful today.

PRATT AND TUCKER INSURANCE, Pittsburgh, PA   2001 to 2002
Marketing Production Coordinator
- Hired by Marketing Manager for new position as her assistant; took over management of small accounts.
- Marketed new and renewal P&C commercial policies through standard and excess and surplus lines markets.
- Directed negotiations with underwriters and consistently obtained comprehensive coverage at competitive premiums.
- Established daily communications with producers for developing and implementing sales strategies.

PARK CITY INSURANCE, Pittsburgh, PA   1992 to 2001
Personal Lines Underwriter
- Provided underwriting decisions on risks and gave technical underwriting advisory support to sales, service, and claims.
- Analyzed markets, resources, and processes; participated in identification and development of recommendations for management of loss trends, regulatory restrictions, and competitive issues.
- Displayed technical knowledge of coverages, programs, guidelines, and rating plans; continually enhanced proficiency in technical knowledge.
- Trained numerous employees on underwriting programs and served as the underwriting expert during new employee orientation classes.
- Started as a Member Relations Specialist and a Special Programs team member; in 1998, promoted to Underwriter.

THIRD NATIONAL BANK, Pittsburgh, PA   1990 to 1992
Assistant Bank Manager
- Selected for and successfully completed Management Training Program in Personal Banking.
- Assisted Branch Manager in day-to-day operations; performed customer services duties.

Page 2 of 2

ANTHONY RUIZ

101 Barber Street, Greenville, SC 12345   (123) 555-1234 anthonyruiz@unknown.com

HEALTHCARE MANAGEMENT SPECIALIST

Management: Highly experienced Practice Administrator and ACMPE Certified Medical Practice Executive. Opened Neurosurgery group; coordinated expansion of Cardiology and Neurosurgery groups.

Skills: Proven skill in change management implementation of workflow processes and technology systems. Adept in medical practice administration, organization, and supervision.

EXPERIENCE

SOUTH CAROLINA NEUROSURGERY ASSOCIATES, Greenville, South Carolina   2005 to present
Practice Administrator
- Accomplished opening of a Neurosurgery practice within a one-month timeframe:
  - Located and leased interim facility.
  - Set up computer systems (Electronic Medical Records, Peachtree Accounting, and Mysis practice management system), network configuration, and telephone system.
- Coordinated office relocation, expansion, and remodeling in 2007.
- Performed buy vs. lease analysis and made recommendations for office relocation.
- Instrumental in growth of practice: Patient numbers grew from 0 to 8,000 since opening in 2005 with average of 3,000 active at any one time, and $4.7M annual receipts for 2007.
- Maintained A/R collections at a high of 89% of net receipts (national average = 52%).
- Trained, oversaw, and audited staff on use of surgical claim coding, CPT, and ICD-9.
- Recruited and negotiated contracts for two surgeons and nurse practitioner.
- Collaborated with Director of Neurosciences Program, Neurosciences Marketing Manager, and CEO in the development and opening of three clinics in rural South Carolina.
- Sustained low clinic overhead costs at 32% of net receipts (national average = 45%).

COLUMBIA TEAM HEALTH, Columbia, South Carolina   1995 to 2005
Administrator
- Liaison between practice and hospital, maintaining ongoing and positive relationships between physicians and hospital's executive committee.
- Steering committee member of Cardiac Program, servicing 70% of South Carolina.
- Coordinated design and construction of new facility (9,650 sq. ft.).
- Facilitated new processes in Total Quality Management (TQM) and Teamwork.
- Grew outreach program from 0 to 14 clinics; situated, staffed, and marketed the program.
- Supervised 18 staff members in office with RN, PA, and four cardiologists.

EDUCATION, CERTIFICATIONS & MEMBERSHIPS

Certified Medical Practice Executive - ACMPE   2002 to present
A.S., Business Management, Columbia College, SC   1995
Continuing Professional Education: 1995 to present
  MGMA Med Series - Management Education & Development (160 credit hours)
  MGMA, Parker Institute - Group Practice Governance Leadership Group (32 credit hours)
  University of South Carolina - Business courses
Memberships:
  American College of Medical Practice Executives (ACMPE)   1994 to present
  Medical Group Management Association (MGMA)   1994 to present

BRENDA R. LINCOLN

123 Lexington Ct. • Lindsay, NV 12345 • (123) 555-1234 • blincoln@unknown.com

OBJECTIVE

Senior Business Analyst position within a regulated environment
with a focus on the Healthcare and Pharmaceutical industries

SUMMARY OF QUALIFICATIONS

- More than 10 years' experience combining technical expertise in software development with economics background and business acumen within the healthcare field.

- Adept at building positive relationships and communicating effectively with both clients and colleagues, with particular skill in translating across technical and nontechnical arenas to ensure client understanding and satisfaction.

- Strong organizational abilities with astute attention to detail to ensure top quality in meeting client requirements; able to keep projects on track and achieve success within scope, budgets, and deadlines.

- A driven and dedicated leader and team member who takes initiative and learns new skills, systems, and processes quickly.

PROFESSIONAL EXPERIENCE

2002-pres.   **RESEARCHINTENSIVE, INC.,** Lindsay, NV
Associate Director, Systems Compliance   *2005-pres.*
Associate Director, IVR Programming   *2005*
Manager, IVR Programming   *2004-05*
Manager, IVR Production Support   *2003-04*
CIS Analyst/Senior Analyst, IVR   *2002-03*

- Actively participated in Corrective Action Plan (CAP) and 21 CFR Part 11 analysis to address federal regulations related to the pharmaceutical industry.

- Initiated and conducted compliance review of all project documentation for products used by physicians in clinical trials of new pharmaceuticals.

- Worked closely with Interactive Voice Response (IVR), Data Management, and Biostatistics departments to ensure compliance with internal SOPs.

- Analyzed issues and discrepancies for each review and worked closely with team members to redefine priorities, resolve specific issues, and develop additional staff training to ensure proper compliance in the future.

- Completed eight reviews for each department per year. Wrote reports and quarterly summaries of findings for senior management.

- Directed a team of up to 16 programmers and analysts in IVR development. Created and implemented change orders for existing systems and plans for six new systems per month, including timelines, requirements, and cost estimates. Supported 50 active projects simultaneously.

- Defined and documented user requirements for internal projects. Created development, installation, and testing plans, and consistently met stringent deadlines, quality standards, and CSV requirements.

-continued-

- Oversaw Computer System Validation (CSV) efforts for in-house development and OTS software, including Inform, Captiva, Remedy, and LiveLink.
- Member, IVR Change Management Committee, 2003-present; Committee Chair, 2003-04. Worked with cross-functional committee members to ensure accuracy and completeness of all documentation prior to production.
- Member, Risk Assessment Committee, 2005-present. Reviewed RFPs and protocols for clinical trials to determine optimal approach for building a system to meet user requirements, including timelines and potential risks.
- Conducted periodic demonstrations of system functionality and proposal defense presentations to clients.
- Identified and anticipated special problems and developed recommendations for the client for specific design adjustments and improvements.
- Hired, trained, and directed team members. Conducted performance evaluations and maintained all training records.

1993-02   **HIGHHEALTH HEALTHCARE (FORMERLY HEALTH COMPUTER SYSTEMS),** Lindsay, NV
Senior Software Analyst   *1999-02*
Programming Supervisor   *1997-99*
Programmer/Analyst   *1993-97*

- Directed projects, trained users, and supported office management system for physicians, clinics, and healthcare facilities nationwide, including diagnosis, scheduling, billing, budgeting, accounting, reporting, and database administration.
- Developed customized software components to address the specific needs of managed care and urgent care environments.
- Tracked and maintained new software releases, installations, and revisions to ensure accuracy and consistency for 70+ diverse versions available in the field.
- Won President's Award for Outstanding Performance as Programmer/Analyst.

1991-93   **PRINCETON UNIVERSITY,** Princeton, NJ
Research Assistant, Economics Department & Business School

- Conducted extensive research for project involving both Economics and Business School Professors.
- Created computer questionnaire to assess health concerns of a diverse array of individuals in the Princeton area and beyond.
- Recruited and trained outside organization to conduct surveys to wider audiences and significantly increase participation in the project.
- Gathered, reviewed, and synthesized data, worked closely with professors to determine optimal types of data analysis, and presented analysis reports.

EDUCATION / PROFESSIONAL DEVELOPMENT

M.A., Economics, Princeton University, Princeton, NJ, 1992
B.S., Economics, minors in Mathematics & Computer Science, St. Albans College, Green, MT, 1990
Additional training through ResearchIntensive:
FDA Audits and Computer Software Validation

AMY MOORE

290 Carson Avenue • Tampa, FL 12345 • (123) 555-1234 • amymoore@unknown.com

OBJECTIVE

A Project / Program Management position within a Healthcare setting

SUMMARY OF QUALIFICATIONS

- 10+ years of progressive responsibility and leadership in project and program management within a medical center environment.

- Independent and creative, able to prioritize effectively, coordinate across functions and departments, and think "outside the box" to achieve program and project goals within budgets and timelines.

- A dynamic team leader, able to establish rapport and provide training and coaching to foster excellence in team members. Skilled in building strong relationships with physicians, staff, and patients from diverse backgrounds.

PROFESSIONAL EXPERIENCE

2003-pres. **MILTON, KRAVITZ & BERKOWITZ,** Tampa, FL
Real Estate Sales

- Developed business plan and successful marketing strategies. Achieved over $30M in annual sales.

- Collaborated with web designer to create website, achieving significant web presence and building momentum for the brand.

- Established strategic partnerships with industry magazines and organizations and coordinated marketing and publicity events to increase market presence.

1992-03 **PORTSIDE MEDICAL CENTER,** Tampa, FL
Senior Project Manager	*1998-03*
Operations Manager	*1995-98*
Facility Manager	*1992-95*

- Developed and implemented a Patient Satisfaction Program to assess quality of care for 45,000 patients in a multi-specialty facility.

- Designed surveys for each patient population, evaluated medical groups and specific physicians, synthesized data, and prepared final report for Medical Director and Quality Management Committee to inform and enhance the Pay for Performance process.

- Recruited, interviewed, hired, trained, and supervised 75-100+ Nursing, Medical Assisting, and Administrative staff. Trained work teams in customer service, maintaining a high level of physician satisfaction.

- Established hospital-based programs to promote community health awareness and hired healthcare professionals to lead each program. Programs include: Smoking Cessation, Diabetes Care, Nutrition, High-Risk Pregnancy, Children with Asthma, and Pharmacy Clinic.

- Oversaw new business development and conducted due diligence to assess viability of acquiring medical practices.

-continued-

- Guided integration of new physician partners into the medical center. Educated new physicians and their staff in policies and procedures, and established a timeframe for their transition into the medical network.
- Conducted audits of physician charts and developed measurement tools to assess levels of compliance with medical center policies and regulations. Coached physicians on processes.
- Coordinated upgrade of practice management software and trained staff in the use of KIP Medical Management system.
- Reviewed and analyzed community standing, reputation, and contractual relationships with healthcare plans and providers within the community.
- Received President's Award for Outstanding Quality Performance, presented by the medical center CEO.

COMMUNITY SERVICE

2004-pres.   **Dade Charter School, Dade County School District**
- Event Chair, Annual Fundraiser: Secured donations; selected site, theme, and entertainment. Coordinated 75 volunteers and oversaw this highly successful event, with 300+ attendees. Event raised $75K, setting a record for the school.
- Initiated eBay fundraising campaign as a new revenue stream, created charitable website, and raised $20K through online donations.
- Coordinated and executed annual giving campaign, with proceeds over $250K.

EDUCATION / PROFESSIONAL DEVELOPMENT

B.A., Summa Cum Laude, History & Anthropology, University of Miami

Computer proficiency: MS Word, Excel, Project; WordPerfect; IDX Medical Management Software

Florida Real Estate Sales License #12345678

Healthcare

Kayla J. Wong
(123) 555-1234
kaylajwong@unknown.com

JOB OBJECTIVE

An Executive / Administrative Assistant position within a healthcare setting

SUMMARY OF QUALIFICATIONS

An efficient, detail-oriented and well-organized professional with more than 10 years of progressive responsibility in Executive / Administrative Assistant positions within the NYMC healthcare system. Known for collaboration and teamwork, as well as working independently with minimal supervision. Flexible, able to prioritize effectively to complete simultaneous tasks and projects within tight deadlines. Skilled in quickly learning new systems and applications.

PROFESSIONAL EXPERIENCE

2008 – Current   **New York Medical Center,** New York, NY
Family Support & Operations Enhancement Department
Administrative Processor III
A limited interim appointment ending on March 22, 2009.

- Process and maintain departmental personnel records.
- Maintain and assure confidentiality as it relates to all personnel matters and interaction with Human Resources and temporary personnel agencies.
- Support the orientation of new employees and maintain schedule to ensure meetings occur as necessary.
- Audit and process all invoices prior to final approval, negotiate with vendors to resolve disputed invoices, and track departmental expenses against budget.
- Review and report departmental expenses and monthly budget; maintain purchasing contracts, including consultants, maintenance contracts, and other outside services.
- Independently resolve building, office, and administrative issues. Support data collection efforts necessary to maintain multiple databases, including the Applications Support (AP) system and the performance portal website.

2005 – 2008   **Manhattan Pediatric Hospital,** New York, NY
Family Administration
Assistant to Pediatric Director

- Performed calendaring for meetings with agenda/log/file preparation and triage phone calls to appropriate personnel.
- Planned and organized the Executive Director's daily, weekly, and monthly activities. Communicated on behalf of the director with MPH senior leadership, staff, faculty, and other departments.
- Managed the capital contingency fund for the fiscal year.
- Processed purchase orders, check requests, accounts payable invoices, travel vouchers; handled payroll, new personnel paperwork, and retreat arrangements for Pediatric Administration.
- Maintained filing system, ensured smooth day-to-day operations, and used discretion and confidentiality in all matters, skillfully resolving issues in the Director's absence.

-continued-

Kayla J. Wong
page two

Office Manager, Family Social Work Department

• Provided overall coordination of the Pediatric Social Work office, to include administrative and analytical duties for the social workers and the director, payroll, CCS billing, and collecting statistics for the database.

Administrative Research Assistant, Planning & Development Program

• Maintained Director's calendar, handled meeting preparation, acted as liaison on behalf of the Director with physicians, staff, and MPH senior leadership. Maintained filing system and assisted with administrative and analytical projects.

• Provided support to Perinatal/Pediatric Outreach Program, including filing, creating flyers and posters, preparing materials, and coordinating with the manager to set up outreach education classes.

1995 – 2005   **New York Medical Center,** New York, NY
Medical Plan Records & Contracting
Program Coordinator/Contract Assistant

• Coordinated daily resolution of facility issues for NYMC's 2300 Peterson facility, in accordance with NYMC Design & Construction and the property management team.

• Coordinated routine maintenance and repairs, identified and assessed facility improvements, and provided regular communications to 300 building occupants regarding both emergent issues and long-term improvements.

• Provided administrative and analytical support to managed care contract staff responsible for transplant and professional contracting.

• Managed the data entry of several Access databases for Transplant and Medical Group Operations, including the Individual Deal Database and the Transplant Database. Updated the monthly Active Contracts Report, Hospital Rate Matrix, Professional Matrix Grid, and Contract Updates.

• As Acting Office Manager/Executive Assistant to Associate Director, handled payroll, accounts payable and ordering supplies, calendaring meetings, conference planning, expense reports, and other administrative duties and projects as needed.

Administrative Aide to CFO, Medical Center Administration (Interim role)

• Performed heavy calendaring, file management, and front-line reception on the phone and in person with the medical center and the campus staff. Acted as a liaison to the CFO's direct reports in finance.

Data Entry Manager, Information Technology, TAC Project

• Supervised and trained a group of six to seven staff members to assist the TAC Team in the system changeover from HealthData to TAC, including inpatient and outpatient visits, insurance information, and daily reports. Audited reports to confirm data accuracy.

Team Leader, Patient Registration

• Pre-registered patients over the phone for outpatient visits, securing all demographic, insurance, and financial information for multiple practices located at MIT and Bourne.

• Provided assistance to the supervisor and staff with registration and insurance protocol training/issues and acted as team leader in supervisor's absence.

NORA P. QUINN, RN CNP
norapquinn@unknown.com - (123) 555-1234
57 Worth Avenue, Avon, CT 12345

SUMMARY   *Experienced Nurse Practitioner specializing in Obstetrics and Gynecology
with broad expertise in private practice, clinical trials, and academic
medical settings & Aesthetic Medicine*

WORK   Aesthetic Nurse Practitioner, 2008-present
EXPERIENCE   Thomas P. Kelley, MD, FACS
Center for Plastic Surgery, Avon, CT
  - Consultation and clinical provider of laser services utilizing Cutera
  - Proficient in injection techniques of dermal filers and Botox
    administration

Aesthetic Nurse Practitioner, 2006-08
Regina Cuthbert, MD, Medical Director
Clearview Clinic, Hartford, CT
  - Consultation and clinical provider of laser services utilizing Cutera
    and Luminus
  - Proficient in injection techniques of dermal fillers and Botox
    administration

Nurse Practitioner, 1999-08
Medical Center for Women
Paulette Morse, MD, Director, Obstetrics & Gynecology Private Practice
West Hartford, CT
  - Provided primary healthcare for women of all ages, including
    obtaining a health and medical history, performing a physical
    examination, and constructing a problem list
  - Counseled individuals regarding family planning, prevention of
    sexually transmitted diseases/vaccination protocol for HPV,
    menopausal medicine, and sexuality issues
  - Provided appropriate pharmacotherapy for select women's health
    and gynecologic and obstetric conditions
  - Proficient in surgical procedures: IUD insertions, endometrial
    biopsies, and insertion of laminaria

Nurse Practitioner, 1999-study end
University of Hartford, Hartford Medical Center
Leo Finley, MD, Principal Investigator, Hartford General Hospital,
Gynecology Department, Clinical Trial for Nationwide Study on
Dysfunctional Vaginal Bleeding
  - Screened, enrolled, and followed clinical trial subjects
  - Provided data and source documentation
  - Ensured protocol compliance
  - Reported and monitored adverse events
  - Maintained comprehensive regulatory documents

NORA P. QUINN, RN CNP – continued

Clinical Research Nurse, 1997-98
Tyler Medical Center, Chicago, IL
- Recruited patients in Premature Prevention Program
- Interviewed and obtained specimens by venipuncture, cervical cultures
- Reviewed patient charts, and collected and reported data from ante-partum through post-partum
- Provided follow-up with mother and newborn
- Performed Dubowitz examinations on newborns and recorded results

Nurse Practitioner, 1990-96
Outpatient Clinic for Obstetrics & Gynecology
St. Paul's Medical Center, New York, NY
- Assessed and managed common and complex women's health problems, including PCOS, pelvic pain, abnormal vaginal bleeding, sexually transmitted diseases, abnormal pap smears
- Provided prenatal through post-partum care
- Provided health maintenance education and counseling
- Supervised and trained Nurse Practitioners and Physician Assistants students during clinical internships

Nurse Practitioner, 1986-90
Ford Health Service, New York, NY
- Coordinated, provided and triaged primary care for student population
- Offered counseling and contraceptive services, STD prevention and treatment
- Prepared and implemented lectures for students on various health related subjects

EDUCATION/ LICENSES
California Nursing License and Nurse Practitioner Furnishing Certificate, current

NAACOG Certification – Obstetric/Gynecologic Nurse Practitioner, 1985-current

NAACOG Certification – Menopause Clinician, 2003-current

State University of Auburn Medical Center/Planned Parenthood of New York, Women's Health Care Nurse Practitioner Program, 1985

Bessemer City College, ADN Nursing Program, 1980

Page 2 of 2

Healthcare

KATHLEEN CANFIELD
10 Thames Street, Apt 2E
Hartford, CT 12345
(123) 555-1234
kathleencanfield@unknown.com

EDUCATION
B.S. Nursing, Brooks College, Norwalk, CT, 2009

B.A., Sociology, University of Rochester, Rochester, NY, 1993

HIGHLIGHTS OF QUALIFICATIONS
- Self-directed and energetic, with a drive to excel. Strong organizational skills.
- Able to learn new skills quickly; effectively handle multiple tasks.
- Ability to work independently, as well as motivate and contribute in a team environment.

PROFESSIONAL EXPERIENCE
2009-pres.   Hartford County Hospital, Intensive Care Unit
Nurse Technician
- Support diagnostic procedures by assisting with vital signs, naso-oral suctioning, preparing and positioning the patient, Capillary Blood Glucose testing, catheter insertion, and bladder scanning.
- Participate in technical nursing treatments:
  - Assist physicians and nurses in care and treatment of the ill who are receiving medical, surgical, psychiatric, or outpatient treatment.
  - Observe and report to the primary nurse, changes in patient behavior, attitude, bodily complaints, and appearance.
- Enter specific information onto the patients' charts, such as blood sugars, vital signs, and I/O's.
- Perform direct patient care, including patient education and duties aimed at increasing the comfort and spirit of the patient.

2004-2008   PHOENIX MEDICAL CENTER, Phoenix, AZ
Anesthesia Technician, 2005-present
- Under direct supervision of Anesthesiologist, perform direct patient care including assisting in line placement, intubations, assembling monitoring lines, and interpreting physiological information.
- Assist anesthesiologists with specialized equipment and supplies, management and maintenance of anesthesia equipment.
- Monitor line preparation for complex surgeries using aseptic technique, including adult cardiac by-pass, heart and liver transplants, and pediatric cardiac surgeries.
- Assist with invasive procedures and fiber optic airway management.
- Utilize working knowledge of anesthesia related equipment to effectively troubleshoot problems with equipment.

-continued-

KATHLEEN CANFIELD
PAGE TWO

2004-2008   **PHOENIX MEDICAL CENTER**, Phoenix, AZ (continued)
- Distribute necessary and appropriate anesthesia supplies and equipment for surgical patients.
- Order and maintain disposable and nondisposable anesthesia inventory; stock anesthesia medication.
- Independently facilitate surgical schedule by managing surgical suite anesthesia set-up and room turnover.

Circulatory Support Technician, 2004-05

- Maintained constant lines of communication with up to 4 perfusionists, 11 anesthesiologists, and multiple OR nurses and technicians.
- Performed autologous blood recovery using cell-saving machinery during various operations, including orthopedic cases, open heart surgery, and liver transplants.
- Charted records, performed inventory management, assisted perfusionists with specialized equipment and supplies, and maintained specialized equipment.
- Monitored patients on the Thoratec Dual-Driver, Heat-mate, and TLC-II ventricular assist devices.
- Assisted perfusionists by assembling and priming the Heart-Lung Machine for cardiac by-pass.
- Assisted cardiologist with the percutaneous insertion of the intra-aortic balloon pump (IABP) in cardiac catheterization laboratory, as well as monitoring the device to ensure proper timing of the balloon.
- Assisted anesthesiologist with offsite anesthesia cases in MRI, Radiology, X-ray, CT Scan, and Cardiac Catheterization Laboratory.

1999-03   **UNIVERSITY OF DALLAS,** Dallas, TX
Recruiting Coordinator, 2002-03   *Women's Basketball Coach, 1999-02*

- Evaluated prospective student-athletes to determine program eligibility, including athletic and academic performance. Worked closely with Head Coach to develop strategic plan and outreach materials to attract candidates.
- Supervised graduate assistant and administrative support staff. Acted as a liaison between student-athletes and Head Coach.
- Planned and coordinated community service and fundraising projects, working with organizations such as Northwest Church, Kinsey Corporation, and local elementary schools.

Healthcare

Andrew Carpenter

65 Hovis Street
Charlotte, NC 12345
andycarpenter@unknown.com

Home (123) 555-1234
Cell: (123) 555-5678

Emergency Medical Technician (EMT)

SKILLS

- Licensed to drive all types of emergency vehicles.
- Basic training in Wildland Fire with S130/S190 Certificates.
- 20 hours basic pump training and operations.
- Incident Command Systems 100, 200, and 700.
- 16 hours basic vehicle extracation.
- Currently on the hazmat team at the awareness level.
- Continuing EMS education.

WORK EXPERIENCE

Mecklenberg County Fire Dept.   2005 - present
Firefighter/EMT
- Member of 28-person fire crew, which serves a residential and commercial area stretching approximately 40 sq. mile.
- Provide patient assessment and care according to local protocols.
- Perform daliy station duties, including testing and maintaining equipment.

USA Medical Services, Atlanta, GA   2004 - present
EMT
- Conduct patient care and run medical reports for diverse populations including non-English speakers and the elderly.
- Provide nonemergency transport of patients from facility to facility.

Athens Energy, Inc., Athens, GA   2003 – 2004
Meter Reader

EDUCATION

Peachland Community College, Peachland, GA   2004
EMT Basics

Tri-City Tech, Atlanta, GA
Firefighter I & Firefighter II

LORETTA NASH

9282 Bigelow Avenue
Albany, NY 12345
123-555-1234
lorettanash@unknown.com

MEDICAL TRANSCRIPTIONIST

◆————— SUMMARY OF SKILLS & QUALIFICATIONS —————◆

- Over 20 years of experience as a highly productive Medical Transcriptionist.
- Known for high accuracy rate of 99% and speed of over 2,000 transcribed lines a day.
- Skilled working as Acute Care Transcriptionist and transcribing for ESL doctors.
- Latest technology skills involve platforms, Dictaphone Word Client, and Escription Voice Recognition.
- Knowledge of medical transcription guidelines and practices in accordance with *Book of Style*.
- Motivated, self-disciplined, deadline driven; work very well with little to no supervision.

PROFESSIONAL HISTORY

Northwoods Hospital, Albany, NY   2005 to Present
- History of excellent evaluations as work-at-home Medical Transcriptionist for suburban hospital.
- As Acute Care Transcriptionist, daily workload includes History and Physicals, Clinical Resumes, Operative Notes, Consultations, Progress Notes, and Cardiology Procedure Notes.
- Transcribe for state-of-the-art Orthopedic physicians.
- Utilize highly developed skills transcribing for ESL doctors of a wide variety of nationalities.
- Involved working with latest technologies: Dictaphone ExText System's Dictaphone Word Client and Escription Voice Recognition Platform.
- Proficient working with 3rd edition of *Book of Style for Medical Transcription* (Association of Healthcare Documentation Integrity).

Geneva Medical Center, Geneva, NY   1998 to 2005
- Worked both at the hospital and at home as a full-time, Acute Care Medical Transcriptionist.
- Experienced with multi-specialties including Hematology, Oncology, and Infectious Disease.

Buffalo General Hospital, Buffalo, NY   1995 to 1998
- Worked as Acute Care Medical Transcriptionist with background transcribing Psychiatric Reports.

MediRecords (Owner/Contractor), Buffalo, NY   1989 to 1995
- Performed transcription for variety of medical professionals; transcribed Child Protection Team Physicals.

EDUCATION & MEMBERSHIP

Certificate Program in Medical Information Coder/Biller (Part-Time Studies)   2007 to Present
Albany Community College, Albany, NY

Current Membership:
Association for Healthcare Documentation Integrity (AHDI), Central New York Area Chapter

Kate Warren

Paramount College • 44 Main St. • Cambridge, MA 12345
123-555-8888 • kwarren@unknown.com

JOB OBJECTIVE
To obtain a research position with a biotechnology or pharmaceutical company in the research and development division.

PROFESSIONAL EXPERIENCE
PARAMOUNT COLLEGE, Cambridge, MA, 2008-present
Research Assistant
- Collaborated on research to assess potential angiogenic factors.
- Performed migration and proliferation assays; maintained cell cultures.
- Applied synthetic organic chemistry to produce 13-HODE, using purification techniques including TLC and HPLC.

THE CANCER RESEARCH LABORATORY, Greenville, ND, summer 2008
Research Assistant
- Isolated and partially characterized gene on mouse chromosome 13.
- Utilized techniques including PCR, cloning, gel electrophoresis, DNA extraction and purification, Southern blot, and phage library screening.
- Drafted final paper and presented results at Summer Student Symposium.

HILLSDALE HOSPITAL, Hillsdale, MN, January 2007
Medical Technology Intern
- Completed rotation through hematology, urinalysis, chemistry, microbiology, and blood bank.
- Observed patient procedures.
- Learned to perform and interpret tests used for medical diagnostics.

EDUCATION
Paramount College, Cambridge, MA
- B.A., Biochemistry/Chemistry, anticipated 2010
- In addition to introductory courses, completed two semesters of organic chemistry with experimental organic chemistry lab, one semester physical chemistry with lab, advanced inorganic chemistry with lab, and microbiology with lab.

AWARDS
Paramount Foundation Award recipient, 2007 and 2008
Dean's List, Fall 1997-Fall 2008
Presidential Scholarship (based on GPA)
Crooper Scholarship (awarded the top 10% of entering class)

AFFILIATIONS
American Chemical Society
Beta Beta Beta National Biological Honor Society

MARTIN HERSCH

221 Oak Road, Allen, TX 12345

123.555.1234 > martinhersch@unknown.com > linkedin.com/martinhersch

OBJECTIVE: Position as CTO/VP of Product Development for Advanced Tech

HIGHLIGHTS OF EXECUTIVE QUALIFICATIONS

- Over 15 years in successful executive positions within the technology industry.
- History developing and selling a variety of innovative web applications, enterprise software, and integrated suites for quality assurance, manufacturing, distribution, and education.
- Creative designer and marketer able to maintain a continuous focus on industry trends.
- Results-oriented executive manager with direct involvement in R&D, product development, marketing, customer sales, and company operations.
- Hands-on experience in corporate startups, turnarounds, and reorganizations.

PROFESSIONAL EXPERIENCE

President   2001 to Present

WICKHAM CORPORATION, Dallas, TX

Develop and support Swiftware suite of supply chain management software.

- Substantially increased customer base from one in 2001 to 25 clients today; customers included Gadgetz, PetTown, Blankenship Books, A-Z Video, and Car Car Auto Parts.
- Repositioned firm from service-based to enterprise software, product-based company.
- Created products in Swiftware suite and developed marketing plans to penetrate markets.
- Directly involved with sales and closing client contracts ranging from $100K to $1+ million.
- Expanded business in an aggressive and highly competitive market.
- Reorganized internal operations of company including retraining and hiring new personnel.

Chief Operating Officer   2000 to 2001

GROW MORE, Plano, TX

Designed and marketed web-based educational software for corporate clients.

- Partner and shareholder of startup company; involved in locating/raising funding.
- Oversaw operations, product design, and website development.

Chief Technology Officer, Inspection Division   1997 to 2000

PMT CORPORATION, Dallas, TX

Managed Inspection Division, formerly Morgan Controls, developing and marketing state-of-the-art quality assurance systems for manufacturing and distribution.

- Developed and sold machine vision and control systems to large international customers, some of which included Baylor Products, Lyons Steel, National Steel, Quell, Inc., Bosch.
- After merging Morgan Controls with PMT, continued with full management responsibility of this profitable and growing division.
- Spearheaded the introduction of numerous machine vision products with direct involvement in design, development, marketing, and sales of systems.
- Planned, acquired, and integrated Croma, a Montreal-based software company.

Chief Executive Officer   1990 to 1997

MORGAN CONTROLS, Dallas, TX

Developed and marketed machine vision controls, products for manufacturing quality assurance.

- Founded company, wrote business plan, and raised over $2 million in startup capital.
- *Inc.* magazine's #182 of "500 Fastest Growing Privately Held Companies" in 1996.

Technology

MARTIN HERSCH
Continued

- Achieved year-over-year profitability and grew company to over 100 employees.
- Directly managed product development utilizing technologies: Windows, Sun, UNIX, LINUX, NT, C, C++, and Java.
- Established strategic alliances with large corporations in the U.S., Europe, and Asia, including
- Babcock and National Steel.
- Negotiated merger of Morgan Controls with PMT, winning shareholders' support for plan.

Vice President, Operations   1990 to 1991
TIMELY SOLUTIONS, Austin, TX
Developed and sold supply chain automation for warehouse and distribution.
- Increased product development efforts and improved existing products.
- Enhanced sales/marketing, effectively expanding customer base by 40-50%.

Project Manager/Design Engineer, Integrated Automation   1986 to 1989
ADELSON/POORMAN, Austin, TX
- Managed multiple projects for new, growing division of multinational corporation.

Design Engineer, Manufacturing Automation   1984 to 1986
ROSENTHAL INTERNATIONAL, Provo, UT
- Wrote software for complex automation processes for automotive manufacturers.

EDUCATION & TECHNICAL SKILLS

BSEE Degree, University of Michigan, Flint, MI
Additionally involved in graduate-level work in Digital Signal Processing

Relevant Continuing Education
- Java, University of Michigan
- Microsoft.Net Master, University of Michigan
- Ecommerce Fundamentals, San Francisco State University
- ASP.Net 2.0, Trainex Corporation

Technical Skills & Knowledge
- Platforms: Windows, Unix
- Internet Apps: Web Services, ASP.NET, HTML, Ajax, SOAP, Flash Remoting
- Languages: C#, Java, Flash Action Script, JavaScript, SOA, XML, HTML
- Databases: SQL Server 2005, SQL Server 2000
- Programs: Windows Workflow Foundation, Microsoft Project, Microsoft Office (Word, PowerPoint, Excel, Outlook), Macromedia (Dreamweaver, Flash, Fireworks), Adobe Photoshop, AutoCAD
- Hardware/Firmware: Xilinx, PCI

Beth Crawford

99 Big Sky Avenue · Cheyenne, Wyoming 12345 · (123) 555-1234 · bcrawford@unknown.com

Marketing Professional in the High-Tech Industry

QUALIFICATIONS

Experience: Over 10 years' management experience in marketing, with over 5 years in the technology industry.

Reputation: Highly regarded for building strong partner relationships and generating innovative solutions that achieve quantifiable results. Thorough and committed; exceptional organizational and team leadership skills.

MARKETING ACCOMPLISHMENTS

2003-2009   Tech World, Cheyenne, WY
MANAGER, STRATEGIC MARKETING *(2008-2009)*

- Collaboratively developed strategies with senior management that drove market leadership in the Bandwidth Trading market.

- Developed consistent, well-positioned marketing messages in seamlessly coordinated executive briefings, conferences, trade shows, and customer meetings.

- Spearheaded production of major marketing videos, DVDs, online campaigns, and internal sales launch to support sales team in applying Tech World's marketing message and increase product sales.

- Orchestrated the Industry Communications Financial Summit 2008, focusing on advising industry professionals on critical telecommunications finance issues. Achieved over $28M in addressable revenue.

MARKETING PROGRAM MANAGER *(2003-2008)*

- Planned and executed inspiring and well-attended seminars on Lucent products, collaborating with product groups to develop content; identified speakers and industry experts, and created outbound marketing materials.

- Generated over $1.5B in expected revenue and 15,000 leads.

- Coordinated innumerable logistics, ensuring that complex scheduling and presentation technology flowed smoothly at key industry tradeshows.

- Managed direct marketing campaigns, which resulted in over 4% response rates and the highest number of qualified leads achieved to date.

- Developed seminar programs through direct mail, online marketing and telemarketing, launching solutions and exceeding projections by 100%.

1997-2003   **MARKETING CONSULTANT**

- Team-developed marketing plan for **Big Ideas Communications** that evolved into the focal point of venture capital solicitations for this reliability and scalability software company.

- Oversaw software upgrade marketing campaign for **Martinsville Publishing Company,** increasing net sales.

- Served as the interim Direct Marketing Director of **Green Thumb Products** and re-launched $5M catalog business.

EDUCATION: BA, Political Science, University of Wyoming, Laramie, WY

Technology

GRAHAM PHELPS

123 Provence Drive • New Orleans, LA 12345 • (123) 555-1234 • gphelps@unknown.com

OBJECTIVE

A senior IT project management position, with a focus on

System Administration   Manufacturing Engineering   Customer Support

SUMMARY OF QUALIFICATIONS

- 10+ years of progressive responsibility in IT for global organizations.

- Highly analytical, with particular skill in maintaining a strong customer focus while providing expert technical problem solving.

- A dynamic project manager, skilled in creating realistic project plans, prioritizing and delegating effectively, and tracking progress to ensure accurate, on-schedule completion.

- Experienced in building solid relationships and communicating articulately to build bridges between customer needs and engineering/technical team requirements. Fluent in Japanese.

PROFESSIONAL EXPERIENCE

1995-pres.   **NOTABLE GRAPHICS INC. (NGI),** U.S. and Asia locations

Global Product Support Engineer, New Orleans   *2007-pres.*

- Conduct in-depth analysis and offer technical support and guidance to 150 System Support Engineers (SSEs) worldwide. Provide third-level support to U.S. customers and second-level support to international customers.

- Consult with engineering team members when necessary to resolve complex technical issues. Manage customer relationships, expectations, and escalations, effectively balancing customer needs and engineering requirements.

- Maintain strict adherence to customer turnaround times, consistently achieving on-time completion of system repairs.

- As Support Expert, prepare and deliver dynamic, interactive presentations to educate frontline support team on new products.

Manufacturing Test Engineer, New Orleans and Tokyo   *2002-07*

- Designed and implemented test processes for mid-range desktop product and high-end server proprietary software product, serving as primary contact among Quality, Field, and Support teams for all issues during system manufacturing.

- Worked closely with Production Schedulers to prioritize tasks and projects, allocate resources, and ensure on-time completion and ISO9001 compliance.

- Met regularly with Quality Group to identify, analyze, and resolve discrepancies and problems with components. Utilized the Integrated Product and Process Development (IPPD) approach to improve the quality of new products while reducing costs and time-to-market.

- Project-managed 15-member Engineering Group in Tokyo, including Mechanical, Quality, Test, and Board-level Engineers. Delegated and matched team members with specific tasks to achieve optimal performance.

-continued-

GRAHAM PHELPS
PAGE TWO

- Trained team members on the production floor for upcoming builds, and acted as liaison between Engineering, Planning, and Finance departments.
- Facilitated conference calls between the U.S. and Japan manufacturing and engineering groups to address problems and keep current with technical issues.
- Prepared test procedures and documentation in both Japanese and English for high-end systems and desktop products.
- Received 2004 Employee Excellence Award for outstanding performance, the only native English speaker to ever win this award.

Field Technical Analyst / System Support Engineer, Boston, MA   *1995-02*
- Provided ongoing technical support, responded to SSE questions, and traveled to customer locations where necessary for escalation management.
- Promoted to Field Technical Analyst based on excellent performance.

1987-95   **PRIMARYTECH,** Boston, MA
Network Analyst / System Administrator   *1992-95*
- Primary System Administrator to the Vehicle Analysis Branch at Boston Tech Research Center. Supported numerous networked systems, resulting in increased efficiency, productivity, and communication.
- As Network Analyst, responded to user questions and quickly diagnosed and resolved network problems.
- System Administrator for the Network Support Office's Sun computers.

Programmer   *1987-92*
- Lead programmer on the Simulation, Monitoring, Analysis, Reduction, and Test System acceptance team for a U.S. military support contract. Designed and tested bug fixes and system upgrades.
- Designed and coded C programs and Bourne shell utilities to support the Cray systems, the world's fastest supercomputers at the time.
- Received two Outstanding Achievement Awards for work in support of the project.

EDUCATION / PROFESSIONAL DEVELOPMENT

B.S., Computer Science, Louisiana Tech, New Orleans, LA

Completed Kempner-Tregoe Project Management Training

Technical skills: Unix, C, shell scripting, PERL, Linux, JavaScript, PHP, MS Excel, Word, and PowerPoint

Former member, IEEE

Technology

PAULA WHITE

16 Oaktree Road • Boston, MA 12345 • (123) 555-1234 • paulawhite@unknown.com

User Experience/User Interface Architect

SUMMARY OF QUALIFICATIONS

- User Interaction Designer with extensive experience in all phases of the development lifecycle
- 5 years experience in usability analysis, architecture, design, and testing
- Knowledgeable of various industries, including telecommunications, healthcare, government, and HR as a result of over 10 years IT consulting experience
- Competent in HTML, CSS, XML, and JavaScript
- Solid understanding of technology constraints and "geek speak" due to previously working as a developer myself
- Great with clients and willing to travel to client sites
- Skilled with Visio, Dreamweaver, and MS Office Suite applications

EMPLOYMENT HISTORY

1997- 2008   Holt Corporation
For over 10 years, worked all over the country for this Fortune 500 IT consulting firm. Worked directly with clients in several industries as my career has progressed toward my goal of becoming a senior consultant with a specialization in User Experience Architecture.

Project History

2008
User Experience Architect, internal project
- Lead User Interface Architect for an internal capabilities management and knowledge share initiative
- Conducted usability analysis on over a dozen internal division websites and their associated SharePoint and Wiki sites
- Conducted interviews with users to determine their goals and needs; monitoring website statistics to validate interview results
- Updated site architecture and language to reflect organizational goals and user needs
- Conducted usability tests to validate improvements made over past year and set direction for future updates

2005 to 2008
User Experience Architect, project for People Systems, with implementation for Basix Health
- Lead UI architect for a comprehensive human resources portal
- Developed Key User profiles and detailed Key User Tasks based on analysis of business requirements
- Created information architecture and navigational structure for both manager and employee self-service portal sites
- Managed complex data and event interactions among seven back-end systems
- Created wireframes for transactions and coordinated the work of other UI Designers to ensure a cohesive and consistent user experience

- Designed and executed usability tests of prototype system
- Managed work of graphics designers and front-end developers to ensure quality and consistency with project vision

2004 to 2005
User Interface Designer, project for State of Massachusetts
- Designed user interface for the user account management within a state government's online business forms processing portal
- Designed the user and data interface for this system with a separate eCommerce payment system so that transition between systems would be seamless for users

2004 to 2004
User Interface Designer & Developer, project for KCD
- Improved and updated the design of an employee time management system for a large telecommunications corporation based on heuristic evaluation

2003 to 2003
User Interface Designer & Developer, project for Health Systems of Maine
- Worked as part of a team to create an online enrollment system for a major healthcare organization's benefits management project
- Designed navigational structure to walk users through complex transactions

ACCREDITATION

Certified Usability Analyst, granted 2007 by International Training, Inc., certification # 2007-5555

PROFESSIONAL MEMBERSHIP

Usability Professionals Association member since 2005

EDUCATION

1997   Boston University, Boston, Massachusetts
B.S., Math
Graduated with honors
Awarded Phi Beta Kappa honor society membership

PROFESSIONAL DEVELOPMENT

Current   Boston University – *Taking online course on AJAX*

Krantz Business School – *Taking class in Adobe Illustrator*

2007   Roanoke University, Roanoke, Virginia
Completed course in Cognitive Psychology

2006 –2007   International Training, Inc., Boston, Massachusetts & Roanoke, Virginia
Completed four-course series for Reliable Business Practices

Technology

Taylor Thompson

16 Fifth Street   Atlanta, GA 12345   (123) 555-1234   taylorthompson@unknown.com

Database Developer, Statistical Analyst, Visual Basic Programmer
Automation and Streamlining, Pushbutton Solutions

PROFILE

- Microsoft Certified Solution Developer (MCSD).
- Dashboard interface development, process streamlining and automation, and full life-cycle development to simplify maintenance, eliminate repetition and error, and save time and money.
- Adhere to best practices in building technical requirements, data structures, development tools, and supporting documentation. Thorough and meticulous.
- Research deeper implications of data to ensure its most effective interpretation.
- Maintain superior client relationships. Ensure that communication around job parameters remains clear and focused. Responsive, reliable, and flexible.
- **Programming languages:** VB6, VBA, VBScript, and VB.Net; **Databases:** Teradata/BTEQ, SQL Server, Oracle, Access, and Excel.

RECENT PROJECT HISTORY

SECOND BANK, Consumer Deposits Group, Atlanta, GA   2008-09
- Created user-friendly application that generates automated FRTC-executed scripts to streamline Teradata database management and monitor national marketing campaigns.
- Designed and implemented an interactive dashboard that gives users greater flexibility and capacity in managing, refining, organizing, and executing macros and queries.
- Built one template to report at five levels of geographic scale, ranging from entire sections of the United States down to individual branches, and saving time and resources.

OPTIMAL BUSINESS SOLUTIONS (OBS), Accounting Department, Athens, GA   2008
- Significantly decreased file sizes, cut recalculation times, and stopped Excel from locking up with errors and premature terminations by replacing "lookup" formulas with links to Access queries.

COBALT SYSTEMS, Financial Forecasting, Savannah, GA   2006-08
- Accelerated accurate financial forecasting by developing push button tools to maintain open-to-buy, divisional daily sales, and top-down planning applications, which reduced the time spent per week by planners from two hours to 30 seconds.
- Expedited cross-referencing and analysis by migrating top-down planning data from 27 spreadsheets into a single Access data source.

BIGELOW TECHNICAL SUPPORT (MacKiver, Benetech), Savannah, GA   2006
- Facilitated ease of project scheduling and monitoring at MacKiver by providing integrated feedback on daily, weekly, monthly, and quarterly jobs, DTS packages, stored procedures, and views. Used SQL Server's management facility to direct users to unfinished and pending jobs.
- Designed custom reusable filters for Benetech's forecasting department that allowed end users to dynamically select criteria by location, product, wholesaler, and retailer.

SECOND BANK, Atlanta, GA   2005-06
- Simplified monitoring of maintenance schedules for ATMs throughout the United States.
- Automated selection of daily, weekly, semi-weekly, monthly, and quarterly ATM reports, using functions and stored procedures (SQL Server, Oracle), DTS packages (SQL Server), and web-based reports. Accelerated query execution and reduced report generation time from 25 minutes to three.

Taylor Thompson, Page 1 of 2

Taylor Thompson *(continued)*   (123) 555-1234   taylorthompson@bamboo.com

KELBERT INDUSTRIES, Peachtree, GA   2005
Lead Programmer/Data Analyst

- Collaborated with nine-member international trade team to consolidate nine data feeds into a single Access database, greatly expanding analysis and metric-generation capabilities.
- Tailor designed SAP/R3 business objects to automate data acquisition and report generation, delivering solutions in 1 percent of the time it had taken the SAP/R3 programming team.

SOUTHERN BANK OF PEACHTREE, Peachtree, GA   2004-05
Lead Programmer/Database Developer/Statistical Analyst

- Developed Access and Excel applications to enable financial analysts with potential loans of over $1m to analyze a thousand portfolios and pool risk grades to a single Access document.
- Translated calculations from Microsoft Excel to Visual Basic code with 100% accuracy.

PETERBOROUGH, INC., Atlanta, GA   2004
Lead Visual Basic Programmer

- Upgraded Microsoft Word survey templates used and migrated the results to a web-based XML database. Significantly improved previous work design by streamlining code, improving search routines, and reducing the data-migration time by a factor of 10.

INDIVIDUAL CLIENTS, Atlanta, GA   2002-04
Database Analyst/Programming Consultant

- Designed and developed data-cleansing procedure and converted a lengthy data gathering and distribution procedure for A1 Analytics, a data mining company, into a simple pushbutton process, delivering product in one-fifth the time.
- Developed SQL Server database to improve collection of Amazon referral fees for a lyrics website.
- Developed Excel-based predictive models enabling Digital Eclipse, manufacturer of video games, to calculate individual item pricing using total revenue, total clients, and attrition rates as starting factors.
- Automated procedure to download 10,000 strategic patents into Access for a patent company. Extracted top 100 inventors as most likely source of new business.

THURSTON'S BIG AND TALL, Atlanta, GA   2002
Lead Database Analyst/Visual Basic Programmer

- Designed and implemented a critical SQL Server management tool that tallied sales information from surveys at over 1,000 stores across the United States under tightly timed and budgeted working conditions.
- Developed Excel-based, dynamically formatted line items, color-coded to enable top executives to determine, at a glance, which stores met sales goals.

EDUCATION & CERTIFICATION

Certified Java Programmer, University of Atlanta
Microsoft Certified Solution Developer (MCSD): Visual Basic 6.0
Sun Certified Programmer for the Java 2 Platform 1.4

B.A., English, Peachtree University, Peachtree, GA

Technology

Kerry Wainwright

123 Porter Street, Denver, CO 12345
(123) 555-8888, kwainwright@unknown.com

SUMMARY

More than 10 years' programming and application development experience, including:

Dynamic database-backed websites	Real-time data collection
Content Management Systems (CMS)	Web crawling

COMPUTER SKILLS

Languages/Technologies
- Java, J2EE, JSP, EJB, AJAX, C, C++, PERL, JavaScript, XSLT, XML, XHTML, HTML, SGML, and various UNIX/LINUX shells.

Software
- Databases: SQL, ESQL, ODBC, JDBC, MySQL, Oracle, Access.
- Platforms: Windows XP/2000/NT/95/3.1, VAX-VMS, various UNIX flavors (Redhat Linux, Solaris, HPUX), Mac-OS.

EXPERIENCE

WEB PROGRAMMER/SOFTWARE ENGINEER
InterRef, Denver, CO, 2004 - present
- Developed Java applications for the data-warehousing infrastructure.
- Developed database-backed web servlets for customer website utilizing XML, XSLT, AJAX technologies.
- Managed data storage and distribution systems via website t ools, RSS, XML, etc.

CONTRACT SOFTWARE ENGINEER
Seamless Systems, Denver, CO, 2003
- Managed several MySQL databases (design, creation, transaction programming).
- Developed features for websites and Content Management Systems, using Java, PERL, JavaScript, and/or XSLT.

SENIOR SOFTWARE ENGINEER
RiteInfo Inc., Boulder, CO, 2002 - 2003
- Designed and built Internet and real-time newswire data acquisition and processing.
- Developed news service system on Linux, including a real-time messaging system.
- Built applications to crawl customer websites.

SENIOR SOFTWARE ENGINEER
Spectrum Technology, Denver, CO, 1996 - 2002 (acquired by RiteInfo, Inc. in 2002)
- As part of the original start-up team, developed and built various systems, including data aggregation, processing, testing, loading, and staging systems.
- Developed original systems and test ing tools for real-time news service.
- Developed data management system (structure, processing and management tools, and data warehousing system).

PROGRAMMER
WINSCO Publishing, Denver, CO, 1992 - 1996
- Developed data conversion programs and production process and test tools, written in C.
- Provided production support to teams building CD-ROM and Internet products.
- Built and maintained tools and performed troubleshooting of production processes.

EDUCATION

B.S. in Electrical Engineering, University of Utah, Salt Lake, UT, 1991

MAUREEN TEETON

14 Blakely Avenue
Los Angeles, CA 12345
123-555-1234
maureen@unknown.com

teetondesign.com
linkedin.com/maureenteeton
twitter.com/maureenteeton

WEB DESIGNER

- ✓ Five years experience designing websites; recent projects include database-driven and content management sites.
- ✓ Solid visual design skills; fluency in design and development software.
- ✓ Comfortable with client interactions and team collaboration.

TECHNICAL SKILLS

CSS	Flash	AJAX
HTML	Javascript	AdobeSuite
XHTML	MySQL	CodeIgniter
D HTML	Document Object Model (DOM)	

PROFESSIONAL EXPERIENCE

2009-pres. **BioTech Inc., Los Angeles, CA**
Lead Web Designer
- ✓ Conceptualized and managed the design and development of a database-driven site, which involved a content management system.
- ✓ Front-end development included hand coding of html, flash design and development, and use of Adobe suite of applications.
- ✓ Designed and developed interactive projects such as banner ads, response forms, flash movies, ecommerce, and html emails.
- ✓ Collaborated with usability team to produce user-centered design.

2006-09 **BooksGalore.com, Ventura, CA**
Web Designer
- ✓ Maintained and upgraded database-driven site for this mega online bookseller.
- ✓ Worked on team to develop site's book club blog, using content management system.

2004-06 **Bellwether Publishing, Santa Barbara, CA**
Graphic Designer
- ✓ Designed book covers and promotional material, working primarily with technical manuals and textbooks.
- ✓ Assisted in annual update of cover art of the Who Done It series, which incorporated the well-established brand logo of 21 years.
- ✓ Assisted in expanding publisher's website to include author videos and webinars.

EDUCATION

BA, Graphic Design, Minor, Web Design, 2004
Pacific School of Graphic Design, Los Angeles, CA

PROFESSIONAL GROUPS - CURRENT

Web Dudes
IT Online
LinkedIn web-related groups

Technology

Katie Baird, Certified Virtual Assistant
Website Development & Maintenance and Project Management

1567 Shoup St.
Prescott, AZ 86305
928-445-4724

ktcosmos@looseends.net
blog.looseends.net
linkedin.com/in/katiebaird

EXPERTISE
- Website planning, production, and maintenance
- Photography and graphic design
- Strong written communication and organization skills
- Software: WordPress, Adobe CS2 (including Photoshop, Adobe GoLive, Adobe Acrobat, Bridge, InDesign, Dreamweaver), QuarkXPress
- Hardware: Macintosh

EXPERIENCE   1996 – Present, Virtual Assistant, Loose Ends, Prescott, AZ
- Design websites, brochures, website ads, and newsletters.
- Develop and implement special projects and P.R. materials.
- Photograph events, people and products for inclusion in print and web design projects.

Clients include:

Yavapai Exceptional Industries	Royce Masonry
West Yavapai Guidance Clinic	Intuitive Cartography
PrescottWeddings.com	Whipstone Farm
Higgins Surveying	Innovative Medical Associates
Temple B'rith Shalom	Dr. Kenna Stephenson, M.D.
MexicoBeachHomes.com	

1976 – 1996, Middle School Teacher, Phoenix, Arizona and Prescott, Arizona

EDUCATION   B.A., Arizona State University, Tempe, Arizona

AFFILIATIONS   International Virtual Assistants Association (IVAA), 1998-present
Remote Professionals, 2004-2009
Women In Networking, Board of Directors, 2000-2006
Prescott High School Career Center, 1997-2005
Yavapai College Career Skills Program, 1999-2001
Yavapai County Big Brothers & Big Sisters, 1997-2004
Yavapai College Graphic Design Department Advisory Board, 2001-2002

"My favorite thing is to go where I've never been." — Diane Arbus, 1923-1971

RYAN SEYMOUR

123 Pillar Street, #1
Kansas City, KS 12345

(123) 555-8888
rseymour@unknown.com

Multimedia Developer and Web Designer

- Self-motivated technical/creative professional.
- Enthusiastic and cooperative team member.
- Advanced knowledge of computer systems and applications.
- Quickly and intuitively comprehend complex systems.

PROFESSIONAL EXPERIENCE

2001-present   Web Design and Multimedia Consultant

www.reliefinsite.com, 2001-present
- Redesigned and added video content to a comedy website, increasing traffic 20%.

www.themansion.com, 2001-present
- Created informational website for Island Mansion and Spa, increasing business and reducing event coordinators' workload.

www.experthere.com, 2002-2005
- Created prototype website for Internet consultant startup to attract venture capital.

www.ress.com, 2002
- Updated and added video to Regional Energy Services website.

1993-2001   Kansas Automobile Club (KAC), Kansas City

Multimedia Developer, 2000-2001
- Consulted with internal departments on corporate Internet and Intranet website multimedia projects.
- Created RealAudio website cataloging KRGO radio spots, which increased the effectiveness of company website.
- Created KAC website for *Auto magazine*, working with creative directors and writers.
- Developed Instant Info website, providing local information and maps to KAC members.
- Digitized corporate video for Intranet distribution, reducing costs and promoting employee communication.
- Designed, illustrated, co-wrote, and published booklet that supported frontline decision making, improving customer service and company efficiency.
- Created and maintained MS Access database of marketing projects and a calendar of marketing events for executive staff. Saved money by eliminating redundant campaigns and improving the planning process.
- Created and maintained MS Access database of over 6,000 KAC employees' phone numbers, titles, and addresses for company phone book. Created PDF phone book and HTML version for the Intranet, saving printing and distribution costs.

—Continued—

Technology

Ryan Seymour

Kansas Automobile Club (continued)

Supervisor, Client Services Technical Support, 1996-1997
- Supervised hardware and software support specialists. Created computer user-groups, which improved employee knowledge and efficiency.
- Oversaw newsletter supporting computer users.

Presentation Support Specialist, 1993-1995
- Worked with the executive staff to create multimedia, including digital video, 35mm slides, and overheads to support their business presentations to the Board of Directors.
- Created animated video, informing managers-in-training about Information Services and promoting better relations with internal clients.
- Produced video that documented workflow of claims adjusters, resulting in new and efficient claims procedures.

TECHNOLOGY AND APPLICATION EXPERTISE

BBEdit	Painter	SoundEdit	Lingo
Dreamweaver	Final Cut Pro	Acrobat	ShockWave
PhotoShop	MediaCleaner	Distiller	MS Access
Illustrator	RealMedia	Director	Mac/Win/NT

EDUCATION

MA, Creative Writing, Kansas State University, Kansas City, KS
BA, English, Hollindale State College, Priceline, KS

Paul Boyette

45 Westlake Road, Denver, CO 12345
123-555-1234, paulboyette@unknown.com

Technical Writer and Editor

CAREER SUMMARY

- More than 10 years' experience as a technical writer and editor
- Effectively communicate technical information to both technical and nontechnical audiences
- Additional experience in freelance writing for national magazines and public relations
- Conducted classroom and online training

PROFESSIONAL EXPERIENCE

Senior Technical Documentation Specialist

Barkley Corporation   **Denver, CO**   **2005 –2009**

Contractor for the U.S. Army Environmental Command (Fort Collins, CO):

- Wrote/updated help files for various applications with RoboHelp/MadCap Flare
- Wrote/updated Quick Start Guides, User Manuals, and training materials for the Army Environmental Command (AEC)
- Created online tutorials with Trivantis Lectora
- Wrote, recorded, and edited narration sound files for tutorials with Adobe Audition
- Facilitated classroom sessions for two training courses
- Documented processes involved in creating tutorials/help files as SOPs
- Recognized with Special Achievement Certificate (4th quarter 2008)

Senior Technical Editor

Green Industries   **Aspen, CO**   **2002 –2005**

- Contractor for the Centers for Medicare and Medicaid Services (CMS)
- Created and updated training material for CMS
- Edited presentation templates
- Interfaced with CMS Subject Matter Experts (SMEs)

Senior Technical Editor

Brainerd Technology Group   **Longmont, CO**   **1999 –2002**

- Hired as Technical Editor, promoted to Senior Technical Editor
- Created and updated training manuals and presentations
- Maintained editorial standards for training team, along with occasional presentations about editorial style
- Created and edited presentation templates
- Trained in Instructional Design

EDUCATION

B.A., German Language, University of Alabama, June 1986

SOFTWARE SKILLS

Microsoft Word, PowerPoint, Excel, Paint, Visio, Trivantis Lectora, MadCap Flare, Adobe Audition (Microsoft Windows 95/98/2000/2003/XP/NT)

Technology

Tawny Hall

123 White Drive • Westchester, NY 12345 • (123) 555-8888 • thall@unknown.com

JOB OBJECTIVE: Technical Writer

SUMMARY OF QUALIFICATIONS

- Four years' experience writing easy-to-read instructions for technical services, products, and safety procedures.
- Known for quick technical comprehension and clear translation.
- Proficient with Windows and Macintosh word processing applications.

EDUCATION

Bachelor of Science   Leedings College, Westchester, NY
Technical Writing Certificate   Unity Community College, Jamaica, NY

RELEVANT ACCOMPLISHMENTS

WRITING AND EDITING
At Chrysler Bank

- Created Standard Operating Procedures for various responsibilities and tasks.
- Cut customer response time and initial analyst training time by creating an Access database to organize frequently accessed information.
- Designed and implemented a training program for technology phone support.

At Unified Alarms

- Wrote brochures, featuring technical capabilities of wired and wireless systems.
- Reduced customer response time by simplifying complex technical instructions.
- Analyzed process and developed instructions for downloading data from PCS to remote microcontrollers.
- Prepared business proposals for technical installations for up to $25K each.
- Edited manual to demystify instructions for entry-level users.

At Camway Communications

- Cut training time by creating concise instructions and worksheets for operators.

At Leedings College, chemistry, physics, and digital logic classes

- Using scientific third-person format, wrote research and analytical reports.

TECHNICAL
At Chrysler Bank

- Install and troubleshoot phone, pager, and telecommunication networks.
- Provide hardware and software support of bank's computers.

At Leedings College, technical classes

- Programmed in Pascal and Basic; debugged computer programs.
- Built electronic boards, using digital logic diagrams and Boolean formulas.

WORK HISTORY

2001-present   Help Desk Specialist, Chrysler Bank, Westchester, NY
1999-2001   Phone Operator Manager, Camway Communications, Inc., Jamaica, NY
1998-1999   Technical Writer, Unified Alarms, Ltd., White Plains, NY

Index

More Help from Susan Ireland

It isn't easy to make a career move on your own. If you're stuck, get help from a professional on Susan Ireland's Job Search Team (provided at an hourly rate) or purchase her do-it-yourself resume software. These tools are available by telephone (call 510-524-5238) or online (go to SusanIreland.com).

Resume Writing Service

Have your resume done by one of the professional writers on Susan Ireland's Resume Team. These writers have composed thousands of resumes, and they're experts at working with gaps in employment, career changes, age discrimination, and other difficult issues.

Resume Critique Service

If you've already written your resume, get it critiqued to be sure you have the most effective job search tool possible. A professional resume writer from Susan Ireland's Team will examine your resume, give you a critique, and answer your resume questions. (Believe me, they pack a lot of information into each critique session!)

Ready-Made Resumes Software

No more staring at blank pages or fumbling with formats. Ready-Made Resumes software by Susan Ireland helps you figure out what to write, and the resume templates come in a variety of layouts. Access this affordable program at SusanIreland.com.

Career Counseling

If you're having trouble figuring out how to proceed in your existing career or how to make a career change, get advice from a professional counselor on Susan Ireland's Team. She'll help you define your talents, understand how to optimize them in your career, and create long- and short-term career plans.

Job Search Coaching

A coach on Susan Ireland's Team can help you develop your job hunt strategy and motivate you through the process of conducting your job market research, cold calling, interview preparation, effective follow-up, and salary negotiations.

Learn more about these services and tools by going to SusanIreland.com or by calling 510-524-5238.

These are exclusive offerings by Susan Ireland and are not connected with Penguin Group (USA) Inc. or Alpha Books.

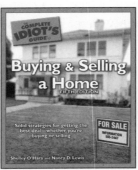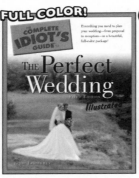

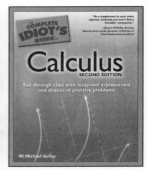
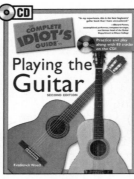